P9-BJL-182

VOICES OF LATIN ROCK

PEOPLE AND EVENTS THAT CREATED THIS SOUND

ISBN 0 634 08061-X

Copyright © 2004 by Jim McCarthy with Ron Sansoe

All rights reserved. No part of this book may be reproduced in any form or by any electronic or mechani-
cal means including information storage and retrieval systems without permission in writing from the
publisher, except by a reviewer, who may quote brief passages in a review.

Published by Hal Leonard Corporation
7777 W. Bluemound Road
P.O. Box 13819
Milwaukee, WI 53213

Hal Leonard books are available through your local bookstore, or you may order at
www.musicdispatch.com, or call Music Dispatch at 1-800-637-2852.

   Library of Congress Cataloging-in-Publication Data

McCarthy, Jim, 1953-
  Voices of Latin rock : people and events that created this sound /
[Jim McCarthy with Ron Sansoe ; foreword by Carlos Santana].-- 1st ed.
     p. cm.
  Includes bibliographical references.
  Discography: p.
  ISBN 0-634-08061-X
  1. Rock music--California--History and criticism. I. Sansoe, Ron. II. Title.
  ML3534.M439 2004
  781.66'089'68720794--dc22
                         2004026527

Printed in the U.S.A.

First Edition

Visit Hal Leonard Online at **www.halleonard.com**

AUGUSTANA LIBRARY
UNIVERSITY OF ALBERTA

VOICES OF LATIN ROCK

PEOPLE AND EVENTS THAT CREATED THIS SOUND

DEDICATION

TO THE SPIRIT OF JOAQUIN ZOPILOTE VILLANUEVA, A.K.A DR. BROWN.
THE AUTHORS WOULD LIKE TO THANK:

For opening this door: Gregg Rolie, Carlos Santana, Neal Schon, David Brown,
Michael Carabello, Jose Chepito Areas, and Michael Shrieve;

Also: Herbie Herbert, Johnny Zopilote Villanueva, Rico Reyes, Dougie Rauch, Coke Escovedo,
Arcelio Garcia, Jorge Santana, Pablo Tellez, Abel Zarate, Richard Bean, Abel Sanchez, Greg Errico,
Karl Perazzo, John Santos, and all the other "angels" from the Mission who aren't around to read this.

Dr. Bernie Gonzalez, Kitsaun King and everyone at Santana Management,
Chuy Varela, Pete Gallegos, Jim Marshall, John Szabo, Ray Cotter Jr.,
Julio Sanchez, Rudy Ramirez.

A SPECIAL THANK YOU:

To the late Rudy Rodriguez and his brother George Rodriguez for the great photos.

And to Hal Leonard Corporation.

JIM MCCARTHY WOULD LIKE TO THANK:

Those in recovery along the road who shone their light;
Andrea, Danny B., Phil F., Marty P., Sandie, and Craig: thanks for sharing.
To special friends: Landy Barney, Luis, Miguel Plaza, Nigelito and the Beulah crew.
E.T. and Marian for extra help with rarities.
Growing up in comic times: Brendan, Pete, and Brett.
Tracey, Steph, Che, and Chavells for keeping me alive.
To Laura Nyro for her unique musical beauty.
To Marvin Gaye for deep soul, especially the *vulnerable* sessions.
Abdul Mati Klarwein for visual hallucinations.

RON SANSOE WOULD LIKE TO THANK:

My brother Bob Sansoe and his wife Sandy; Kate, Matt, and Mike.
Also, Rich Sansoe and his wife Dorothy; Chris, Andy, and the rest of my family;
Kira K.; Aloha sister Sher on the island.

ALSO AVAILABLE BY JIM MCCARTHY

Godspeed: The Kurt Cobain Graphic (co-authored with Barnaby Legg),
Omnibus Books, 2003.
Eminem: In My Skin (co-authored with Barnaby Legg),
Omnibus Books, 2004.
Tupac Shakur: One Nation Under The Gun (co-authored with Barnaby Legg),
Omnibus Books, 2005.

RESPECT IS DUE....

I would like to thank the following people for generously consenting to be interviewed. Some went on to a second (or more) bout in order to have their brains picked further. Others kindly made invaluable contributions of different kinds, pictures, information etc.

In no particular order they are: Arcelio Garcia Jr., Pablo Tellez, (thanks for the ministry Pablo), Richard Bean, Tony Menjivar, Pete Garcia Jr., Gabriel Manzo, Abel Zarate, Johnny Valenzuela, Leo Rosales, Michael Shrieve, Abel Sanchez, Dr. Bernie Gonzalez III, Chris Wong, Jorge Santana, Percy Pinckney, Carlos Santana, Al Perez, Neal Schon, Amber Schon, Joel Selvin, Raul Rekow, Karl Perazzo, Jeffrey Trager, Angela Davis, Ben Fong-Torres, Roberto Quintana, Michael Carabello, Fred Catero, José Simon, Benny Velarde, Pete Escovedo, Gregg Rolie, José "Chepito" Areas, Adrian Areas, Jim Welch for Rolie band shots, Armando Peraza, Mauricio Aviles, Jan Cameron, Diane Black, Olga Brown, Neftali Santiago, Claude"Coffee"Cave, Ric Wilson, Lou Wilson, Carlos Wilson, Wilfredo Wilson, Ray Cotter Jr for super photos, Julio Sanchez for great photos behind-the-scenes, Jorge Bermudez, Johnny Cortade, Greg Errico, Rachel Milstein, Debbie Busalacchi, Brian Rohan, Wil-Dog Abers, Raul Pacheco, Asdru Sierra (the last three from Ozomatli), Manny Martinez, Ray Martinez, Mumia Abu-Jamal, Herbie Herbert (for enduring repeated interviews) Glendon Miskel, Willie "G" Garcia, Johnny "Zopi" Villanueva, Dora Tellez, Robert Lazaneo, Gregg Landau, John Santos, Gregg "Happy Sanchez" at Secret Studios, Gerald Matoi, Bill Perasso, Dolores Huerta, Ruben Arellano, Roberto Hernandez, Peabo Rodriguez and Bill Walker at Thump Records, Joan Chase, Bob Sansoe for Mission Street and SF Parks and nocturnal pictures, Doug Tracy, Joe Bean, Cesar Ascarrunz, DM Reed, Willy Lizarrago, Jim Cassell (Berkeley Agency) Etienne "ET" Houben, (thanks ET for invaluable help with photos/discographies) Martin Cohen of Latin Percussion, Oscar Estrella, Tom Poole, Victor Pantoja, Jesse "Chuy" Varela for going the extra mile with "interview" transcripts, Gibby Ross, Neil Norman of GNP Crescendo, Daniel Deaguero of Night Beat Records, Pete Gallegos at the Mission High School (thanks for valuable editorial assistance), Manny Valdez, Lynn Fouts-Rainey, Jim Susoeff, Jack Leavitt, Randy Bachman, Rudy and George Rodriguez for their excellent photographs, Victor Alemon for some great early pictures, Ron Reisterer for the excellent photos, Jim Marshall for Attitude pictures, Eric Minton for the Alberto article, Bueno for the Word, Bryan Andrews at Rhino Records, BLU Magazine for deep insights and reprints, The Mission Cultural Centre, The Mission Archives, Angel Lara at Accion Latina, Pedro Tuyub at El Tecolote, Marvin Gaye for the spiritual soundtrack music, Mandrill supplied the world groove, Richard Mann for his Apple Mac and Quark expertise and design skills.

Last but certainly not least, I'd like to thank Ronnie Sansoe for shepherding this project with patience, good humor, attention to detail, and for co-ordinating all these interviews. Maximum props go out to Chiori Santiago for her el fabulistic editorial overview.

MAIN MENU

SIDE ORDERS

MAIN MENU

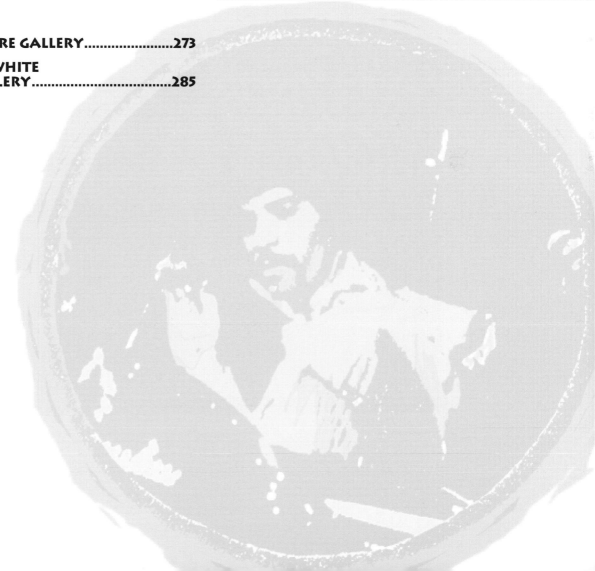

DESSERT

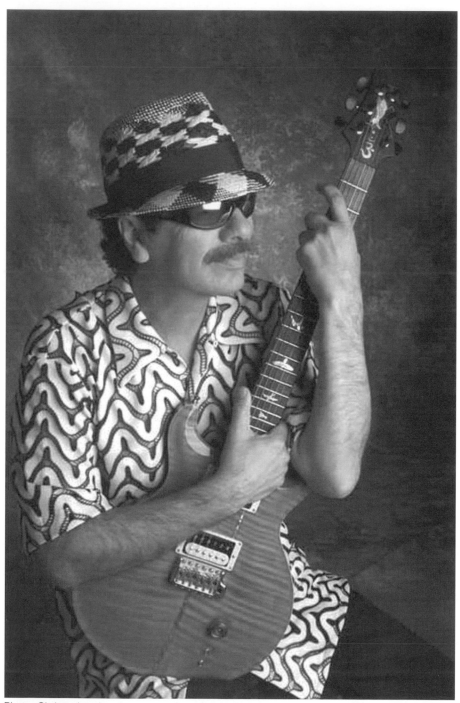

Photo: Christopher Jacobs

FOREWORD BY CARLOS SANTANA

Back in the early sixties, when I was in high school, there was a band contest sponsored by some local radio stations. It was held in a high school gym, and I remember going there and it seemed like an army of bands were there—hundreds of drums and guitars as far as you could see. Out of a thousand bands, half got eliminated right away. We stayed because we had something different. We were playing the blues. Later we were able to stand out because we picked up the Afro-Cuban rhythms, and no one else was playing rock and roll in 3/4 time.

I'm into people seriously changing their skins. That's what was happening back then. There was a lot of racial tension at the time, but a few people were trying to keep a more spiritual frame of mind. Bill Graham had a healing thing going on at the Fillmore Auditorium with the mixed music bills. In that environment, Santana was born. I never liked purity in music; it can sound like background music in a restaurant. For us, music was more of a matter of sounding like a street mutt, like a dog that's bred with everything. This is our contribution to the world: we gave birth to Chicano music, to a sound that is very alive today.

The other day I went down to Precita Park, where it all started. There was a band there; the guitarist was a young Mexican American-Indian guy with a mohawk. He was really getting inside his guitar. A part of me wanted to walk over and ask to sit in, but I said to myself, no. This isn't your time anymore. Just enjoy it, because this is the future. It brought back the way we started out, just jamming in the park.

I want to thank the creators of this book from the bottom of my heart for having the passion and interest to document our stories. The people in the book really opened up to Jim McCarthy, and I'm not sure we would have done that for anyone else. I also want to thank the women in our lives, our wives, mothers, and daughters, for being there when we created this music. They stood with us, side by side, while the guys were out on the road. We couldn't have done any of it without their help.

I'm grateful this book was written, because it's a chance to take us back and bring us forward. If our history can challenge the next wave of musicians to keep moving and changing, to keep spiritually hungry and horny, that's what it's about.

Landy and Denton, Hanwell, West London. 1971. Landy morphing from skinhead to Afro head, while Denton still favors the sheep-
skin coats and loafer shoes popular amongst the reggae and Motown listening skinhead fraternity.

INTRO:
RUDIE GOES AFRO;
SKIN GOES LATINO

Jim McCarthy and Landy
Gray, London, 1970.

How did a first generation Irish kid, living in England with no immediate connection to Latin rock music, come to write a book on Santana, Malo, Latin rock, and the surrounding musical scene?

My journey began around 1967 with an infatuation with American soul and R&B music. I can remember, as a kid, listening to "Save the Country" by the Fifth Dimension (penned by the glorious Laura Nyro) under the bed covers, my tiny transistor radio picking up the distorted signals of the pirate station Radio Luxembourg. Hearing the song's swirling organ sound was an early peak experience. As teenagers, my friend Landy and I would check out a lot of new stuff from stateside. We were skinheads[1] listening to Motown, Trojan reggae, ska, and bluebeat. Landy's trips to Washington DC yielded 45-rpm James Brown imports on the King label and Marvin Gaye's

We listened to Aretha Franklin blowing out the fuses at Atlantic with a series of single releases and also the excellent *Live at the Fillmore* album, recorded the same night as King Curtis's historic live Atlantic album set, catching them both at their peak. The Norman Whitfield-produced Temptations stuff, along with Sly Stone, was a revelation. We spent months listening to Donny Hathaway's "The Ghetto." Lewd early reggae in the form of "Wet Dream" by Max Romeo and "Pussy Price Gone Up" vied for my ears with Free, Jimi Hendrix, the BarKays, and Curtis Mayfield. Landy, Ronnie Doctrove, Gary Frazer, and I, when money was short, would think nothing of walking from Hanwell, West London to Soho, Central London (about a 20-mile round trip) to see Mongo Santamaria, or to go Upstairs at Ronnie Scott's, where the club played all the latest funk records. We considered other kids who were just listening to pop hits as complete wankers. Landy and I were turned onto early Latin music by Curtis, a Trinidad-born bongo player living in West London who, after getting us well spliffed up on ganja, would play us *Herbie Mann at the Village Gate*, with its

Photo: Jim McCarthy

Curtis: Trinidadian bongo player, Ealing, London 1971. First brush with a "real life" percussionist.

truly hypnotic drumming featuring Ray Mantilla on conga, Chief Bey on African drums, and Rudy Collins on traps. That was the first time I can really remember getting "zoned out" on the drum. Another favorite was *Mas Ritmo Caliente* by Cal Tjader, a lurid red vinyl LP issued on the Fantasy label. This was a precursor to Santana and the Latin rock vibe and featured the heavyweight percussion of Mongo Santamaria and Armando Peraza with the timbales of Luis Kant, Al Torres, and Willie Bobo. As a result, Landy mutated from Jamaican Rude Boy to an Afro-American style, and I adopted a London Latino stance inspired by American fashion and attitude.

My first brush with any form of Latin-based rock music was Santana's debut album. The music seemed then (and still does) very underground and uncompromising. It took awhile to fully register where the group was coming from, but that album opened a floodgate of musical connections and pleasure that has never abated. I can remember shelling out extra money to buy *Santana 3* on import days before its UK release. It was an album of savage intensity made by a band of enigmatic individuals about whom little was known in my part of the world.

Imagined against this aural backdrop, America seemed a glamorous faraway place where some extraordinary music was being pumped out. The most immediate connection to this book came from a desire to find out about the lives of the community from which this music sprang. I was reminded of a quote by Santana's original drummer, Mike Shrieve, in which he said, "One has to meet with one's mentors in order to move on and fully form one's own creativity." Shrieve himself was the starting point for a series of connections. I was then engaged in writing commissioned articles for the now-defunct *Real World* magazine. I started out by calling *Modern Drummer* in New York, where I was given a contact to reach him. When I eventually called him in New York, his wife Cindy gave me his number in San Francisco. At that time he was working on the film soundtrack for

Photo: Chris Cuffaro, Courtesy Michael Shrieve

Michael Shrieve, New York, circa 1991.

Photo: Jim McCarthy

Mike Carabello, in his studio, 1991.

Bedroom Window with Dr. Patrick Gleason (the synthesizer whizz who played on the *Mwandishi* and *Sextant* albums by Herbie Hancock). Initially bemused, Mike graciously answered some questions over the phone and, over time, we swapped live Santana and solo Shrieve tapes (including unreleased material) and other newly released Shrieve import CDs. Shrieve also introduced me to original Santana conguero Michael Carabello.

A trip to the States in 1991 led me to stay at Carabello's house in Marin County, California. Together, with Shrieve and Chepito Areas, he had forged the early Latin rock rhythms as Santana's first boiling percussion section. We spent time listening to rare reel-to-reel tape of *Abraxas* outtakes, unreleased, unedited Santana cuts, and Luis Gasca material. In a series of coincidences (certainly guided by a Higher Power), I met Jeff Trager, who ran the BreakThru music promotion company in San Francisco. I asked Jeff what had happened to Malo (a bad-ass Latin-rock band I'd much admired in my Latin-lovin' days back in London). He informed me he was off to see them rehearse that night at Townsend Street Studios in San Francisco; did I want to come?

Later that night I sat and watched as Arcelio Garcia Jr., Malo's leader and vocalist, put the band through its paces. I sat in respect, checking out the hot percussion of Tony Menjivar and Roberto Quintana and Wayne Carter. That night I met Ron Sansoe. Sansoe was managing Malo's publishing catalogue; he was immediately intrigued by the idea of a history of Latin rock. This book is the result.

Voices of Latin Rock: People and Events That Created This Sound has three areas of focus. First, it traces the stories of the prominent Latin rock bands Santana and Malo, examining in detail Malo's four pioneering releases for Warner Bros. and Santana's first three on the Columbia label, and the ways in which both reflect a wide spectrum of Latin influences. This music also makes connections to all the main influences of the time; traces of jazz, (particularly Miles Davis's), Motown R&B, New York Latin, the Beatles, English blues guitar, and the "psychedelic" experience prevalent in San Francisco at the time, were all stirred into the pot.

Secondly, the narrative puts the bands within the framework of the San Francisco Mission district's Latin community and its cast of characters, particularly those from the other bands that provided the elemental impetus to evolve this musical form. This small, volatile, and passionate pool of musicians created an explosive sound that has been little documented compared to the more mainstream "white" music of the period. It also frames the urban Latin music scene within the broader turbulent events of the period. The blending of cultures that characterized the Mission district and the highly charged political consciousness and activism of the late 1960s and early '70s established a robust platform upon which the music known as Latin rock was launched.

Third, the book touches on wider aspects of the American music business, which in those early, riotous times did not serve the Latin rock genre (with the exception of Santana) as well as it might have, due to a lack of understanding of the music's cultural and crossover significance. This book mostly concentrates on the period between 1968 to 1975. After that, Latin music, apart from the genre known as salsa, became submerged or repressed as the music business blanketed the world with disco. Even Santana, which prospered throughout the late 1970s and '80s, came under extreme pressure from the Columbia label to use outside producers in attempts to mold them into the producer-driven product of the time. Partly directed by "advances" in studio technology and the increasing corporate approach to selling "product," the music business's focus shifted from an emphasis on the creators' vision to a more corporate, coke-addled, overblown style in which, as Mike Carabello puts it, "the truth had become airbrushed."

Looking to the future: Santana, just as the first wave of international success was about to explode.
(L to R) Carlos Santana, David Brown, Gregg Rolie, Mike Carabello, Jose "Chepito" Areas, Michael Shrieve.

What the record industry failed to realize was that Latin rock was a totally new art form. It was, and still is, Latin soul music—a musical interpretation of what it was to be Latin and living in the US; a way of echoing a generation's proud cross-cultural identity. The music coming out of the Mission was as relevant in conveying a regional attitude to the rest of the world as were the Merseybeat bands that shaped the Liverpool sound, the psychedelic music of San Francisco's Haight Ashbury, or the soul music of Detroit's Motown records. This was music as tight as the great Motown acts, as slinky as the best R&B and as cocksure as it comes, both caressing the listener and flaunting its controlled aggression, delivered by players at the top of their game. The music's intensity not only emanated from the decibel level of the cranked-up amplifiers, but more importantly, from a human fire rippling up from the music's African origins, the drum.

Voices of Latin Rock: People and Events That Created This Sound is the lyric, the words, stories, and memories of the musicians who devoted their lives to playing their passion.

Annual 24th Street Merchant's Festival, 1987

Photo: Courtesy El Tecolote

LA MISIÓN

Mission Dolores

Photo: Bob Sansoe

Photo: Courtesy El Tecolote

18th and Mission, 1972

Photo: Courtesy El Tecolote

Director Bob Rojas in front of LULAC office
(League of United Latin American Citizens).

The mission is a reminder that California indeed was once part of Mexico and ruled by Spain. Until the last half of the 19th century, the territory was an outpost of quiet haciendas operated by Mexican landowners known as "Californios." In 1848 the Treaty of Guadalupe Hidalgo ceded the land of California to the United States. The following year, gold was discovered 90 miles to the north in Coloma, touching off a migration that established San Francisco as an international city. Fortune-seekers arrived from all parts of the United States as well as from Europe, China, Chile, and Mexico (miners from the state of Sonora were especially adept at grinding gold from the granite mountains of the Sierra Nevada).

People flocked to the port city to reinvent themselves, whether through fortune or folly. It's important to understand that San Francisco, and the Mission district, have always been places of new beginnings. In the 1940s, the neighborhood was mostly Irish and Italian. During World War II, African-Americans from the South migrated to help in the war effort. Together, they helped build the shipyards across San Francisco Bay in Oakland and Richmond and the Naval shipyards at Hunters Point.

In the 1950s and '60s, Mexicans seeking jobs and Central Americans escaping war and persecution moved into the affordable apartments in old Victorian buildings standing cheek-to-cheek along Harrison, York, and 24th Streets. "Mission Street was known as the Miracle Mile," recalls San Francisco concert producer Mauricio Aviles, who arrived from El Salvador as a boy of ten. "I had never seen such lights—it seemed as if all the lights in the world were on that street, and all night the streets were full of people," he recalls.

In the late 1960s, the Hispanic population predominated in "the Mission," as it's commonly known today, although the cultural palette remained diverse. The Spanish spoken in the streets contained the inflections of a dozen territories—Nicaragua, Guatemala, Puerto Rico, Cuba, Argentina, and Peru. Michael Carabello remembers:

Mission Districts Dominguez Bakery located at 24th Alabama, with its famous murals painted on its wall.

Photo: Bob Sansoe. Digital enhancement: Richard Mann

"Growing up in the Mission was great, for the simple fact that there was a balance of Russians, Italians, Mexicans, Puerto Ricans—real multicultural. The hot spot for Latin people was around 24th and Folsom streets. Arcelio [Garcia, later a singer with Malo]'s mom ran a great restaurant, the best for Puerto Rican food. She made the best pasteles, rice and beans, and pork." In the blare of jukeboxes in bars and restaurants, it was not unusual to hear traditional Mexican rancheras, Central American cumbias, Puerto Rican mambos, and Argentine boleros co-mingling with good old rock and roll (cover renditions of American hits by Mexican groups such as Los Teen Tops were immensely popular with Spanish-speaking listeners). "Stuff like Los Tres Aces were monster sellers," recalls Bill Perasso, who worked Latin, jazz, and R&B releases for radio. In the late sixties, doo-wop groups could be heard on street corners and at lowrider gatherings.

The Bay Area is home to several prominent universities, and the Mission district in particular, with its cheap rents and laid-back ambience, was a magnet for artists, painters, and poets, in addition to a large community of musicians. The result was a rich stew of intellect and ideas, which both fed and were fed by the political questioning of the time. San Francisco State University and, across the bay, the University of California Berkeley and Merritt College (the Black Panthers' stomping ground) ignited high levels of political consciousness and activism, beginning with the Free Speech Movement in 1964 and continuing through the Vietnam War protests. The concept of changing the status quo to make the world a better place was expressed in the region more avidly that anywhere else in the country. This magical time of convergence—of art, politics, ethnicity, pride, and struggle—gave birth to the music known as Latin rock.

9

Malo group in one of many transitions in personnel.
(back) Richard Kermode, Jorge Santana, Tom Poole,
(middle back) Arcelio Garcia Jr, Leo "Pepe" Rosales, Raul Rekow,
(middle front) Richard Spremich, Tom Harrell, Mike Heathman,
(front) Abel Zarate, Pablo Tellez.

Photo: Rudy Rodriguez

MUSICAL CONVERGENCE:
THIS IS OUR TIME

Carlos Santana and Mike Carabello with Santana, give it up at the Family Dog, San Francisco, 1969.

Photo: Joan Chase

"Convergence" means to meet, to intersect, and to form links. The enduring appeal of what has been dubbed "Latin rock" was born of the explosion of sound and energy that emanated from the Latin community in San Francisco's Mission district in the 1960s. The beginnings of the Latin rock bands lie at the end of San Francisco's psychedelic, acid rock era, when a more urban sound was simmering in the blue collar Mission district and Oakland, across the water from San Francisco in the East Bay. A growing interest in Chicanismo and Spanish-inflected alternative music gave rise to the Latin rock genre and spawned not only Santana and Malo but also a number of other great acts, such as Azteca, Sapo, and Soul Sacrifice (which would become Dakila).

Photo: Joan Chase

David Brown, Santana's bassist, modelling the knitted headgear popular with West Coast hipsters, such as Sly Stone, Larry Graham, etc.

11

Tito Puente, "El Rey del Timbal" in action.

Ray Barretto, "Mr Hard Hands" on congas.

Photos: Courtesy El Tecolote

Mongo Santamaria, poses with conga drums.

The stories of Santana and Malo intertwine as both bands drew on the same mercurial Mission talent pool that existed in a parallel but self-contained universe alongside the acid rockers of the "flower power" scene. During this period the depth of musical convergence, in which many musical forms collided, was astounding. In Santana's music alone you can hear references to English blues via Peter Green and Eric Clapton, Latin dance via Ray Barretto and Tito Puente, African via Olantunji, funk via James Brown, English R&B via Spencer Davis, jazz via Gil Evans and Miles Davis, with traces of Brazilian, salsa, and much more combined in the gumbo. I would need another book just to deal with this topic; however, some examples should provide a flavor of the times. For a period in the USA it seemed that ideas about racial divisions were breaking apart and that consciousness, at least in the young, was being lifted. In California especially, LSD, marijuana, and other mind-altering substancess were opening doors of perception, at least for a certain segment of the populace. A "counterculture" was embracing the black struggle, to a degree, and multiracial bands such as Sly and the Family Stone, Jimi Hendrix Experience, War, and Mandrill were at the forefront of a musical melting pot, which simmered despite America's emerging racial power struggles.

Bay Area native Sylvester Stewart, aka Sly Stone, started out as one of the hippest radio disc jockeys in the region. He also played guitar with Bobby Freeman, who had a big hit with "Do the Swim" in 1964 and a huge hit with "Do You Wanna Dance" in 1958. Sly quickly became known for his electrifying performance style. "He pushed the envelope as far as performing," says Michael Carabello. When Carabello was still working at the Three-Minute Car Wash on South Van Ness Avenue in San Francisco, Stone was hanging out with the likes of jazz pianist Earl "Fatha" Hines. Sometimes he'd bring Carabello along for a visit, thus establishing an aural connection that would show up later in the Santana band's love of jazzy riffs and blues compositions. With his own band, Sly and the Family Stone, the ex-DJ would create some classics of seventies-era soulful rock and roll, including "Everyday People" and "Dance to the Music," plus the monster funk of "Thank Yo Falettinme Be Mice Elf Agin."

Motown was heavily influenced by Sly Stone's multiracial slant on funk, particularly in the Norman Whitfield-produced "psychedelic" soul sound of the Temptations, Rare Earth, and Undisputed Truth, among others. The funky drumming of Clyde Stubblefield and Jabo Starks (James Brown's dual funk machine), twinned with the outrageous bass of Bootsy Collins, fueled many variations, such as Bernard "Pretty" Purdie's locked-up drum funkisms backing such luminaries as Aretha Franklin, King Curtis, Les McCann & Eddie Harris, and Wilson Pickett. With his trademark three-choke lick on the hi-hats, Purdie brought a monster groove to the funk. In turn he influenced Oakland-based Tower of Power, with their team of Francis Rocco Prestias's and David Garibaldi's bass and drums. They took the funk into an outer mathematical zone, always changing accent but always on the one. Tower of Power would famously assert "What Is Hip"; check *East Bay Grease, Back to Oakland, Urban Renewal,* or *In the Slot* albums for the full re-definition of funk.

The musicians of Santana's generation undoubtedly were influenced by the Cuban and Puerto Rican dance music coming out of New York. The hits of their parents' generation became an ample source of songs that could be recast as electrified rock; the addition of Caribbean rhythms was borrowed directly from the bands of Tito Puente, the brothers Charlie and Eddie Palmieri, Ray Barretto, and others. Santana popularized and internationalized the music of Tito Puente with their reworking of his "Oye Como Va" on *Abraxas* in 1970. A flashy timbales player and vibraphonist, Puente was already a veteran of the New York salsa scene; he was known as the first to set his drum kit in front of the band, thus underscoring the importance of the rhythm section in Latin music. When Carabello and Chepito Areas brought Puente's tune "Oye Como Va"[2] to Santana's repertoire and rock audiences, they formed a link to Puente and his East Coast brothers, opening the door for the international embrace of this music (Stevie Winwood, for example, played guitar at the Fania All-Stars salsa gig in 1976 at the Lyceum, London). In addition, the early sixties boogaloo beats popularized by Mongo Santamaria and Ray Barretto (from Tito Puente's band) included such songs as "Soul Drummers," "Acid," "Hard Hands," "Watermelon Man," and "El Watusi" (an English pop chart hit in 1963), illustrating how Afro-Cuban rhythms and American pop music could be successfully combined, paving the way for Latin rock's fusions.

Cal Tjader's influence ranks as a precursor to the Santana and Malo and Latin rock wave. Vibraphonist Tjader started with George Shearing and recorded several 10-inch discs with jazzman Dave Brubeck. He became fascinated with the structure and syncopation of Latin rhythms and formulated a smooth, lyrical jazz that became known as the "West Coast Latin" sound. In 1952 he hired timbalero Benny Velarde, a Panamanian who'd arrived in San Francisco

---

[2] Chepito Areas, with The Aliens, had already included the song in their sets at Mission district clubs.

Photo: Unknown

Cal Tjader, exponent of cool West Coast Afro-Latin jazz; many great percussionists went through his ranks — Mongo Santamaria, Pete Escovedo, Willie Bobo, Armando Peraza, etc.

Photo: Courtesy Nat Cohen at Latin Percussion

Willie Bobo, bandleader and timbalero, played with Tito Puente, Cal Tjader, Santana in 1971, and fronted his own bands.

at age sixteen and graduated from Mission High School (alma mater of most of the members of Malo and Santana and other renowned students and graduates, including Maya Angelou, the world famous poet and writer).

"At that time there were few Latin percussionists in California," Velarde says. "Me and Tito [Puente] and Willie Bobo, who was in Tito's band, were good friends in New York in 1951. I was in [Tjader's] original group from 1952 to 1957. At the time we were doing mambo and guaracha music." In 1954, Fantasy Records contracted with Tjader, beginning a relationship that led to more than 30 records. Tjader signed with Creed Taylor and Verve in the early sixties to record more great sides, including "Soul Sauce (Gauchi Guara)," a hip favorite amongst the Latin and acid jazz fraternity. Latin musicians such as Candido Camero, Armando Peraza, Tito Puente, Eddie Palmieri, and Benny Velarde played with him over the years. Tjader's slant on Latin-based jazz is one of the roots of Santana's music.

Later, the musicians themselves began to cross over. During the late 1970s and early 1980s, Santana's roster included Cuban bongocero Armando Peraza (of Cal Tjader's band) and timbaleros Orestes Vilato (previously with Ray Barretto) and Pete Escovedo, who'd honed his chops in Oakland with the Carlos Federico band. Both Hadley Caliman and Luis Gasca were on Tjader's front line as horn players and straddle both the Latin jazz and Latin rock periods. Michael Henderson was the young bassist brought into Miles Davis's band after working with Stevie Wonder and on Miles Davis's *On the Corner* sessions. He was also found popping up on *Blessings in Disguise*, an unreleased solo album by Santana's Mike Shrieve. For just one example of how one musician impacted three totally different, hip musical areas, listen to the deluxe edition of Marvin Gaye's *Let's Get It On* for the

Benny Velarde, one of the first percussionists.

Photo: Courtesy Benny Velarde

Photo: Courtesy Pete Escovedo

Pete Escovedo, vocalist, percussionist, fronted the Escovedo Brothers with brother Thomas "Coke" and Phil on bass.

Gregg Rolie, Santana vocalist and keyboardist/arranger, developed a highly original Hammond B3 organ sound as both soloist and for the big Lesley-driven sound for Santana's melodic/rhythmic attack.

instrumental "Mandota," in which Marvin's music heads into Santana territory with dreamy guitar atmospherics courtesy of Hamilton Bohannon's band, anchored by the redoubtable bass of Michael Henderson[3].

The early Santana band spearheaded Latin rock's initial wave. Named after guitarist Carlos Santana, the band's first self-titled album was released in October 1969, just as the freewheeling, acid-dropping sixties drew to a close. It featured a fusion of Santana's hot electric guitar solos, Gregg Rolic's bluesy organ and lead vocals, a three-prong Latin percussion section featuring Mike Shrieve on traps, José "Chepito" Areas on timbales and Michael Carabello on congas, and an underpinning of David Brown's sturdy bass. The tracks included extended instrumentals such as "Persuasion," a rocking remake of "Jingo," a West African chant popularized on Michael Olatunji's *Drums of Passion* (a popular selection in the African dance classes then proliferating in the Bay Area), and tough, street-smart music such as "Soul Sacrifice" and the hit "Evil Ways." The rhythm palette had a sensuous, body-shaking feel drawn from the deep roots of Afro-Caribbean percussion. It was, for rock and roll, both highly original and rhythmically uncompromising. Overnight, Santana's music made a lot of rock music's more monotonous 4/4 rhythms seem redundant.

Malo also arrived in this first blaze and expanded the textures and rhythmic possibilities of this hybrid music, which incorporated elements of Latin, Cuban, funk, blues, rock, soul, calypso, pop, and flat-out scorching acid guitar. The use of hot guitarists with a base rooted in the blues, but also heavily influenced by the psychedelic space rock of Jimi Hendrix and Sly Stone, cemented the music's appeal to the broader white audience, and grew popular alongside their San Francisco contemporaries, such as the Grateful Dead, Jefferson Airplane, Country Joe and the Fish (and others too humorous to mention). Whereas some of these bands had a stoned, laid-back approach to their craft, Santana and Malo had no such reservations.

"Latin rock had a huge influence on a whole generation of people," says music producer Gregg Landau, who had watched the scene develop and played with the Quintana brothers in a group called The Ghetto. "Salsa was more danceable, if you had learned the steps, but Latin rock was more linked to the earlier Chicano rock scene. Outside of California, people didn't quite get the Latin rock thing. It was a cultural hybrid way before the 'world music' scene was being mixed up. San Francisco and Los Angeles had it, the Southwest, Texas, Arizona, and Mexico—places where people speak Spanish and English. New York was a different kind of fusion. You still have a style that's particular to the Bay area. There wasn't a lotta room for the middle ground. You either made it or you didn't."

---

[3] Marvin Gaye had also introduced the conga drum to the *What's Going On* album and guiro and tumbao patterns in the "Right On" track on that same album.

VIVA TIRADO / EAST L.A.

Other acts in the 1970s and beyond would incorporate elements of the Latin sound to great effect. Mention should be made here of the highly influential El Chicano band from East Los Angeles. Evolving from the VIPs and under the management of Eddie Davis, they scored a US hit with Gerald Wilson's "Viva Tirado." Charting at No. 28 on the *Billboard Top 100* in May 1970, it was apparently the first US single to simultaneously chart in all popular music categories. Bobby Espinosa's carousel organ-playing drove the top layer of this continuously exciting band, along with Mickey Lespron's and Jerry Salas's guitars, Freddie Sanchez's bass, the percussion of Andre Baeza and Rudy Regalado with the trap drums of John De Luna. Espinosa's Hammond B3 keyboard approach, along with that of Santana's Gregg Rolie, must be singled out for their highly individual influence on the nascent Latino rock scene.

As did Santana, El Chicano had an ongoing line in groovy cover versions. Their *Celebración* album featured "Senor Blues" by Horace Silver, "In a Silent Way" by Joe Zawinul (obviously inspired by Santana's live sets), and a great Latinized version of Cream's "I Feel Free." Their *Cinco* album featured diverse covers of "El Cayuco" by Tito Puente, "Ahora Si" by Ray Barretto, and "Little Sunflower" by Freddie Hubbard. Releasing nine albums on MCA Records, their initial run lasted well into the late seventies.

Bobby Espinosa, another original Hammond/keyboards player, whose solo organ sound drove the El Chicano band.

Freddie Sanchez, Mickey Lespron, and Andre Baeza of El Chicano in the middle of an interview.

El Chicano main men, Top: Andre Baeza
Front left: Bobby Espinosa
Front right: Mickey Lespron

All photos on this spread: Courtesy El Tecolote

Additional purveyors of Latinismo included Mandrill (featuring the mighty Wilson brothers from the Bed-Stuyvesant area of New York on hot cuts "Mango Meat," "Hágalo," and "Cohelo"), War, and the jazz-Latin fusion sound of Caldera, along with artists such as Earth, Wind and Fire, Gato Barbieri, and Sergio Mendes. In East Los Angeles, The Village Callers made an earlier version of Sonny Henry's "Evil Ways," which later became an international hit after being lifted as the first single from Santana's debut album. Thee Midnighters and Cannibal and the Headhunters ushered in the later sound of Macondo (who grew out of The Romancers group), Yaqui, Tango, Redbone, Queztal (who now have re-releases on Arista out in Japan), El Chicano, Tierra, and more recently Cruzados, Los Illegals, and Los Lobos. In England, Osibisa were the dopester's delight. Their heavy fusion of African rhythms allied to catchy riffs supplied a cool backdrop to whatever high was happening in the audiences in the early seventies. There were a few other bands influenced by Santana's success. Gonzales, regularly found Upstairs at Ronnie Scott's Jazz Club, had a nice slant on the Latin although it never really broke out beyond the London club scene. Cuban bands like Irakere were Ronnie Scott's regulars, blowing the crowds away during sold-out, two-week stints. Paz, Cayenne, and Spiteri blended salsa, funk, and jazz-fusion in the tight homegrown scene. Batti Mamselle, featuring the young and outrageously talented drummer Richard Bailey (who went on to play on *Wired* by Jeff Beck and with Jan Hammer), was a stew of Trinidadian steel drums, hooked to a fantastic rhythm section. A superb live act, they lasted long enough to record the *I See the Light* album on Cube Records in 1974 before collapsing, as the initial scene in Britain and the States for Latin-style fusion was beginning to wane.

Arcelio Garcia Jr vocalizes and Mike Carabello plays timbales as guests on onstage with the Limbo band at the Nite Life, 1970.

Photos on this spread: Johnny Valenzuela

MY LOVE: THE MALIBUS

Mission Street was the center of the world for Michael Carabello and Arcelio Garcia. "Everything was six blocks away in any direction," Carabello recalls. "I knew Arcelio from the San Francisco Boys Club, the Mission branch. We hung out there. We both went to Bryant Elementary School. Seals Stadium for baseball was nearby, where Joe DiMaggio used to play.

"Arcelio's mother had this restaurant and my stepdad hung there; he played guitar and everybody knew everybody. All the Latin baseball players would go there to eat–people like Orlando Cepeda, like José Pagan, Roberto Clemente, who played for the Pittsburgh Pirates. The Alou brothers, they all hung there for the Puerto Rican and Cuban food. Arcelio was such a great baseball player. He was ready to play the majors at age fourteen. We used to sneak into the San Francisco Giants games all the time. He was my connection to the Giants and the San Francisco Seals. He was getting inspiration from all these great baseball players. His brother Pete played great too. His other brother, Ramon, was into horse racing."

Arcelio Garcia Jr sings on with Limbo at the Nite Life.

Photos: Richard Bean collection/Percy Pinckney

An earlier incarnation of Malo plays Battle of the Bands in 1971. (L to R) Ismael Versosa on organ, Richard Bean on timbales, Carlos Gomez on rhythm guitar, Jorge Santana on lead guitar, and Dave Guzman plays drums.

Malo featuring rare picture of Arcelio Garcia Jr playing trumpet, Carlos Gomez on guitar, and Richard Bean plays saxophone. Jorge Santana is behind Bean in background.

Malo jumping for joy at Bernal Heights, San Francisco, 1970. (L to R at back) Dave Guzman, Ricky Parker, Richard Bean, Arcelio Garcia Jr., Ismael Versosa, Carlos Gomez (front), Pablo Tellez, and Jorge Santana.

Carabello and the Garcia brothers played on the Horace Mann Junior High School teams. Not only was Garcia a whiz on the diamond, he attracted attention off the field as well. Childhood friend Johnny Valenzuela recalls a scene at the Latin baseball league's annual picnic. "We were eleven years old, playing baseball for my dad; they had a team in San Francisco. We would go the annual picnic. In 1965, I think, I was at the picnic, and all of a sudden, I hear this music and this voice and there he was, singin' [tunes by] James Brown and Question Mark and the Mysterians. There was this dynamic young Latin guy, doing splits on the floor, just doing a show at this simple family picnic. Arcelio was a consummate performer—he had a crowd around him, around the pool."

Arcelio so enjoyed his role as entertainer that he failed to attend to school grades. His mother would quiz him about the D and F grades that covered his report cards, which he ingeniously explained away as an indication he was Doing Fine, or D F-ing, as he called it.

An injury put a stop to Garcia's hope of a sports career. "At first I wanted to be a ball player and I played till I got hurt," he says. "It's funny how it all started because after I got hurt, these friends of mine were singing and hanging at the house. They were buggin' me to sing, because their baritone had just gone to jail. I'm saying, 'I can't sing.' We started foolin' around, singing on the corner; we did a couple of talent shows. I was just singing background. We were singing in front of my house one day, on the steps; this guy pulls up in a car, comes up, listens to what we were doing and approaches me: 'Do I wanna be in a band?' This guy's name was Mauricio Salinas and he was leading a band called the Fabulous Malibus. He started teaching me how to hold my notes, and I guess the rest is history."

Arcelio's brother Pete remembers those early days with the Malibus: "We were hanging out at Lucky Alley, singing a cappella, with Mauricio and Jimmy Salinas. Then they started off playing in a little garage, just five guys fooling around. Mike Carabello lived at our house for about three years—my mom 'adopted' him. We all used to hang in a Latino gang called the Barts [who covered the territory from Potrero Street up to Mission Street]. The band started playing at the Mission YMCA[4] dances. I can remember we won every Battle of the Bands contest. The last major Battle of the Bands we played, in I think 1970, the Intruders were on the bill; they'd had a couple of hits out there but we beat them. We also played with another band called Freddie and the Stone Souls.[5] At that time the Mission district also hosted a large black music scene at places like the Little Bo-Peep before the neighborhood's ethnic

changeover to a more Hispanic community. [Freddie and the Stone Souls] were one of the hottest acts around—that was Sly Stone's brother—but we ended up with top band. We took it all."

Malibus promo picture

Pete Gallegos, a long-time Mission district resident, recalls: "The Malibus played the high school dances. They were a straight-up R&B group. Arcelio had his hair greased back. He had a conk with a do-rag to keep your conk in shape, or all that grease is gonna' get messed up. [The do-rag] could also be used to wrap around your knuckles, if you wanted to hit somebody."

By that time Mauricio Salinas had gotten married and joined the Army. Garcia took over as lead singer of what was now called The Fabulous Malibus. Bass player Billy Areno and guitarist Mauricio Areno were the next to be claimed

---

[4]   Young Men's Christian Association

[5]   At that time the Mission district also hosted a large black music scene at places like the Little Bo-Peep before the neighborhood's ethnic changeover to a more Hispanic community.

by the now escalating war in Vietnam. After they too enlisted, Garcia tried several replacement bassists with no success. Then he ran into Pablo Tellez.

Tellez had arrived from Central America with his family in 1966. He had formed a small group, The Gettyups, with another high school friend, and had been performing for about three years when he met Garcia.

"For many years I tried to develop something unique, something of my own, different ways of plucking the bass," Tellez relates. "My influences were very much the Motown sound, the cleanness and sharpness of the bass playing. Also, on the Latin side what really got me was the playing of Cachao [Lopez, a Cuban bassist who co-led the orchestra Las Maravillas de Arcaño with his brother Orestes Lopez]. Somehow I felt that the Latin playing of Cachao, mixed with the Motown sound, kinda fit, so I started trying to develop a unique sound of my own. I was a very rhythmic player but I also liked that cleanness of the notes—to be really definite but at the same time not to be so strict, to have a mood of its own, rhythmic, melodic, but a staccato style of playing."

Tellez was staying with his parents, but eventually he and Garcia became roommates, sharing an apartment on 20th Street for the next three years. The bassist would become central to the Malo sound. Garcia also brought in a new percussionist, Ricky Parker. With Ismael Versosa on keyboard, Carlos Gomez on guitar, and vocalist Richard Bean from the original Malibus configuration, the group was ready to go mano-a-mano with the competition.

Richard Bean, a typical Mission mix of Scottish, Portuguese, French, and Indian, had played in various bands such as The Dynamics (which featured Carlos Santana during their 10th grade at Mission High), Jet (with Jorge Santana), The Righteous Ones, and Wizard (with Abel Zarate), and Casanova (with Mike Judge, a creator of "Beavis and Butthead"). "I got involved in music when I was fourteen years old. I played sax at Pelton Junior High and also Horace Mann. My brother Joe also

The Dynamics at the Spanish Club dance, December 18th 1964. (L to R) Carlos Santana (guitar), Richard Bean (saxophone), Danny Haro (drums), Gus Rodriguez (bass), and Andy (sax).

Photo: Courtesy Richard Bean

Righteous Ones promo pic.

Photo: D. Margonon, Courtesy Richard Bean

Ismael Versosa, Billy Areno, Mayor Joe Alioto, Richard Bean take some photos at Youth For Services Center in 1968.

played saxophone in junior high. One of my first bands was The Righteous Ones; Abel Zarate was in that band with me. We were doing Top 40 stuff. We were pretty popular, doing the Stones and Animals material. After this I joined the Malibus. They had a singer called Tommy Guadalupe and there was Marty Gonzalez, the guitar player, and his brother Jimmy was the drummer. The bass player was Billy Areno and I was playing sax. Tommy decided to battle his own band, called the Continentals, an Asian band, against the Malibus. We were the Hispanics, right! We did battle at the Mission Y [against] our own singer in the other band. So I started to learn the songs and we battled them and we beat them. Tommy wanted to come back but that was the end of that."

Percy Pinckney was the Malibus' first manager. "I ran up on the Malibus in the early days. I personally really liked Arcelio. I had a house in Daly City and they practiced in my basement. Of course, the neighbors were calling the police about the noise and giving me the blues. They were very irate and wanted to ban us.

"I bought their first set of instruments. I liked the fact they were real serious about practice. I'd have about five or six songs; they'd practice over and over. We created our own events, like dances at the YMCA. I was able to get them on TV, and through two weeks on 'Happening 68' they got some national exposure. They got right through to the finals. Arcelio was smart, a bit more mature; you put him up before a crowd, he'd want to get it on! They'd be doing shit like 'Cold Sweat' by James Brown, 'It's Not Unusual' by Tom Jones, 'Your Precious Love' by Jerry Butler, stuff like 'Ain't Too Proud to Beg' by the Temptations—incredibly versatile repertoire."

As Richard Bean remembers: "We were involved in Youth for Service and we went on the Battle of the Bands, [and] on a TV program called 'Happening 68' that was hosted by the Dave Clark Five. We made it to the finals and this was with bands from all over the States. We had gold sequined jackets; we thought they were the coolest—they sparkled pretty good. Arcelio was doing all the James Brown-type moves; he was a real great front man. We lost to a girl band from Texas called the Heartbeats.

"Percy Pinckney was the Malibus' manager at the time. He was quite a character[6]. He loved the ladies. He had girlfriends all over the place, fighting over him. He was a debonair guy; he wasn't the best looking guy but the girls sure loved him. We had a road manager called Mike 'The T-Bone.' Percy decided we needed to put out a single. The band changed: Billy Areno was still on bass and Ricky Parker had gone. Ismael Versosa came in on keyboards; he was also from the Mission.

---

[6] Pinckney was no stranger to show business. He had been in a group called The Imperials and was cousin to Bobby Freeman, the black rocker whose first hit was "Do You Wanna Dance" in 1958.

"We started to learn this tune, 'My Love.' I wrote the words. I'd already written 'Suavecito' in algebra class, during eleventh and twelfth grade—I flunked [algebra] twice. Originally they were poems; it helped that I was in love at the time. I think Percy got Youth for Service to spring for [the recording]. We all got 45 copies of the single and Percy was selling these at the gigs."

As happens so often in the entertainment business, just as the group was about to break through they left their first manager, lured away by bigger and better promises. "They fell through the crack with somebody else," Pinckey says. "He conned them away from me. I think in the long run, they were poorly managed and promoted; that hurt them more than anything else."

The Righteous Ones, who specialized in playing all the "head music" from England.

All photos on this spread: D. Margonon, Courtesy Richard Bean

Richard Bean with The Righteous Ones.

Carlos Santana, developing the bridge between the blues, soul, Latino-rock, and Afro-Cuban with the young Santana band.

Photo: Joan Chase

EVERYTHING IS COMING OUR WAY

Photo: Courtesy El Tecolote

Don Jose Santana, father of
Carlos and Jorge Santana.

The Santana family arrived in the Mission early in 1963 after a journey that took them from the poverty of rural Mexico to the border town jive of Tijuana. Family patriarch José Santana was a seasoned mariachi who supplemented the family's income by playing at weddings, baptisms, and quinceñiera parties. José's son Carlos was often pressed into service. His father gave him an L5 Gibson electric guitar when he was twelve. "I first got involved with music through my father," Carlos says. "He was a musician and his father before him was a musician. My father taught me the guitar, violin, and how to read music. The first thing I heard as a child was Trio Los Dandys and Cuco Sanchez, music like that. Then later on in Tijuana, I learned about Chuck Berry, T-Bone Walker, BB King."

Jorge Santana in the early Malo days.

Photo: Rudy Rodriguez

Recalls younger brother Jorge: "With a big family, four girls and three boys, we always played music… we had musicians in the household, so we were exposed to music all the time." The Santana boys' school was the border city's streets, strip clubs, and bars, all of which offered valuable lessons in la vida loca of a musician's life.

"Tijuana is a pressure town," says Carlos. "The pressure of living there, trying to cross the border, the music on the street and lifestyle, it's like the *Star Wars* cantina. It really is like that."

When he moved his family north, Don José found a vibrant mariachi scene at The Sinaloa Club, a restaurant cabaret on Market Street, at the weekend dances at the Centro Social Obrero and the now-defunct Mariachi Club at Mission and Army (now named Cesar Chavez Street). Don José Santana helped anchor the Mexican presence in the Mission district when people still held mariachi masses at Mission Dolores Church.

Meanwhile, his children were growing up in the cultural melange of the Mission district's America and its musical soundtrack. "When I was younger, I was very narrow minded; I was just into straight-ahead black blues. I thought jazz was boring cocktail music," Carlos Santana recalls. "Then when I got to San Francisco, I discovered Gabor Szabo. He is a spellbinder. His music is such an inspiration, so melodic, so spacial and intimate. Gabor opened my ears to other musicians—Miles Davis, Wes Montogomery, and many others.

"I respect all the music I heard before the blues. When I heard the blues it was more naked. Strangely enough we used to work in strip joints playing the blues. We'd play for an hour and then the strippers would do their thing for an hour. All the music I heard before that was always coated with plastic, whether it's from Hollywood, Las Vegas, or Mexico City. Don't get me wrong; there are a lot of people who play the blues like Cuco Sanchez, Los Indio Tabajaras, and many others that is not plastic. [But] anytime I saw people playing and singing stiff in tuxedos, to me it was plastic, where the blues was just naked.

Photo: Courtesy El Tecolote.

Mission students hanging out after school

"For me the blues were what punk music is today. Punk people would rather listen to their music than to Barry Manilow. The blues was our way of being punks. For us the epitome of being a rebel was to listen to John Lee Hooker or Muddy Waters, not to Fabian or Frankie Avalon. The 1950s and 1960s gave birth to a lot of renegades. The blues epitomized the hippest thing, along with certain jazz musicians like John Coltrane and of course Miles."

Richard Bean, a vocalist with the Malibus, remembers playing with Carlos Santana while in tenth grade. "I think it was Top 40 stuff, a five-piece band called the Dynamics. Danny Haro was the drummer and Gus Rodriguez was the bassist. They both worked at La Palmas, the market. Me and my friend Andy Vargas, who played sax, we hung out there all the time. Carlos was looking for a couple of horn players. Carlos was a pretty humble guy and very talented even then. We performed at a Mission High School dance. Gus and Danny weren't that serious and Carlos was upset about it and the band broke up; it lasted only a few months. I had taken up vocals with the Malibus."

As did the Malibus, Carlos's band drew notice at organized competitions such as the Battle of the Bands sponsored by radio station KYA. "I remember walking into the gym at St. Ignatius High School," says Carlos. "It seemed like an army of bands were there. Out of a thousand bands they eliminated five hundred straight away. They all sounded like three things: The Rolling Stones, The Beatles, and Van Morrison. We stayed in the heat with [a vocalist named] Joyce Dunn, who went to Lowell High School. We didn't have a vocalist then, so we backed her. The rest of the band was Gus Rodrigues and Danny Haro. We were playing blues, stuff like 'Steal Away' and 'Heatwave.' This was around 1964 or '65."

At the time, Carlos was a student at Mission High School, but most of his education was gleaned at the Fillmore Auditorium, the rock palace operated by promoter Bill Graham, who was booking national rock and blues acts as well as introducing some exciting local musicians.

"I had some fine teachers at Mission High School, but they were few and far between," Santana says. "I used to cut school a lot and go the Fillmore. Being at the Fillmore was the ultimate PhD—seeing Charles Lloyd, John Handy, Bola Sete, Jimi Hendrix, Muddy Waters, The Young Rascals, The Doors, Buddy Rich. The Fillmore was real education. If you hung out at the Fillmore for a week you didn't have to go the Berklee School of Music if you really listened and learned what they're doing. That's where I got my main education I think."

It was at the Fillmore that Carlos got his break. The young guitarist was quickly making a name for himself at impromptu gigs at street fairs and "Summer of Love" festivals.

"A friend asked Bill Graham if I could sit in on a jam night. It was Michael Bloomfield, Grateful Dead, Jefferson Airplane, Quicksilver Messenger Service—a lot of bands were just jamming because Paul Butterfield didn't show up and Charles Lloyd had already did his thing. So my friend tells Bill Graham that I'm a kid from Tijuana who loves BB King, who can play. So he pointed me to Bloomfield and said, 'If it's cool with him, it's cool with me.' Bloomfield looked at me and said, 'Go ahead; there's my guitar.' So I grabbed it. Michael and Bill heard me and they started asking questions and got interested in my band. That's where we hooked up with Bill. He always believed in us. I guess it reminds him of New York's Spanish Harlem and he claims

Mike Carabello fused his own original street slant on Afro-Cuban conga styles and represents the first Latin *conguero* to achieve international fame.

Photo: Joan Chase

our music [as his own]. I'm very grateful to him. He's my brother."

Although the young guitarist's talent was evident from the start, the sound that would become Latin rock took some time to evolve. As do many budding artists, Santana emulated his heroes, and his first efforts consisted of covers of his favorite blues artists. Fortunately, each musician who cycled through the band contributed concepts and attitude that would be fundamental to the Santana sound. Not until band members began to mix the wail of the blues with the rhythms they heard—and played—in the streets, did they hit upon a gold mine of originality.

"It took time to build the band because, at that time, I was playing mainly songs by Paul Butterfield from the *East West* album," Carlos says. "Our sound or identity was not right. But the next time I played at the Fillmore, it was with our own group and our own vision. We had learned a lot from a lot of people to make our own sound.

"We used to go Aquatic Park and check out the conguero players and saw how the congas affected people. So we figured if we played some blues with some Afro-Cuban or street conga drums it would make people do different things. We mainly called it the Santana Blues Band because we couldn't think of a better name and everybody in the band agreed that my name had a ring to it. I was playing blues 24 hours a day it seemed like."

Photo: Joan Chase

David Brown added a heavy bass style and played in the many styles needed to stoke the fire of Santana's rhythm section.

The original Santana Blues Band included Carlos, organist Gregg Rolie, Danny Haro on traps, Gus Rodriguez on bass, and Michael Carabello on congas. Carabello had met Carlos at the Aquatic Park jam sessions. When Carlos was hospitalized with tuberculosis in 1967, Carabello brought him a tape player and recordings by Gabor Szabo. Once Carlos latched on to an idea, he could pursue it with something close to obsession, Carabello found.

"I had one conga drum and we'd play 'La Bamba' and 'Chim Chim Cheree' in 6/8," he says. "Santana just rehearsed every day, all the time, birthdays, holidays. First we rehearsed on Potrero Hill, in a garage below these apartments. We brought plywood to put on the floor, because it was just dirt. You could barely stand up in this place."

Carabello stopped rehearsing while Carlos was in the hospital. Marcus Malone, a "showboat" player from the Aquatic Park scene who contributed an African underpinning to the band's sound, replaced him.

"The band didn't embrace the Latin thing until Gregg Rolie and I started hanging out with Marcus Malone," says Carlos Santana. "We met him through Stan Marcum and Ron Estrada, who were our first managers. They found him at Aquatic Park. Marcus was a street mutt, just like Santana's music.

"We were embracing Eddie Harris, stuff like Les McCann. Then we started integrating the Olantunji thing with Gabor Szabo. We were listening to Big Black, Chico Hamilton—but we felt there were too many blues bands. We were doing *Mary Poppins* songs and with the congas our music sounded very distinct, rather than [like] Mike Bloomfield or Jefferson Airplane. We were doing 'My Favorite Things' in three-quarter time, and that stood out immediately in San Francisco. Nobody was doing that except for maybe the Grateful Dead.

"We hooked up with David Brown around then, we found him at a club on Grant Street in North Beach and we wrote 'Soul Sacrifice.' When we found Michael Shrieve it really gelled. Gregg Rolie was totally into the Beatles and the Stones. Carabello was into Jimi Hendrix and Sly Stone. David Brown liked Albert King, Otis Redding; he liked the Stax stuff. Michael Shrieve was into John Coltrane and Miles Davis. I was into blues, John Lee Hooker, Eddie Palmieri, and Tito Puente. This is what we brought to the table.

"We transcended a lot of groups in San Francisco. I don't say that arrogantly, but they were like a car that only had one or two gears— folk and rock. But we had many, many gears, man! When you start going up the hill, you need a lot of gears."

Photo: Coni Night Loon Beeson

Marcus Malone, with Santana, before being jailed for murder. Pictured is Bob "Doc" Livingstone, whose drum seat was taken over by Michael Shrieve.

The group began climbing the hill in earnest, although their lack of experience didn't impress everyone. When they opened for Frumious Bandersnatch at the Straight Theater on Haight Street, road manager Herbie Herbert remembers he wasn't moved by their sound. "They were very Afro at that point. This is when they had Doc Livingstone on drums and Marcus Malone on congas. Doc Livingstone and I were good friends; we used to hang out at our communal house in Lafayette. I wasn't that impressed by Santana at first."

Malone was the first of the original band to crash and burn just before the re-named Santana band recorded its first album. Malone had grown up in Hunter's Point and lived with his mother on Potrero Hill. "If you closed your eyes and dreamt up Hollywood all the way, it was Marcus," says Herbie Herbert. "He was a quintessential pimp: superfly clothes, Cadillac convertible, big hat, and two babes on his arms at all times. Totally Gangster Lou—if he were cruising the streets of Compton or Watts today, he'd be like Mack Daddy. He would always be the last one to show for the gigs, but he was a great entertainer."

Malone's mackin' image would finally get the best of him. He was visiting a girlfriend one night when her husband came home to find them together. In the ensuing struggle, Malone defended himself with a knife; the husband was stabbed. Malone was arrested on assault with intent to kill. When the other man died after three successive operations at in San Francisco's County Hospital, Malone's charge was changed to first degree murder. He stayed in jail until 1973.

Michael Carabello was living on Florida Street in the Mission. He'd often stop by the home of a Santana roadie to play congas. "He says, 'Did you hear what happened last night? Santana's conga player got busted for attempted murder. Why don't you go see them?'" Carabello re-joined the band just in time to record the first album.

Another key element in the band that would be Santana was drummer Chepito Areas. "The supreme metronome," Carlos calls him. Before coming to the states from Nicaragua, Areas was already a seasoned musician who'd toured with

A rare shot of Jose "Chepito" Areas, seen here playing trumpet.

Photo: Joan Chase

his uncle's band Los Satelites de Nicaragua. Music producer Gregg Landau, who lived in Nicaragua for ten years, notes that the band reflected a sound typical on that country's airwaves, but as yet unknown on California's West Coast. "On the radio there they had a different take; [you heard] real traditional Cuban music on the radio. Chepito had that, plus funk, Brazilian, plus his 6/8 timings from traditional Nicaraguan bullfight music. Los Satelites were a clone of that Cuban band Sonora Mantancera; they toured all over Europe."

Areas's first instrument was trumpet, but he was equally at home on all manner of percussion—"Very simply, he was the best musician with perfect meter," Gregg Rolie would later say. According to Jesse "Chuy" Varela, a well-known DJ and host of KPFA-FM's weekly lowrider show, "La Onda Bajita," Areas first won Bay Area recognition "doing Perez Prado stuff" on the horn. "He had also played with Cesar Ascarrunz. Cesar had a band called Cesar y sus Locos [the house band at his North Beach nightclub, Cesar's]. Cesar was from Bolivia; a piano player, he was into the Cal Tjader thing, and that's when people started to realize how talented Chepito was."

Later, Areas joined the Aliens, a Top 40 cover band with a solid following at the Nite Life, an old Nickelodeon theater-turned-club owned by Johnny Cortade. "Benedict Arnold and the Traitors were one of my first bands. They drew a large crowd. Over in Marin County, I heard [a group with] Frank Zavala—he was the singer; Chepito was there, Julio Savalo was the manager, and they were called the Aliens. People lined up around the block to see them," remembers Cortade. "In the Mission they were the hottest."

In addition to lead singer Frank Zavala, the Aliens consisted of brothers Mike and William Guillermo on guitar and vibes, Areas on trumpet and percussion, and a conga player named Willie Colon (not to be confused with the New York trombonist of the same name). What captured listeners were their references to the Latin jazz coming out of New York and influencing the California jazz scene.

"People were looking for their cultural identity," says Pete Gallegos. "The Aliens introduced some Tito Puente, some Cal Tjader with the vibes. They had straight-up rock guitars. They had funky cumbia influences. You could be in the Nite Life and dance to a straight-up cumbia, followed by Creedence Clearwater, like 'Born on the Bayou' with congas. Everybody just went with the flow."

"The Aliens had a rhythm like Santana did but they didn't have the guitar like Carlos Santana would play," says Pablo Tellez. "They had a nice, beautiful, round fat sound; a beautiful band to listen to. Cliff [Anderson, on congas] was excellent and very knowledgeable about salsa-style beats, and we also had him in the Malibus. He was a great showman and really great fun on stage. Chepito really knew what a solo meant, and he had the power to carry it out."

Johnny Valenzuela, a young percussionist who later played in a Santana cover band called Soul Sacrifice recalls the Aliens as "about the best unsigned band. We kept hearing about this great little player; people were saying this guy blows everyone away. I heard they were better than Santana. Then I hear they'd lost their timbales player to Santana."

Photo: Johnny Valenzuela

The young Johnny Valenzuela plays timbales in a cool outfit.

Carabello was instrumental to Areas's inclusion in the Santana band. "I was at [the now defunct amusement park] Playland at the Beach. We'd go there to play drums; it was quite competitive. We were introduced to Chepito, who sat in and it was, 'Oh my God, this guy plays his ass off!' I was living with Carlos and Gregg [Rolie] then and took them to see Chepito playing at the Nite Life. Chepito and Carlos spoke Spanish to each other very well." Johnny Cortade remembers Carlos Santana coming into the Nite Life after that, carrying his tape recorder and standing in front of the stage, "checking them out."

Like Marcus Malone, Areas's personal style was as wild as his playing. Herbie Herbert (who would become Santana's road manager) remembers him "fresh off the fuckin' boat, acne, short, slicked-back pachuco-style hair, couldn't hardly speak a word of English. Here's the guy, a monster musician." And according to Gregg Rolie: "When Chepito first came in [the band], he was driving a Cadillac, [had] pinkie rings with a pompadour." But he took his job seriously, insists Johnny Villanueva, who worked alongside Herbert as road manager. Areas was "the best trap drummer in Central America… always an hour early for rehearsal."

David Brown, Santana's original bassist, brought an African-American facet to the band's music. Brown lived in the Bayview area of San Francisco, and shared the same neighborhood and a church upbringing along with Sly Stone. Like Arcelio Garcia, Brown was a young athlete, recalls his younger sister Jan Cameron. "He won first place in the All-City High Jump Championships in high school. Later on he became a second-degree black belt in karate. Also he was an avid archer. He was also really into cars and he used to ride Harleys a lot with the local Hell's Angels."

Brown's father was a Baptist minister. His grandmother played piano in the church and the whole family sang in the church choir. As he grew older, he took on the bass parts. He was well versed in the gospel idiom, but he was exposed to jazz as well. His uncle, Oscar Preston, was a local jazz pianist, and keyboardist Billy Preston (who played on the Beatles' "Get Back" sessions) is a second cousin. According to his sister Jan, Brown loved doo-wop, and formed a local band called the Soul Distributors when he was 14 years old. He was playing in clubs in San Francisco's North Beach area, backing touring acts such as the Four Tops, when Santana manager Stan Marcum heard him and invited him to join the band.

David Brown and sister Diane.

Photo: Jim McCarthy

Photos: Diane Black and Jan Cameron

David Brown's first band, The Soul Distributors, 1966.
Back: David Brown, Paul Harris (with glasses), Leotis Foster.
Middle: Horace Richmond, Michael Greer. Front: Steve Marshall.

Michael Shrieve, Santana's original drummer, was a trailblazer in this musical melting pot. His fiery blend of jazz and rock drumming chops, coupled with his appealing street urchin appearance, made him a natural personality for Santana's line-up. Shrieve had developed an early gift for the drums: "I was already playing a lot of jazz and R&B, five nights a week, in a fifteen-piece soul band at the Nairobi Lounge in Palo Alto. We'd back BB King, Etta James when they came through. Then I'd do organ quartets."

Shrieve later played with a folk-rock outfit called Glass Menagerie, also in Palo Alto, south of San Francisco. He'd been offered a slot with Jefferson Airplane in 1969 (his first experience in an actual airplane found him flying to Los Angeles with Jorma Kakouken and Paul Casady when the Airplane was recording *Bathing at Baxter's*). Happily for Santana, things didn't work out between Shrieve and the Airplane. At a New Year's Eve gig in 1968, Santana drummer Doc Livingston had tumbled off his drum stool while playing, apparently drunk. A few weeks later, the band gave him his marching orders. Shrieve happened to be in the same studio complex where Santana was rehearsing and was invited to sit in a jam session. After playing all night, the chemistry was obvious. He was in.

Michael Shrieve

Organist Gregg Rolie co-founded Santana with Carlos and brought a complementary but different blues/fusion sensibility—a completely unique Hammond organ sound plus arranging skills and a confident lead vocal style to the young band. He took a roundabout route to the music business. He was living in suburban Palo Alto and planning to become an architect when the full force of the Vietnam War and the protests that followed prompted a complete change of direction. "I made a decision. I dropped out of school [to pursue music]. I gave myself five years to do it. Moving to San Francisco was a total change.

"When I first moved up to the Mission with the Santana band, we went to Aquatic Park and watched the conga players. It was a very enjoyable experience. It was never mean-spirited. I remember spending a lot of time getting Chepito's breaks down; I came from rock and blues music, so Latin breaks were difficult at first. My Hammond B3 style was a conglomerate of Jimmy Smith, violinists, slapping on the keyboard. My rig was just the loudest, like a foghorn. Says Mike Carabello: "Gregg had that big sound, not like the Doors, with their stupid, shitty little organ sound."

Adds Gregg, "It was an interesting culture clash joining Santana, meeting the guys in the band; we came from such different backgrounds, nobody understood anybody.[7] The guys in the Mission were more hardcore than I was used to. When I first showed up, they thought I was rich because I had a car. The music in the middle held it all together."

Gregg Rolie

Photos: Joan Chase

Noted Michael Shrieve: "Me and Gregg were curious objects to Carabello and Chepito when we first arrived in the Mission, [but] even though I came from the suburbs and looked like I was twelve, I was around a lot of black folks." So he had no trouble fitting in.

LA RAZA

"'Lowrider' is a generic term for people who fix their cars in a certain way," explains Pete Gallegos. Lowriders often, but not always, belonged to car clubs that operated as a loose fraternity. Characteristics of a lowrider vehicle generally include a suspension rigged for a bouncing effect and perhaps a lowered, or "chopped," frame so close to the ground the bumper almost scrapes the asphalt, attention-getting details such as wild paint jobs, chrome hub caps, and other personal touches, as on the ride belonging to Andy Pacheco, cousin of Jesse "Chuy" Varela: "He had a lowrider Corvair, man, that was a rare thing. He had a little record player that he had hooked up to the cigarette lighter. We would play 45s in this great car—a pearl-white Corvair with baby moon rims. Real nice upholstery, fur along the dash. Then as we got older, in high school, I got a '57 Chevy. I kept it stock and clean. That was the car that took us to the Fillmore, Winterland, and the gigs."

"There was a time when the lowrider scene got so big there were cars from 24th to 20th Streets [along Mission Street] just bumper to bumper," Gallegos recalls. "Cars coming down Mission from Daly City, cars from 16th Street coming up Mission; it became quite an event. People would be hanging all over on the street."

Photo: Courtesy El Tecolote

Lowriders

Through it all, Latin rock was the background music linking drivers and admirers, gangs and civilians. "We were aware of the market place, the lowrider scene in San José, the scene in Oakland," says Bill Perasso, who favored working one or two cuts from an album to appeal to a specific audience. Stores that blasted the music to reach the crowds hanging around outside helped his efforts. "In the Mission, the major record store was Musica Latina. Gene Kelly ran a store called Music 5 on Market Street; he had all the hip Latin records like Willie Bobo, Joe Cuba, and stuff from New York that sold through black radio. So in the Mission, music would be playing on outside street speakers; you'd get a lot of walk-in trade. It was hard at times to sell the West Coast-based Latin music, particularly in New York. People didn't understand it."

"Before Carlos and Malo, we were isolated into our own community," says Varela. "Malo did these benefits and we'd be there. We started to get enlightened. It was tribal. As the band evolved, Arcelio would be, for us, the bad-ass street dude that took no shit. Jorge was another great voice on the guitar. Francisco Aguabella was a real deep force, and Leo's playing would kick your ass. As the thing got bigger we'd cruise Story and King streets in San José. Thousands of people would cruise and we'd be playing Malo on our eight tracks. We were around seventeen then. The other place was Mission and 24th; also there was 23rd in Richmond and A Street in Hayward.

"After a while we were hippie lowriders. Sapo's 'I Can't Make It' was part of the soundtrack. We'd go to Dolores Park, see the drummers hanging out, people like Marcus Gordon—he was a Trinidadian guy and he came from Spanish Harlem. He brought that Willie Bobo stuff, but he had seen the real rumba scenes in the '60s with Carlos 'Patato' Valdes in New York. Also, the awakening was happening with the Black Power movement allied to Africa, and one of the things that came from that was the bata drum. Those black cats were playing bata first. One of the things Aguabella did was to play five congas at the same time; it was orchestral. It hipped people to fusion and jazz."

Photo: Courtesy El Tecolote

Constant tension between Latin youth and S.F. Police.

Francisco Aguabella

Photo: Courtesy El Tecolote

"When Santana and Malo impacted, it really changed the Mission," says Gallegos. "This is our culture, our neighborhood pride; it was such a thrill for people to hear what we were groovin' to every weekend. The fact it was in Spanish validated the language."

"After Carlos got into spiritualism, Malo really connected through the coasts," says Varela. "The lowrider wars began. The police wanted us to stop cruising'; they'd kick your fuckin' ass, man! After this it got hard everywhere—in San José, in LA; they closed Whittier Boulevard down, which was one of the main lowrider hangouts."

"Parking became prohibited; no left or right turns," adds Gallegos. "It became a battle between the police and lowriders. It was a standoff. Effectively, they shut it down. You always had clashes with the community and the police back in those days. I'm not sure if it's any better now."

Arcelio Garcia, Jr.

Photos: Rudy Rodriquez

STREET MAN

Arcelio Garcia Jr.

By 1969, the Malibus were building a following with their hybrid mix of James Brown and Latin percussion. In the process, they also created some unlikely alliances between Mission district gangs. Their first manager, Percy Pinckney, became acquainted with the band via his role as a Youth For Service worker. "We were a multiracial agency. We would try and unite the black, Latino, and Asian gangs, to stop the turf wars. [I was] intervening in young people's lives—people who'd got in trouble with the law, or were on probation.

Richard Spremich: Malo drummer

Night Life in the Mission after dark.

Photos: Courtesy El Tecolote

"There was a number of Mission Street gangs then, or 'clubs' as we called them. There was a gang group from Hunters Point, real bad boys called the Buccaneers. There was the Brave Bulls from out of the Fillmore district, and the Warlords from the Mission. One Asian gang who was notorious was called the Wah Chings. There was the White Shoes—they were considered the bad boys; they were a white gang. Arcelio Garcia was a member of the Barts. At that time the Mission was controlled by heavy gang activity. The gangs were turf motivated; Mission High was one of the battle scenes.

"[The Malibus] changed that culture, as it existed back then. They played a major social role in bringing these clubs together at these dances we held at the YMCA. They were able to attract all the racially diverse groups—as many blacks as Latinos would show up to see them. The crowds got so big, we moved to a bigger venue; and after that, we went on to Cecil Williams's Glide Memorial Church. They let us use the sanctuary there, then they started appearing on radio."

Around this time, Johnny Cortade, owner of the Nite Life dance club, heard the Malibus at a YMCA gig and hired them to play at his venue,

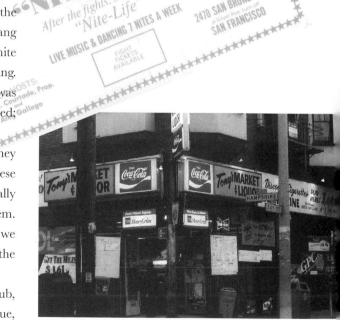

Hampshire and 24th Street in the Mission District.

Chris Wong became Malo's second manager.

Carol Steele: Renowned female percussionist.

Photos: Courtesy El Tecolote

five sets a night, from nine at night until closing time at two in morning, on a six-month contract.

"We played at the Nite Life for about eight months solid," says vocalist Richard Bean. "We rocked the place every weekend." By all accounts, the place rocked with a wild rhythm of its own: "The Nite Life was always packed out," Bean adds. "There could be fights, good-looking women, plenty drinking, you know."

Chris Wong would follow Pinckney as the band's manager as they morphed into their next incarnation as Malo. Wong was working on Broadway when he encountered the group: "I had a deal at Basin Street West to open up in the early hours, as everyone wanted to jam after their gigs. My guest list was a hundred miles long. I had to get opening acts; someone told me about this band the Malibus. As time went on they wanted to get outta playing the Nite Life. I started to get them other jobs. I had called Wolfman Jack to set up some dates in El Centro, and there was point in time when the name had to go—the name 'Malibus' sounded a bit like surfing or something."

The way Richard Bean remembers it, the band's new name came from a fan's acknowledgement of the musicians' bad-ass style—which was about to adopt a more Latin tinge as band members began composing such songs as "Nena" by Arcelio Garcia with Pablo Tellez, Garcia's "Café," and Bean's own "Suavecito," which would be their first hit.

"We did a gig at Chico State, in northern California," says Bean. "Carol Steele [a percussionist] was at one of the shows. She was yelling out Malo! Malo! And the name stuck." ("Malo" means "bad" in Spanish; and in street lexicon, "bad" was about as good a compliment one could get.) The name, as well as the word, was like a rallying cry to the emergent Chicano identity.

As Chuy Varela describes it: "We were lowriders; we listened to the oldies, stuff like The Penguins, Thee Midniters, Rosie and the Originals. Y'know, cruisin' oldies. Malo hit us in high school. The way the music impacted at the time, we were getting really politicized. The whole thing

43

that happened in LA in 1970—the August blow-outs, protests against Chicanos fighting in Vietnam, and the disproportionate deaths that were happening. We got into a lot of protests. The thing that was happening up here was Cesar Chavez and the United Farm Workers union.

"The first Malo gig I recall was at Glide Memorial and it was a benefit for the United Farm Workers union. Basically, Luis Gasca opened the show and then a real loose version of Malo played. Their set was broadcast later on KPFA Radio in Berkeley. KPFA was instrumental in bringing this music forward, as back then, we were trying to acknowledge the fact we were Chicanos, Latinos—a bilingual, bicultural people. We were fighting for certain principles. We were no longer living in our homelands. Radio KPFA started a program called 'Comunicación Atzlan.' That was the first progressive Latino urban culture show." The station was one of the first to introduce Latin bands like Malo.

In the male-dominated world of Latin rock (and the rock world in general), a few female lights shone. Lydia Pense of the funky soul-jazz combo Cold Blood wailed with a vocal intensity similar to a funkier Janis Joplin. Janis had recommended her to Bill Graham, and Lydia and the band ended up being represented by Graham's Millard Talent Agency on Market Street. Two of their albums were released on Graham's Fillmore records.

Their third album, *First Taste of Sin*, featured Coke Escovedo on congas and Jose Chepito Areas on timbales, whipping up a hot gumbo on the cut "Down to the Bone." Linda Tillery was another soulful mainstay around San Francisco, helming the superb Loading Zone, which included future Santana alumni Tom Coster and Dougie Rauch. She showed up on Santana's *3* recording and as recently as 1995, supported Santana at the Fillmore with her incredible Cultural Heritage Choir, who brought it all back to the work songs of the chain gang. A sought-after vocalist and lecturer, she has appeared with Boz Scaggs, Taj Mahal, and Bobby McFerrin, to name a few.

Lydia Pense: lead singer with Cold Blood

Photo: Courtesy Cold Blood Management

Poster: Courtesy Malo Archives

Photo: Rudy Rodriguez

Jorge Santana on stage with Malo.

At the time Wong lined up Malo's first tour, the group consisted of vocalists Arcelio Garcia and Richard Bean, Dave Guzman on drums, Cliff Anderson (a veteran of Chepito Areas's Aliens) on congas, Pablo Tellez (who'd been introduced to the band by rhythm guitarist Carlos Gomez), and Ismael Versosa on the "heavy as hell" Hammond B3 keyboard. They rehearsed at Bean's house on 25th Street, downstairs in the "blue room," where Bean's brother presided over many a party. "Then Jorge came into the band," Bean says. "Eventually Jorge was chosen over Carlos Gomez." "We had tried other guitarists, but it kinda wasn't working out," recalls Arcelio Garcia. "And then we found Jorge Santana. He auditioned. He was seventeen years old and [we thought] Oh man! This guy's great! So we brought him into the group. It was about six months later that I found out he was Carlos's brother."

Jorge Santana had grown up and graduated from Mission High a year after his brother and followed his path into R&B-laced music. According to friend Robert Lazaneo, he displayed impressive chops even as a youngster. "I met Jorge Santana about 1965; Jorge was at James Lick Junior High. I saw Jorge playing 'Louie Louie' with just a drummer. We played together, just making noise. At the beginning [the group] was called Jim and the Gents. We had suits like the Beatles. We started to write together, and the song 'Everlasting Night' that appeared on *Ascension* was written then. We were called Sounds Unlimited Blues Band by then. We gigged 'til late 1969."

Pablo Tellez backstage at Malo show.

Photos on this spread: Rudy Rodriguez

"After school we played in plenty of garages," says Jorge Santana of the four-piece blues band. "I was very influenced by BB King and also the British blues invasion, like John Mayall's *Blues Breaker*, which is one of my favorite albums, where you've got Peter Green as well as Eric Clapton. The song 'The Supernatural,' for Carlos and myself, was the ultimate song, with so much emotion. It'll be in our hearts forever. For me, Cream's *Disraeli Gears* was another big influence. Subconsciously I was also absorbing what Carlos was doing along with Chico Hamilton, Gabor Szabo, and some of Ray Barretto's stuff, and Mongo Santamaria. I also was listening to a lot of West Coast things like Willie Bobo with Victor Pantoja and the guitarist Sonny Henry. The West Coast sound was more of a spacey sound, not so arranged, more free with time and space.

"Carlos Gomez introduced me to the band. They were still called the Malibus and they were already one of the top rhythm and blues bands in the city, playing the YMCA, special events, and the dance halls. [They were] a mixture of Wilson Pickett and The Spinners. I met Richard and Arcelio out on Bryant Street. They were playing in a garage. At that time they had an African-American percussionist called Ricky [Parker], who was with us up to the Nite Life. We were doing about four sets a night. I'll never forget that period. We were also playing the Longshoremen's [Hall] in North Beach."

In addition to chops, Jorge brought contacts. He convinced Chris Wong to take over from Percy Pinckney as the Malibus' manager. He attracted a recording industry secretary, Linda Rogoff, to a Keystone Korner show ("I think she liked Jorge," says Garcia); she in turn brought her boss, Columbia Records producer David Rubinson, to see the band. Rubinson would prove an influential, if problematic, force in band's career. In the meantime, Wong was busy promoting his new charges. He secured a gig at Bimbo's, where they opened for the Escovedo Brothers, Pete and Coke, and the Wolfman Jack appearances in southern California.

"The first tour, we were eleven guys in a U-Haul van," says Wong. "When the rear door closed it was pitch black. We just sat in the back of this coffin, in the dark, 'til it was time to change. We got picked up by Wolfman's people, a big Cadillac convertible with a phone in it; we were so impressed."

Then it was home to rehearsals at the Heliport in Sausalito or in Wong's garage. "We tried to make it into a studio," Wong says. "We had loads of hare-brained ideas of how to soundproof it. I didn't want the whole neighborhood all up in arms, so I put plywood all over the walls, started pouring sand into the gaps—someone told me sand was a great insulator. One night the band is playing and WHOOM! the wall blows out, all this sand flying out of this thing. We had lots of laughs.

"The band was very young and kid-like. Arcelio was always up for everything, a real high-energy guy. Jorge was more introverted but very kid-like. I mean I was supposed to grow up, too; here I was a manager of a band, agents calling me up and all this stuff going on—it amazed me how all this came about. We started to get some good people in, like our secretary Susan Alexander, and then we got Doug Tracy as our road manager [who'd been with Tower of Power and Blue Cheer]. Money started to roll in. I bought a new Mercedes and I got Jorge and Pablo a new Volvo; I think Doug got one also. Arcelio was always the peacock, him being the frontman. They rented a house out in Daly City on Canterbury Street—that's where the name of the publishing company came from. Jeez, it was so foggy up there, we had to count lampposts to find our house. We were up there for about a year; it was like a little family. We were dead close, playing ping pong all the time."

Malo rehearsing at the Heliport. Left to right: Pablo Tellez, Leo Rosales, Jorge Santana, Abel Zarate.

Cliff Anderson: Malibus' conga drummer outside Basin Street West Club.

Carlos Gomez, friend and Dave Guzman, Malibus' guitarist and drummer showing up for Basin Street West gig.

Photos: Courtesy Malo Archives

San Francisco's rock clubs—such as Fillmore West, The Avalon, and The Family Dog—where hippie got introduced to Latin via Santana and Malo, developed national reputations. In addition to the better-known haunts, a host of clubs existed—The Ghetto, The Nite Life, Mr G's, The Matrix, Cesar's on Broadway—as well as later hangouts such as The Yellow Brick Road, The Peppermint Tree, The City, Andre's on Broadway, The Village, The Orphanage, and The Purple Onion (Maya Angelou had her act going there for some time).

Most visitors to San Francisco knew of the legendary clubs along Broadway. "Back then there was El Matador, where Bola Sete, Cal Tjader, Gabor Szabo, Stan Getz, played regularly; they were playing there steady freddy," says Abel Sanchez, who started his career playing at the Galaxy on Broadway. "At Basin Street West, it was the Latin jazz scene, Mongo Santamaria with Armando Peraza. Before he was big, Sly Stone was playing there, Bobby Freeman and people like that. The North Beach Revival club had El Chicano, War, all the other bands played there."

"The club where all the comedians hung out was the hungry i, run by Enrico Banducci," recalls Percy Pinckney. "Richard Pryor, Redd Foxx, and Dick Gregory would appear there; later there was Lou Rawls and Johnny Mathis. Sly Stone was always down at the Condor, on Columbus and Broadway, where Carol Doda, the famous topless dancer, appeared. He dated her for a while. Lenny Bruce could be found peddling his brand of comedy at Basin Street West, where he got famously busted for uttering the 'F word.' James Mamu also played guitar and sang at the Condor. He had a finger missing and used to wear a mask like the Lone Ranger. Another group called George & Teddy [Jerry Martini, Sly's future saxophonist, would sit in with them] were always down there."

Soul Sacrifice with Johnny Valenzuela playing maraccas, live at the Ghetto.

In other parts of the city, "The Bo-Peep was the cocaine dealers club," says Joel Selvin, who covers rock and roll for the *San Francisco Chronicle*. "The Yellow Brick Road was more a squares club for the bridge-and-tunnel crowd,[8] to listen to slick stuff. Tiger a Go Go out by the airport was another big deal. [When] Moby Grape first came down from Seattle, as the Frantics, they'd do the Dragon a Go Go in Chinatown. When they got fired, they grew their hair and became hippies, as a last chance to make it."

Rock music promoter Bill Graham rose to prominence running the legendary rock palace the Fillmore Auditorium, but it originally was owned by a man named Charles Sullivan. He was nicknamed the Vending Machine King, owing to his vast empire of vending machines throughout Northern California. "Sullivan owned and ran it for twenty years," says Pinckney. "He ended up murdered on the street, with fifteen thousand dollars in his pocket. The murder was never resolved. It wasn't a robbery. He was just assassinated. So, Bill Graham walked in and picked up [the business]."

The Mission district club scene really started to thrive in the 1970s. "When Johnny Bajone bought [a neighborhood bar called] Laura's, he changed the name to Bajone's and started featuring jazz and comedy. Whoopi Goldberg used to have a residency there," Pinckney remembers.

Musician José Simon played in a band, Four of a Kind, with Michael Carabello during Carabello's hiatus from Santana Blues Band. With vocalist Rick Stevens, who went on to join the original Tower of Power, the group played covers at topless bars on Broadway in San Francisco, and at The Rock Garden out in the working-class Excelsior neighborhood adjacent to the Mission. "The Rock Garden was a hard club, real party hardliners. The bouncers were two Samoan guys. They kicked the hell out of anybody trying to kick off in there. The Rock Garden was the competition to the Nite Life, and was probably the first rock club in the Mission area. They had Big Brother, Janis Joplin, Mongo Santamaria." Later, the club changed hands and became the Ghetto. "The Ghetto was originally a black club," says Richard Bean. "Then the Latin thing started there. Abel and the Prophets were like the house band. Crackin' was another band from around that time. They were bloods.[9] They used to play at Orphan Annie's in San Mateo."

— LATIN — SOUL — ROCK —

AN ALLEO PRODUCTION — presents a

DO - ME - RIGHT AFFAIR

Come One, Come All, Young and Old — It Will Be An Affair To Remember On A Sunday Afternoon — See You There!

SUNDAY, JULY 18, 1971 — 4:00 PM TO 8:00 PM AT THE FABULOUS GHETTO CLUB
4742 Mission Street, San Francisco, California

Music by the "SOUL SACRIFICE" and the New Sound of the "ANTECA"

Contribution: $2.00 with Ticket; $2.50 without Ticket, Per Person
PAYABLE AT THE DOOR
Minors! Welcome!   (First Come, First Served Basis)   This Is An Invitation!

---

[8] "Bridge-and-tunnel" refers to people from the suburbs, who drove through the Caldecott Tunnel and over the Bay Bridge to reach San Francisco.

[9] Slang term for African-American.

"The hot clubs… were in a radius of about five miles," says Sanchez, who fronted Abel and the Prophets. "We were THE hothouse band on Mission Street. Mr. G's was more like a neighborhood hangout. Club Rhode Island had great black acts—Bobby Blue Bland, Ray Charles, BB King—jamming there. The Matrix was more rock orientated, a Jack Cassady and the Jefferson Airplane scene. The Ghetto club was a high point; we

Photo: Courtesy Abel Sanchez

Abel Sanchez (center) on stage at the Ghetto with his band the Prophets.
Coke Escovedo (right) sits in as guest on timbales.

were there for a year straight every night, which is a rare thing. It was a real mixed crowd, a Latin soul crowd."

Adds Pete Gallegos: "You also had on Mission Street several clubs like Club Elegante, El Señorial (another salsa club), and El Tenampa, which was Mexican. There was the Puerto Rican club on Mission, so on any given Saturday night you could walk within a ten-block distance and hear any Latin [music] you wanted during the late sixties and early seventies."

Another popular dance spot was Cesar's, which opened as a basement club in North Beach and later moved to a larger venue on Mission Street near Army Street (now called Cesar Chavez), where it was renamed Cesar's Latin Palace. Owner Cesar Ascarrunz

The Nite Life on San Bruno Avenue where Malo had an ongoing residency. Appearing this night were the Providers.

Johnny Cortade, Nite Life co-owner, with friend.

Photos: Courtesy Johnny Cortade

managed to book most of name bands from New York and Latin America, despite the fact he was notoriously stingy. "I operated Cesar's Latin Palace for 23 years," he says. "We had everything from Jerry Garcia, the Grateful Dead to Celia Cruz, Tito Puente. When Santana happened onto the scene it was deluxe, super deluxe."

"Cesar Ascarrunz was a trip, man," says Gallegos. "He always had a turtleneck on with a big medallion round his neck. He had this rep for being open all the time, all night long. You weren't supposed to sell booze after 2 A.M.; but he had ready-made rum and coke mixed from the gun. Order a wine, it'd come out of a regular bottle with no label, like water. He was the owner, the doorman, the bartender, and he played piano, too. He ran for mayor a couple of times. He'd say 'I came in second for mayor.' Fact is there were only two candidates running; he'd get, say, 3000 votes and the winner would have 150,000, but Cesar would still be talking about coming in second."

"Cesar used to walk around with a roll of money, but the musicians would get fifty bucks," says Richard Bean. "That used to burn me."

One of the hottest hangouts to showcase the burgeoning and totally fresh Latin hybrids forming in the Mission district was the Nite Life. Recalls owner Johnny Cortade: "The Nite Life was a Nickelodeon cinema and was closed up when I bought it. Benedict Arnold and the Traitors were one of my first bands. They drew a large crowd. Richard Pryor would hang out at the club. Tower of Power would come in at the weekends; Luis Gordon managed them at that time. I had the band the Limbo too; after that we started to go more to salsa."

"The Nite Life was super hip," says Gallegos. "Johnny Cortade and Alex Gallegos, who ran it, they were two young playboys, both of them came up through Mission High. They had matching little blue and white convertible Mercedes Benz cars. Two young, sharp Latinos in 1969, driving around, dressed sharp; it was everybody's dream. Life just seemed to be one big party. I was working in the Nite Life parking lot.

"The Nite Life attracted a big crowd, everything from eccentrics to the guy in the street. One guy, Pat Maguire, pulled up in a gold Bentley with a Doberman pinscher called Diablo in the back. He was a big guy [six foot nine and three hundred-plus pounds, he wore a custom-made tuxedo]. He later worked the door at the Yellow Brick Road, down on the Embarcadero, in the mid-'70s. He would give me ten bucks, point at the dog and say, 'Don't let anyone next to the car as this mother-fucker will tear your head off if he don't know you.'

"There was this other black guy with a process; he looked like a classic pimp but he was different. Instead of driving a Cadillac, he'd arrive with his little MG sports car. The real hip people [were] smoking weed—it was pretty mellow then. A lot of the women would be dressed in go-go boots and mini skirts. Every night there was an after-hours party, every week someone was having a party on 101 Olmstead Street. [Malibus' conguero] Ricky Parker would come in with his gold cane; that was his little fashion statement. He was a player. He had all kinds of girls all the time. There were a lot of players at the club." In a historical irony, Johnny Cortade had auditioned Santana for the Nite Life's Wednesday slot, but "Johnny was saying, it's too loud or something," Gallegos recalls. "They didn't get the slot. I think it was the same year that Carlos shot to the top."

From a musical ghetto along Mission Street between 24th Street to Army Street, following the lowriders' cruising route, Latin clubs eventually expanded outside the Mission. "There was Roland's, The Reunion [on Union Street, which featured a house band led by Roger Glenn, the vibes player in Pete Escovedo's band], and also Sneaky Pete's was doing Latin for awhile," Gallegos says. "Sneaky Pete's had a female mannequin all dressed up, sitting in the corner. [The owner would] have her there so it always looked like there was someone in. It was dimly lit; if you were drunk she looked real. People would buy 'her' drinks." Timbalero Pete Escovedo was a regular, Bean remembers; "You'd run into all the other musicians there, people like Mongo Santamaria."

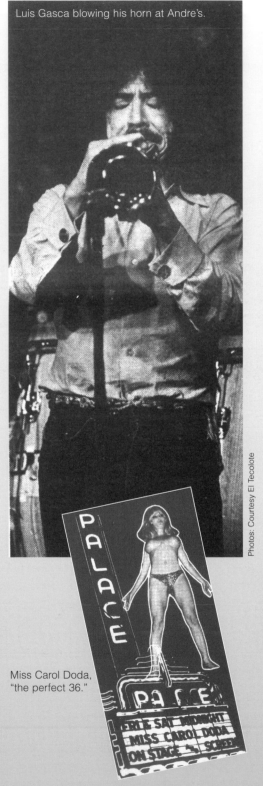

Luis Gasca blowing his horn at Andre's.

Miss Carol Doda, "the perfect 36."

Photos: Courtesy El Tecolote

52

Arcelio Garcia Jr. on stage with Malo

Photo: Rudy Rodriguez

Joel Selvin remembers Luis Gasca and Jules Broussard playing at Roland's. "Another band around was San Pacu, with Rico Reyes, who were managed by Herbie [Herbert], and they were talked about for a moment; they were the kings of the audition shows. Rico Reyes, in his prime, he was very much a ladies man; he had that look—when he sang, the girls would be hitting me up to get his number. They'd pack them in at two bucks a head, but they disappeared."

Early shots of Abel and the Prophets.

Photo: Courtesy Abel Sanchez

53

Santana: San Francisco, 1969

Photo: Joan Chase

WAITING

Santana's first album, released in 1969

The Latin rock scene emerged from a confluence of the Bay Area's cutting-edge music. As one newspaper critic noted: "Malo and Santana came in from the Mission, same as the Sly Stone guys came out of that talent pool around the Mission. Gregg Rolie came out of that Berkeley thing with William Pen & His Pals; The Beethovens were another one, also The Baylanders, who were widely renowned for a version of 'Wipeout.' A lot of people heard 'East West' by Paul Butterfield, dropped acid, and it changed their lives. In the Santana crowd, Stan Marcum was the big jazzbo; he introduced them to Gabor and Coltrane. The Latin rock thing had certain aesthetics: jazz was cool. Being commercial was not.

Photos: Courtesy Columbia Records

"At first no one realized Santana represented this whole new cultural thing. The first time most people saw them was Thanksgiving Eve of 1968 at the Fillmore. The press was there; it was their unveiling. It's a Beautiful Day played, kinda ethereal stuff, and then these hard asses from the Mission came on. No one then realized they were the spike of this huge cultural revolution. There wasn't even a lot of media stampede in that direction, but Santana shot through the hierarchy so fast, and then they were headlining. They were knocking everybody dead."

Santana, although boasting a large local following and headlining at the Fillmore, did not as yet have a record deal in place, although David Rubinson thought they would be ideal for Columbia. At the beginning of 1969, he produced an album's worth of material under the title *Freeway Jam* in a Los Angeles studio. "There was a Santana recording done and a lot of prick teasing," says Jeff Trager, then a young record promoter getting his foot into the business. "Blue Thumb Records got offered Santana with a package of five or six bands, but they passed." Other producers likewise didn't think the band had much potential. Ahmet Ertegun, head of Atlantic Records in New York, was taken to see Santana by attorney Brian Rohan, and famously remarked: "Can't play; furthermore, won't sell."

Trager remembers an aborted attempt to generate a record label's interest. "When I was

Photo: Courtesy Jeff Trager

Nate Thurmond and Jeff Trager with Jeff's Bentley.

first hanging out in the city—I was just getting in the business in 1967—I was hanging out with the Santana guys in rehearsal rooms up on Fillmore Street. They were playing at the Fillmore a lot, to rave responses. I was with ABC Dunhill, A small, successful label. They had Steppenwolf and the Mamas and the Papas. [Santana manager Stan Marcum liked the label, 'cause they didn't have a lot of acts and they were small.] I had the company president, Jay Lasker, send some promotions people up to check out the band. I said, 'They're blowing everyone away!'

"They send up some guy, Barry Gross, with two chicks in see-through shirts. [Gross] was the guy who signed the Grass Roots [a folk-rock group with a slew of hits] and that was his taste in music. When he saw Santana he didn't get it at all. He had no fuckin' clue. He went back to Lasker and said, 'There's nothing here. If you like Tito Puente, great! But it's just a bunch of kids playing Latin music.'

Carlos Santana

Photos: Joan Chase

"It was a typical Santana show. Everyone went nuts. When I brought Gross backstage after the show, the first thing out of his mouth to Stan Marcum was, 'If you're looking for any front money, forget it!' Stan just got up and left him sitting there. Gross was saying, 'Where is he?' I said, 'What do you mean, where is he—he's talking to CBS in the other room.'"

"I personally wanted to be with CBS," Carlos recalls. "It was a matter of innocence. I wanted to be there because they had Miles Davis, The Electric Flag, and Bob Dylan on their roster. I had heard stories about Atlantic from The Young Rascals and other people who weren't happy with the distribution or the royalties. I kept my ears open to that stuff. Consequently, we made more progress because we hooked up with Clive Davis [at Columbia], who was more artist-orientated than cash register-orientated."

Santana's first album on the Columbia label introduced the world to Mission-style Latin rock; and even thirty years later, although suffering from murky production values, it has a immediate visceral appeal. What it lacked in polish was amply balanced by the honesty and sheer adventure of the music.

As Carlos Santana puts it: "The first album was soundwise, no; musicwise, yes. We'd been playing that material for about a year and a half. A lot of people forget we were headlining the Fillmore West without an album out. By the time we recorded it, it was done very fast with people who had no understanding of the music or how it should be recorded. As far as the music, I'm happy because we knew next to nothing except that we could do it. We believed we could play our own music and have some kind of impact on the people. It was street social music. I don't play Mexican, African, or whatever; I just play music, and trying to bring it all back home as they say. I respect it all but I would be bored just playing one type of music."

Jackie Villanueva (left) and Herbie Herbert (right) who made up Santana's road crew along with Jackie's brother Johnny.

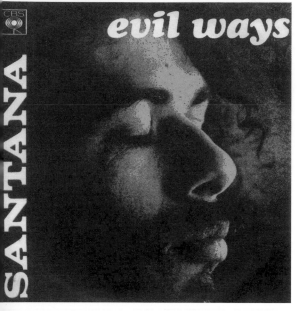

Santana 45 vinyl single sleeve:
released in Africa.

Photos: Joan Chase

David Brown

Santana had asked Alberto Gianquinto, a pianist friend from the Mission, to advise and help with the arrangements. Alberto was straight to the point, came to the studio, told them to cut down on the solos and left them to it. They recorded the album in May 1969, in less than three weeks, working twelve to sixteen hours a day at Pacific Recording Studio. To produce the album, they enlisted the help of Brent Dangerfield, who'd done the band's sound at their Straight Theater gigs.

"The Straight Theater was really freaky and hippie. The guy that mixed the sound, his mouth was rotten—he was such a speed freak, his mouth looked like post-war Dresden; his teeth had all gone," according to their soon-to-be-road manager Herbie Herbert. "He was Brent Dangerfield and they got him to engineer the record. The guy never did anything again in his whole life. He produced that first record; it sounded great. They were already breaching protocol by recording in a non-CBS studio with a non-CBS producer. They made magic on that first record: songs first, performance second, engineers third." Michael Carabello also approved: "I thought Brent did a great, raw job. It was tricky then mixing conga and timbales and trap drums to that sound."

Carlos's was the dissenting opinion. "The sound was horrible. We went to Hippie Hill and got the first hippie we thought could do it. He didn't know shit about sound. It sounds too brittle to me, with no bass. I remember Gregg Rolie, Michael Shrieve, and I hearing it in Cambridge, Massachusetts, on the radio. It was a mix of elation: 'Wow, we're on the radio man!' to 'Wow, it sounds horrible.'"

The self-titled album, wrapped in Lee Konklin's cover artwork featuring a tribal lion's head composed of several hidden pictures obvious upon close scrutiny (David Brown liked the art so much he had the three-sided lion's head tattooed on his body), was a striking debut visually as well as musically. On the reverse were

John Santos at home, Oakland California, 1991.

Photos: Jim McCarthy

photographs of the band in full-bore performance; there were titles of the tracks and little additional information. The design hints at the enigma and totally new slant of Santana's music.

As with all the first Santana recordings, the first side of the album has the feeling of a suite. The opening piece, "Waiting," was a guaguanco adapted by Carabello and Chepito on congas, swiftly followed by Brown's heavy bass, and Mike Shrieve's slicing hi-hat work. The top layer was supplied memorably by Gregg Rolie's sullen, spiky organ and Carlos's stinging guitar work. "We called it 'Waiting' 'cause we felt we were at that time always waiting for stuff to happen," says Carabello.

"Shades of Time," "Savor," and "Jingo" (suggested by conguero Marcus Malone, who'd heard it on Michael Olatunji's *Drums of Passion* album), bleed into one another. "Savor," an earthy rumble in the jungle with Areas's clattering, crisp timbales break and Carabello's primal conga take, are featured on the dawn-of-time "Jingo." "Treat," a Les McCann & Eddie Harris-inspired piece, which featured Gregg Rolie's bluesy piano musings, extended the young band's musical palette. One of several classic cuts on the first record, "Soul Sacrifice," closed the album on a high note. The interplay between Santana and Rolie is fantastic—a really tight organ and guitar arrangement hammered home by Carabello's and Areas's congas and the sinuous drums and bass of Shrieve and Brown. It is a perfect example of the amalgam of old-world guaguanco rhythms and strictly American licks that hit audiences right on the spot.

"Originally the guaguanco would be played on wooden boxes in Havana; they play it differently in Matanzas, the neighboring province," says conguero and music scholar John Santos, who notes that the band had intuitively taken up the percussive banner borne by Cuban drummers such as Chano Pozo, Carlos "Patato" Valdes, Candido Camero, Mongo Santamaria, Armando

Peraza, and Francisco Aguabella, who had arrived in the states in the 1940s and '50s; the latter three lived in the San Francisco area, where they played and recorded with the likes of Cal Tjader and Peggy Lee, and certainly influenced the Santana percussionists. "When Santana came out, it hipped a lot of people to congas," Santos notes.

"We knew we had something going on before the first album was out, because people were copying us," says Carlos. "Everyone was getting congas: Miles, Paul Butterfield, the Stones, Chicago. [Before that], very few people personally would let us in, just Mike Bloomfield, Jerry Garcia, or Bill Graham. The rest of the [San Francisco] groups were very snotty to us. Jefferson Airplane were very snotty towards us; a lot of people couldn't hide what they were feeling. I felt some disgust and disdain. We learned confidence opening for Creedence Clearwater Revival, hanging out with Peter Green, seeing Fleetwood Mac recording in England. Other bands like San Pacu and the Loading Zone were following in our footsteps, getting in the Hammond organs and stuff. Even Jimi Hendrix started getting congas."

The album, released in August 1969, went gold that year and sold two million copies in its initial run. Its first single, "Jingo," peaked on *Billboard* at No. 56 and charted for six weeks. "Evil Ways," the album's second single, hit the *Billboard Top 100* at No. 9, spending thirteen weeks on the chart. The album itself peaked at No. 4 and stayed on the chart for a total of 108 weeks.

Said one fan: "The first Santana album had such a huge impact in San Francisco. The day the album came out, Discount Records on Telegraph Avenue in Berkeley were selling out, the album was so anticipated. It was the big event and was slammed on the radio in the city. Santana were the best-selling band in the world at that moment, selling more records than even the Beatles. They were an unparalleled experience. They were a flash from the ghetto."

Bill Graham pushed the band into high visibility with appearances on the "Dick Cavett Show," "Tonight Show," "Ed Sullivan Show" (where they played a medley of "Persuasion," "Treat," and "Soul Sacrifice"), and the infamous concert at Woodstock, New York, where their playing was a highlight of a later documentary film. "This was all in a couple of weeks of each other," recalls Herbie Herbert. "They were the only act to play without a record; it was unparalleled. Santana went from Woodstock to being in global demand almost overnight.

"I picked up the first record for $3.99; it was just great. Bill Graham offered me the job with Santana; he said, 'Think I can get you $75 a week.' I said, 'Is that what you are recommending?' Bill says, 'You asked my advice, YOU OWE ME NOTHING!' Bill said, 'I've just seen Woodstock; they are going to be a monster.'

"Santana were such street people, so unsophisticated, they were all jockeying for position. There were requests from Japan constantly, [but] it's like, 'We don't wanna go to Japan; we want to be able to smoke our weed. Maybe in Europe, we can have our stash.' When we agreed to play in Africa, the whole band would go somewhere to get inoculated with shots for malaria, cholera, yellow fever—a real pain in the butt! Still, there was a lot of love in the band. Even when they fought internally, they always had a united front against anybody fucking with them."

Santana up against the wall. "...They always had a united front against anybody fucking with them."

Photo: Joan Chase

Santana gear up to create their masterpiece, the *Abraxas* album.

Photo: Joan Chase

ABRAXAS

Fred Catero in the studio.

Photo: Rudy Rodriguez

Santana 45 vinyl single sleeve: released Portugal, 1970.

Courtesy: Columbia Records

CBS

BLACK MAGIC WOMAN / HOPE YOU'RE FEELING BETTER

SANTANA
SANTANA
SANTANA

If ever an album realized a band's early promise, it was *Abraxas*. Santana's second album was recorded at Wally Heider's studio in downtown San Francisco and produced by Fred Catero. "The thing about recording for me is to try and do it live," he says, "I learned a lot from working with Santana on *Abraxas*. I was brought up Spanish and I speak Spanish. You know, if a player says, 'I'm gonna do cascara here' and you don't know what they're saying, that's a big turn off for musicians." Catero's savvy paid off. The disc is a classic: a cool suite of seamless music that takes you on a smooth ride through many moods and rhythms, notably the Latin influence of Chepito Areas in the merengue "Se A Cabo" and Tito Puente's cha-cha "Oye Como Va." The passion and ecstatic soloing captures the psychedelic feeling of the times. The musicianship is tighter and more refined than in Santana, and shows the ensemble at the height of their powers.

Neal Schon, who hung out at the *Abraxas* sessions, joined Santana at the tender age of fifteen.

Photo: Joan Chase

Photo: CBS Records

Gabor Szabo

Photo: John Szabo

"Carlos and Neal had a great guitar sound: those souped-up Fenders with the four Twin Reverbs," Herbie Herbert recalls. "Neal got that sound with the wah-wah pedal, in-line between the guitar and the amplifier, and the pedal open half way. Add to that a Gold Top Les Paul and that aggressive fire—he was so skinny, but he was fearless. Gregg was a franchise player; you could build a team around him."

Mike Carabello's tone poem, "Singing Winds, Crying Beasts," opens the album with an airy, effects-swept piece that captures the musicians' states of mind at the time. "Fred Catero and I got turned onto coke during *Abraxas*," says Herbert. "We'd wonder how the guys in the band kept going. It'd be six, seven in the morning and the band would be, 'Let's cut this!' We're dead on our feet. It's fucking daylight outside. When they were doing 'Singing Winds' at Wally Heider's, Carabello's like rushing around at five in the morning. Fred Catero looks like a basset hound. Michael, Fred, and I are toast; we can't do anymore. Where's this crazy energy comin' from?

"I called Carabello [and asked], 'What are you guys doing, man?' Michael says, 'Oh! We're doing blow, man. You guys ought to try a bump. Here, check this out.' He comes into the control room and says, 'Try this.' Me and Fred didn't feel a thing at first until we got the buzz; after a while you identify the high. Then Fred and I looked at each other, 'Holy fuck, I'm lit up like a Christmas tree!' We were whack."

"Mike Shrieve and I worked on 'Singing Winds,' and then the next day, the band heard it and loved it. It worked out great as an intro for 'Black Magic Woman,'" says Carabello. "Black Magic Woman" was the first cut from *Abraxas* released as a single. Gregg Rolie had brought the song to the band and had to fight to get them to play it, but it hit Number 4 on *Billboard*, becoming their biggest hit.

The track segues perfectly into "Black Magic Woman," which itself was linked with Gabor Szabo's "Gypsy Queen." Neal Schon remembers: "Gabor Szabo was very cool. Herbie [Herbert] was doing Carlos's guitar tech stuff; he set me up with a room and records and I just played and learnt them while they were recording *Abraxas*." Gabor Szabo was a Hungarian guitarist who, at age twenty, escaped the communist uprising and settled in California. He joined Chico Hamilton's quintet, featuring Charles Lloyd, and developed his free, single-note phrasings, chord flurries, and intricate runs on guitar. Szabo went solo in 1966 and recorded the *Spellbinder* album with Chico Hamilton, Ron Carter, and Victor

Pantoja. That album provided Santana with the sound collage on "Gypsy Queen," which bookended "Black Magic Woman" on *Abraxas*.[10]

"Gabor was to the guitar what people thought Miles was to the trumpet," Jeff Trager says. "Nobody knew him 'til 'Gypsy Queen' on *Abraxas*. He never had a paycheck like that in his life. He was revered by musicians and had his own releases out on the Impulse Record label, which was one of the finest innovative labels of all time. They had John Coltrane, Gil Evans, and Ray Charles. Gabor did that original version of 'Breezin,' on Blue Thumb with Bobby Womack, before George Benson. To this day that track ['Black Magic Woman'] is one of the most played on classic rock stations."

The next track, "Oye Como Va," became the second single and hit the charts at Number 13. When Santana recorded the classic Latin hit that Puente had written and recorded, the composer was miffed that such a band would dare mess with his music. As soon as the royalty check came (based on massive sales of Santana's album), Puente discovered the upside of having other people perform his songs. "El Rey Del Timbal" has since preceded the playing of "Oye Como Va" with that little story many times and come to realize that Latin rock music has done as much to promote Latin jazz for current audiences as Machito's music did for an earlier generation.

"Incident at Neshabur," co-written by Carlos and Alberto Gianquinto, was an astounding blend of styles and a fitting explorative piece to round out *Abraxas*'s first side. "We did time changes, colors, and musically, things that were very sophisticated with 'Incident,'" says Rolie. "It was a perfect combination of pianist Horace Silver and [conguero] Big Black, with Aretha Franklin singing Burt Bacharach's 'This Guy's in Love with You.' We'd just combine things we had a passion for." Adds Carabello: "We were very into jamming and taking bits out, like the Stones did in the studio. We had to be very versatile." The tune, Jeff Trager adds, "brought them to another plateau."

Gregg Rolie on stage at the Fillmore West, 1970.

Michael Carabello on stage at the Fillmore West, 1970.

Photos: Joan Chase

---

[10] Gabor Szabo also recorded *Jazz Raga* in 1966, which again featured the awesome drummer Bernard Purdie. Many influential albums followed, such as *The Sorcerer*, recorded live for Impulse. Szabo found time to form a record label with Cal Tjader called Skye Recording Co., Ltd. He went on to also record the cult *High Contrast* with Bobby Womack for Blue Thumb in 1971. "Breezin'," a song Womack brought to the sessions, later became a hit for George Benson, and was briefly quoted on "Song of the Wind" by Carlos and Neal, on the *Caravanserai* recording, in another music-community convergence.

Photos: Joan Chase

Rico Reyes, vocalist and percussionist, who appears on *Abraxas*.

Abraxas's second side featured another eclectic mix of music. Chepito's "Se A Cabo" leads with a razor-sharp performance. Carlos plays a wild, jazzy solo; Carabello adopts his trademark triplet slap on the quinto conga drum here, moving from merengue to add a cooking groove beneath an exhilarating timbales solo by Areas. Two Gregg Rolie tunes, "Mother's Daughter" and "Hope You're Feeling Better," are much more in the rock vein. "Hope You're Feeling Better" starts with Rolie's growling, funky Hammond organ intro, aided and abetted by a furious roll 'round the drum kit by Michael Shrieve. The cut has a dramatic coda with exciting playing by Carlos over a resounding ensemble performance. "Mother's Daughter" (on the Quadraphonic version) features Neal Schon's first recorded licks on the outro. "Samba Pa Ti" is a beautiful piece written by Carlos in which Rolie's sympathetic organ brings it all home to a gentle samba shuffle, over which Carlos solos with verve. The group, apparently, were at loggerheads with Carlos over this tune's inclusion, but level heads prevailed; "Samba Pa Ti" became an instant Santana classic, heeding both its Mexican-American romantic folk and blues roots. "El Nicoya," Areas's tribute to himself, is a short roots piece and rounds out the album with Carabello and Rico Reyes (on vocals and percussion) providing a percussive base for Areas to show off his conga and timbales chops.

Reyes, a friend of the band, appeared as a guest on *Abraxas*, *Santana 3*, and *Caravanserai*. He possessed a soulful, raw voice that augmented Santana's chants and lent the band a further authentic Mission style. He also had a writing credit on "Guajira," a Santana classic. "Rico Reyes was from the neighborhood; a real street-tough little guy," remembers Abel Zarate. "I first met him at Basin Street. He was sitting in with a band called Aum. I didn't get along with him at first, but he was a real sweet guy. He was into Perez Prado, way back then in 1971." Reyes was always pounding rhythms on the desktop, adds Johnny Villanueva, who knew him in high school.

Abraxas featured another startling example of cover art, now a classic of the time. A painting called *The Annunciation*, by Abdul Mati Klarwein, showed the angel Gabriel astride a conga drum, visiting a voluptuous black Mary to announce the birth of Christ. It is an evocative lysergic insight, bordering somewhere between the spiritual realms and hip kitsch. Abdul Mati was a German hipster, taught by Fernand Leger and Ernst Fuchs, whose finely detailed paintings were exhibited at his Aleph Sanctuary in New York. Both Jimi Hendrix and Miles Davis were patrons of his, and in addition to Santana's album, his work graced the covers of albums by Miles Davis, Buddy Miles and Jerry Garcia, to name but a few. *Abraxas* itself went heavenward, flying all the way to Number 1. It stayed on the chart for 88 weeks.

"I think *Abraxas* is Santana's best album," Michael Carabello insists. "We had really captured a sound on there. Fred Catero did some great cross fading—maybe George Martin did some stuff like it with the Beatles, but nobody [did it] like us. Santana had the magic going on. We brought something totally different to the table. We brought an Afro-Latin, Tex-Mex, blues haze to what would later become the style that Weather Report was exploring. Miles wasn't even doing that stuff yet."

After the *Abraxas* recording in July 1970, and before its October release, the band performed a prestigious gig with the Voices of East Harlem and Miles Davis at Tanglewood open air amphitheater in Massachusetts. The date, promoted by Bill Graham, was billed as "The Fillmore in Tanglewood." Davis at that time was soaking up the sounds of Santana, Hendrix, and Sly Stone. His remarkable electric music began evolving from this period of influence—a style which helped make him an icon of progressive US jazz despite his onstage eccentricity.

"Santana attracted a lot of great musicians, which pressured the band to perform at a higher level," says Herbie Herbert. "At Tanglewood, the Voices of East Harlem had already performed, and Miles Davis's greatest band was on stage opening for Santana with no sign of Miles turning up. This was like a symphony orchestra-type gig; Bill Graham was pacing up and down: 'That motherfucker Miles; I'm gonna break his fucking neck.' All of a sudden there's this 'WeeeeeeeeAaaaaOoooooScreeeeech.' Miles, in patched-leather vest in his open-top Maserati, careening to a halt, his horn on the passenger seat, jumps out of the car, straight up on stage and just hits it. Bill and I watched this go down with our mouths hanging open. I reckon if your gonna behave like this, can you at least be Miles Davis. Though Miles walked through the valley, he feared no evil, because he's the baddest motherfucker in the valley."

"It was a gas doing *Abraxas*," says Fred Catero, who remembers how his first Santana production almost grounded Chepito Areas. "*Abraxas* had just come out and Chepito was going back to Nicaragua with an armful of albums. He had 'em wrapped in brown paper. He gets on the plane, clutching this package. He didn't speak English very well. The stewardess comes down the aisle, she sees him clutching this brown paper package. 'Sir,' she says, 'the package will have to go overhead in the compartment.'

"'No, iz alright, I hold it, I hold it!' says Chepito.

"'Sir, it's regulations.'

"Chepito goes, 'No, no, no, oh, it's dynamite!!' So, the plane taxis around to an empty hangar. The FBI come on and pulls him off. Bill Graham had to call them and explain what Chepito was trying to say, that it was a dynamite recording, that he wasn't a hijacker, and they finally let him go."

Miles Davis hanging out with Buddy Miles.

Chepito Areas arrested by the FBI.

Photos: Joan Chase

Photo: Ron Reisterer

INCIDENT AT BERKELEY

During this period in the USA, racial barriers began breaking down, at least in the younger populace. Prior to 1965, according to Carlos Santana, "there was a lot of tension between blacks and whites at Mission High School. The auditorium got burnt, there were lot of fights. I would say Mission was forty percent blacks and about twenty percent white. The [rest were] Latin: Nicarauagan, Salvadorean, Costa Rican, Mexican. The majority of blacks came from Fillmore or Hunter's Point." Students divided along racial lines until later in decade, when the era of "love not war" descended upon the city. "The only people the blacks didn't beat up was the hippies," Santana says. " Hippies were like a neutral zone between whites and blacks. They were like a sanctuary crowd." An element that united each of these warring factions in the late 1960s was music.

Malcolm X and Muhammed Ali

Photo: Courtesy Eddie Palmeri/Chori Santiago

Eddie Palmeiri released the heavily politicised *Live at Sing Sing* albums

Not only was Latin-based music starting to cross over, a counterculture was embracing the black struggle, to a degree. Multiracial bands such as Sly Stone, Santana, Jimi Hendrix Experience, War, Mandrill, and Malo were at the forefront of a musical melting pot in which simmered an emerging awareness of racial power.

In 1965, the country was rocked by rioting in the predominantly black neighborhood of Watts in South Central Los Angeles. The United Farm Workers Union, led by Cesar Chavez, was organizing underpaid field workers in the California valleys and reflected an emerging, politicized Chicano attitude. Set against the backdrop of the Vietnam War, the Oakland-based Black Panther party was formed in October 1966 by Huey P. Newton and Bobby Seale. The collective allied themselves with other Third World revolutionaries and was a strong force in black neighborhoods in the early 1970s. They organized free health clinics, free breakfast programs for children, and defended their right to bear arms under the US Constitution's second amendment. They consequently were targets of police retaliation, and many Black Panther members were shot by law enforcement agents. These included Fred Hampton, who was gunned down along with Mark Clarke in Chicago in December, 1969.

The Black Panthers were aghast that the huge sums of money that poured into the Vietnam war machine could have instead eased the extreme financial impoverishment of communities such as Watts. Eldridge Cleaver, whose prison writings, collected in *Soul on Ice*, galvanized a generation, became the party's Minister of Information and amplified the point by stating: "Black Americans are asked to die for the system in Vietnam; in Watts they are killed by it." Or as champion heavyweight boxer Muhammed Ali, member of the high-profile black organization Nation of Islam, put it: "They want me to go to Vietnam to shoot some folks that never lynched me, never called me nigger, never assassinated my leaders."

Black power advocate Stokely Carmichael had already visited Cuba and North Vietnam in 1967. Newark, New Jersey; Detroit, Michigan; and Los Angeles, California were among the worst hit by violence in the aftermath of the assassination of Martin Luther King, Jr. on April 4, 1968, when black Americans rioted in more than 100 US cities.

Like modern-day African tribal griots, The Last Poets of New York disseminated stark information against the sound of the conga drum.[11] Early rap poems such as *Wake Up Nigger* and *When the Revolution Comes* carried a no-frills message of liberation. Latin acts began playing benefit concerts in support of political and race issues. On the East Coast, Eddie Palmieiri's *Live at Sing Sing* albums (Volumes 1 & 2) featured not only stirring descarga versions of the hits "Muñeca" and "Azucar," but also the poetry of Felipe Luciano, a New Yorker of Puerto Rican origin who also performed with the Last Poets. His contribution was an ode to racial pride entitled *Jíbaro, My Pretty Nigger*. Gil Scot-Heron later carried this mantle with songs such as "The Revolution Will Not Be Televised," and "The Bottle," into the seventies and eighties.

---

[11]   Their albums, *The Last Poets* and *This Is Madness* (with a cover by Abdul Mati Klarwein) were released on Douglas Records in 1970 and 1971, respectively. They prefigured the solo releases by Gil Scott-Heron and were a direct influence on Melle Mel's *The Message*, which moved hip-hop in a more politicized direction.

Photo: Ron Reisterer

Angela Davis: placed on the FBI's Ten Most Wanted list.

Photo: Ron Reisterer, Oakland Tribune

Robert Seale (b. Oct. 22, 1936, Dallas, Texas, U.S.), African-American founder, along with Huey Newton, and national chairman of the Black Panther Party. Seale was one of a generation of young African-American radicals who broke away from the traditionally nonviolent Civil Rights Movement to preach a doctrine of militant black empowerment. Following the dismissal of murder charges against him in 1971, Seale somewhat moderated his more militant views and devoted his time to effecting change from within the system. He ran for mayor of Oakland in 1973, finishing second. As the Black Panther Party faded from public view, Seale took on a quieter role, working to improve social services in black neighborhoods and to improve the environment. Seale's writings include such diverse works as *Seize the Time*.

Photo: Malo Archives

Angela Davis benefit concert,
Berkeley Community Theatre, featuring Malo.

Brown Berets, Chicano Moratorium, August 29, 1970.

Photo: Rudy Rodriguez

The Brown Berets, echoing the Black Panthers in paramilitary uniforms of khaki pants and hats, emerged around 1968. Chicano activists, mostly concentrated on college campuses in the Los Angeles area, they protested the disproportionate number of Chicano soldiers killed in Vietnam, as well as the high unemployment rates at home that kept Latinos at the lowest per-capita income level of any US ethnic group.

Says Pete Gallegos: "The Farm Workers and the Panther movement gave birth to a lot of community activists. The Brown Berets were less militant than the Panthers but they were street soldiers who were proud of their heritage. Back in the early seventies, there was a real distinction between Mexicans born here and those born in Mexico. Those born here coined the term 'Chicano.'[12] As more Latins and Mexicans came in that weren't born here, I don't think they related to that so much, so the term 'La Raza' came in. So [people referred to themselves as] Chicano-Latino or a Chicano-La Raza community"

In 1974, Santana featured a composition on its Lotus album called "Free Angela" by Bayete.[13] It referred to Angela Davis, a member of the Black Panther party, who had gained an international reputation due to her imprisonment and trial on conspiracy charges during 1970–1972. She had championed the cause of the "Soledad Brothers," a group of activists, most notably the young Black Panther member George Jackson, incarcerated in California's Soledad prison. Jackson's younger brother, Jonathan, and two hostages, including a county judge, Harold Haley, died in August, 1970 during an attempt to gain George Jackson's freedom.

George Jackson was killed a little more than a year later in the yard of San Quentin prison during what was characterized as an escape attempt. Davis was accused of supplying Jackson with a weapon. In 1970, Ronald Reagan, then governor of California, cited her Communist sympathies as reason for her removal from her post at University of California-Los Angeles. During that same year, she had been placed on the FBI's Ten Most Wanted List.

---

[12] Originally a disparaging term referring to an American-born citizen's lack of Mexican authenticism, "Chicano" was appropriated by second-generation Mexican-Americans as a badge of pride.

[13] Aka Todd Cochran, an avant-funk keyboardist with whom Mike Shrieve joined forces to create Automatic Man.

"I was singled out as the target of repression and was charged with very serious crimes—murder, kidnapping, and conspiracy—and spent a year and a half in jail, during which time there was an enormous international movement which I would compare today to the campaigns to free Leonard Peltier or to free Mumia Abu Jamal," Davis says today. "It was when the campaign was successful and I was released that people began to look to me for leadership. There was a feeling we were on the cusp of a revolution, which may have inspired people in a way not possible today, since we face such enormous forces that seem difficult to contest." During her incarceration, an international "Free Angela Davis" campaign led to her release in 1972.

Malo appeared in one of the "Free Angela Davis" benefits at the Berkeley Community Theater on February 28, 1972, with Taj Mahal, Herbie Hancock, and poet Maya Angelou. Santana had already been linked with the Black Panthers, playing a benefit (also at Berkeley Community Theater) for the organization on February 6th, 1970. The show was broadcast on KPFA radio, the independent Pacifica station located just down the street. Carlos Santana was quoted as saying it was one of the first band's best shows. The brainchild behind the show, however, was one of the band's worst nightmares.

Pianist Alberto Gianquinto was responsible for arranging the show. A graduate of Mission High School and, like Arcelio Garcia, a real talent at baseball, he was also as unpredictable as a tornado. "Alberto was a very revolutionary cat; he had a beard and a beret like Che Guevara," Carlos says. "I always have fond memories of him; he had a lot of respect. I know some people might have been rubbed differently to him, because of whatever chemicals he was taking."

Alberto Gianquinto was raised in Eureka Valley and had joined the Colt 45s (the National Baseball League team in Houston). He started playing piano at the age of twelve; he also found time to father his first child at the age of thirteen. He had also written his autobiographical anarchist workbook, *Three Steps to Anarchy*. This was a polemnic against politicians and capitalism and the police.

He had seen service in Vietnam and returned home to marry Bonnie Warren (they actually married twice). A gig with BB King led to his re-contact with Santana.

Image: Courtesy Eric Minton

Alberto Gianquinto paying his dues.

Gianquinto toured with Santana in 1970 to promote the *Abraxas* album and was responsible for co-penning "Incident at Neshabur," a tribute to the Haitian revolutionary Toussaint L'Ouverture. The tune musically illustrates one of L'Ouverture's battles against colonial French forces in Haiti.

"'Incident at Neshabur' was a real stretch for the players in the band," says Gregg Rolie. "Carlos gave that song to Alberto as a wedding gift. Alberto used to say there's no wrong notes, there's just good or bad ones." As Carlos remembers it, "[Gianquinto] wrote the part in 'Incident in Neshabur,' which originally he sang, which went, 'Can you do, can you dig, can you do the pimp thing. Go ahead brother, right on.' That was a chant he'd sing. I think he had this fantasy about being a pimp."

"To this day Haitians tell me that 'Touissant L'Ouverture' means so much to them on the third album. I have a friend, Lolo, the leader of Boukman Experience, he's like the Haitian Bob Marley, and it's a very real thing—they're still fighting the struggle," recalls Michael Shrieve. Gianquinto took the revolutionary role seriously, according to Shrieve: "David Brown lived with Alberto, who was loaded to the gills with weapons at his house. Alberto looked like a Mexican revolutionary."

"Let me tell you about Alberto," says Rolie. "One time he came up to my house and he thought pointing his M1 rifle at me was hilarious. He was a shade off."

"There was a lot of crazy stuff surrounding us but we were totally into the music," adds Shrieve. "We did the Black Panther benefit and we were sympathetic because Alberto got us into it. Even though he was white, he was a black revolutionary. David Brown was also into it, on the fringe. He was living with Alberto and felt compelled also, as he was Afro-American."

Santana decided to play the benefit largely due to Gianquinto's influence. "When we played for the Panthers, it was a radical time," says Carlos. "There was lot of tension then. The media was different then. TV today is very selective; it's a Nintendo game. In the sixties they showed people getting their asses kicked. You'd turn on the TV and see a Vietnamese monk pouring gasoline on himself and setting himself on fire. You'd see the FBI shooting up a house full of Black Panthers." The context of social and political revolution was musically exciting, but the reality proved less inspiring. Each player in this drama had a different motivation for joining the revolution—and that didn't always make for a happy ending. The benefit concert proved to be an unhappy chapter in a story that began with good intentions.

Rather than a celebratory atmosphere, the band encountered a massive police presence at the theater. "What I remember is walking in the building and being searched four times before getting to the backstage area, for weapons," says Shrieve. "Then going out to perform, being searched another four times, which I found very offensive." Shrieve also was disappointed by the generally grim audience. Perhaps he'd hoped for a warmer reception at a concert they'd considered a righteous cause.

"I said as much—y'know, who's doing who a favor here? I remember playing to a very stiff, militant crowd. Doing the drum solo I dropped one of my sticks and held my hands up and made some comment. I felt resentful about the cool non-response to the music, which was non-typical and inappropriate for Santana's music. I felt there was no gratitude towards us for lending our talent and time. By the time I left I felt more offended by them than warm."

"For Mike Shrieve and I, it wasn't about black and white, it was about deep or shallow," Carlos says. "We wanted to be around deep people like Miles Davis, Herbie Hancock, Keith Jarrett, and Wayne Shorter. Miles never hung the black thing on us—never! We always knew that our skin was not a threat to anyone and their skin was not a threat to us. We were on a quest to learn as much as we could."

"To me, that Berkeley benefit thing was a fiasco," says Rolie. "You know, I'm Norwegian, so people coming up with 'Viva La Raza' didn't always mean a lot to me. It was a very tense show. It was a high watermark for us though, that black, white, and Latino were so into our sound."

However detrimental Gianquinto's politics may have been to his judgment, they were a driving force behind his sound. "Alberto was into Mao, Che Guevara," says Johnny Villanueva. "It gave him an edge that added to his playing." According to Carlos Santana, "Alberto was an incredible white piano player. He was one of the first whites to go to the South Side of Chicago and actually play with black musicians. At that time it was taboo; you couldn't do that." Adds Carlos: "When black people found out he could play like Otis Spann or Thelonious Monk, it would be, 'This white boy's bad.'"

As the band's schedule ramped up, drugs began to take the place of political activism. In the end, Alberto Gianquinto would become a victim of his own cool. "He was always on his game. He died huddled in a doorway on the streets of Kansas City. Alberto made Charlie Parker look like an upstanding citizen," said a local critic.

Photo: Joan Chase

Santana with Alberto Gianquinto (second from left) outside the Royal Albert Hall, London, England, 1970.

Angela Davis

Huge Cop-Killer Search

6 Youths Wanted in Shooting

GARY LESCALLET   **JOSE MELENDEZ**
Two of the six sought by police

Clipping: Courtesy San Francisco Chronicle

Mission district musicians and artists produced their music, art, and poetry against a backdrop of social turbulence during the 1970s. "Oakland was the predominantly black area, [but] at the time, they had never had any black elected officials; we had Edwin Meese who had worked for ther Nixon administration," Chuy Varela points out. Similar imbalances between race and representation were true of San Francisco and the rest of the Bay Area. "There was so much abuse going on, everybody's ass was getting kicked. There was a case of a Mexican guy, Bardo Benevidez. Bardo was shot in the back, point blank. There was a similar incident later on in San Francisco with Los Siete. The Panthers were deep, man, they said, 'Fuck this, we're gonna protect the community.'"

The trial of Los Siete ("The Seven") galvanized the Latin community and sparked the politicizing of the Mission districts. "Los Siete de La Raza were Toni Martinez, Mario Martinez, Jose Rios, Bebe Melendez, Gary Lescallet, Nelson Rodriguez, and Gino Lopez who defended themselves from harassment by officers Joseph Brodnick and Paul McGoran on May 1, 1969," chronicled Francisco Flores of the Mission district newspaper *El Tecolote*. "The officers were investigating them because they were moving a 'hot' television set into a house on Alvarado St. After the altercation, Brodnick lay dead on the sidewalk of Alvarado St. in Noe Valley."

Headlines in the *San Francisco Chronicle* the next day already proclaimed the youths the focus of a "Huge Cop-Killer Search," although they were merely sought for questioning. Recalls Pete Gallegos: "Nobody knew who did what, but none of the seven had a gun. They were put on trial for murdering a cop. It polarized the community; they felt that the police had targeted the seven without real cause. It was a big trial; it was going on as the same time as the Soledad thing [the trial of 'Soledad Brothers' defendants in the George Jackson case mentioned earlier] was going on."

During the trial, which opened May 19, defendant Rios claimed the police "were calling us punks and hitting us." The group's defense was headed by attorney Charles Garry, famous for defending Black Panther Chairman Huey Newton, and included attorney Michael Kennedy, who charged: "I think my client cannot get a fair trial in San Francisco because racism is permeating this country and permeating the people who will sit on this jury."

Los Siete's (The Seven) trial politicized the Mission District.

76

GARY LESCALLET
No burglary verdict

MARIO MARTINEZ
Still in custody

Clipping: Courtesy San Francisco Chronicle

Cesar Chavez and Dolores Huerta

Photo: Courtesy El Tecolote

The response from Mission district residents, in Flores's account, was "a well-spring of support for Los Siete [that] fostered the beginnings of The Committee to Free Los Siete de La Raza. The group became the mothership for organizing in the Mission. The Committee was born when community members met to plan the defense. A political campaign was launched that included rallies and picket lines, as well as an educational campaign to mobilize community and 'movement' support."

Meanwhile, "Charles Garry maintained that the only person who could have pulled the trigger was the other person with a gun at the scene: Officer McGoran," Flores writes. "His gun killed Brodnick. The officers' reputations as 'brutal' did not help the prosecution's case. Witnesses in the trial testified that McGoran kept marijuana at home in order to plant it on suspects. McGoran's ex-wife testified that he once kicked her out of a car on the freeway." Los Siete were acquitted 18 months after their arrest when the prosecution could not prove "beyond a reasonable doubt" that any of the seven had pulled the trigger.

The trial's influence proved long-lasting. The original support committee served as a catalyst for many other community-organizing efforts around police brutality and other issues where the legal rights of community residents were abused. During the same time period, many other organizing efforts were taking root and growing in the Mission community as part of "El Movimiento de La Raza" or the La Raza Movement. This was an overarching term used to describe community organizing within the Latino/Chicano community. Organizations such as La Raza En Accion Local and others established and operated a myriad of community programs including community breakfast programs, health clinics, legal resource centers, low-income housing, and many other community services which still exist today.

"It was very inspiring, a sense of fighting back," says Varela. "We'd also go to these 'Farm Workers' marches down in the valley. You'd have the Teamsters Union shouting in your face but the Farm Workers were peaceful. The late, great Cesar Chavez, a founder of California's United Farm Workers union in 1962, spent his life battling racial and economic discrimination. A proponent of non-violence, Chavez employed boycotts (such as the famous one against non-union grapes that ran for five years), hunger strikes, street theater, and impassioned speeches in his crusade to improve the lot of migrant farm workers by increasing contract protections, healthcare, and better pay. Chavez passed on April 23, 1993, at the age of 66. His funeral in Delano attracted 40,000 people. On August 8, 1994, he became the second Mexican American to receive (albeit posthumously) the Presidential Medal of Freedom—the highest civilian honor in the US.

Dolores Huerta, who co-founded the United Farm Workers Union with Chavez, helped transform the movement into a political power for radical change. "I think that we as a country and some religions—and I'll blame mine for one, I'm Catholic—have over the centuries done many injustices against people," she says. "There should be some kind of reparations for Native Americans, for African Americans, Asians, and Latinos, and women. People have got to feel a responsibility, become active, and participate." In 1988 she sued the San Francisco police department after a severe beating she sustained while demonstrating against presidential candidate George Bush's stance on pesticides. Today Huerta is secretary treasurer of the union, based in La Paz, California, and works from home.

Dolores Huerta

The forceful activism of the 1960s has perhaps quieted down, but the current culture in the Mission district is filled with complex and difficult social problems. Gentrification split the community in the early 21st century, racism has not abated, and ethnic and economic dividing lines prevail; yet a spirit of social consciousness lives on. In this thriving neighborhood, a sense of possibility and change remains constant. It is one place where a thinker such as Angela Davis might realize a dream to "seek political coalition strategies that go beyond racial lines… to bring black communities, Chicano communities, Puerto Rican communities, Asian-American communities together."

By 2025, Hispanics will make up a quarter of the population of the USA.

Photos: Courtesy El Tecolote

Santana rehearse with Jose Feliciano (third from left) at the Otani Mansion, Hawaii. Third from right is Santana's manager Stan Marcum.

Photo: Joan Chase

SHADES OF TIME

Photo: Joan Chase

Michael Shrieve at the Otani Mansion, Hawaii.

Photo: Joan Chase

Jose Chepito Areas at the Otani Mansion, Hawaii.

Jose Feliciano

Photo: Courtesy El Tecolote

The year 1971 began with promise for Santana. On New Year's Day, the band flew out to Hawaii to play the Crater Festival. They were put up at the Otani Mansion, on the beachfront. "Johnny [Villanueva] and I set up all the band's gear in the house," says Herbert. "It was real comfortable, and anytime they wanted to, they could come in off the beach and play. This is where all those songs with the multiple solos were jammed endlessly, like 'Jungle Strut' and 'Toussaint.' It was so high, I can remember Carlos and Neal rolling on the floor and hugging in fits of laughter. They were played much higher than was ever captured on the third album. When Neal got in the band, it was such a love-fest the way Carlos, Gregg, and Neal would trade solos. They would get so high and just hope and pray they could take the audience there. It was so special to be there."

Shrieve set up his drums in the mansion; "we used to jam in the house with José Feliciano. We'd play 'Light My Fire.' It was a great, fun opportunity." Around this time, the band started their ongoing trend of inviting guests onstage. One show that stands out from this period was at the Los Angeles Forum in early 1971, in which Feliciano joined them for spirited versions of 'Oye Como Va' and a gorgeous extended version of 'Guajira.'

Neal Schon: "...a fifteen-year-old with a lot of smarts" officially joins Santana.

Photo: Joan Chase

The group started the year in high spirits. A new album was being planned, along with a European tour preceded by an appearance in Ghana. Almost immediately setbacks necessitated a number of changes. First was the introduction of guitarist Neal Schon into the band. Johnny Villanueva remembers Neal Schon as a fifteen-year-old with "a lot of smarts; he had played the oboe before the guitar." Herbie Herbert adds: "At a certain point, when they added Neal Schon, it took it to a new high point. After that anyone else was a liability. I'm talking Rico Reyes, Victor Pantoja, and Coke Escovedo. They came in, so blazingly ambitious."

"Bringing in Neal Schon was a good transition," David Brown commented later. "Most bands woulda been uptight; it was like bringing in another wife."

"I started hanging out with Gregg Rolie a lot; his dad lived nearby my folks in San Mateo," says Schon. "Gregg had a piano there. I would cut school to go there and jam. Soon after, he started to take me to Santana rehearsals while they were doing *Abraxas*. I was a 'streety' person; I was a little juvenile delinquent, a mastermind thief. I was too young to work, so I'd steal equipment from music stores that I needed to play. I had a lot of attitude for a kid my age.

"Old Davis was one of the biggest bands on the Peninsula at that time. [They played] good-time rock, songs like 'Road Runner.' I joined them for about half a year and we were playing at the Poppycock in Palo Alto. Our bass player was 'Nine Year' Woodridge; he was friends with Michael Shrieve and Gregg Rolie. He invited them to see us. They hung around and started jamming after the club closed to the wee hours of the morning."

Photo: Ron Reisterer, Oakland Tribune

Carlos Santana on stage at the Soul to Soul show, Accra, Ghana, Africa, February, 1971.

Neal Schon plays live with Santana.

Photo: Joan Chase

"Neal Schon came in out of a band called Old Davis," confirms Gregg Rolie. "We'd just recorded 'Incident at Neshabur' in the studio. Neal came in and ripped a solo on 'Mother's Daughter' and even then his talent was evident. Neal came in after the Berkeley gig, when Derek and the Dominoes were in town, and Neal had already had their offer to join Eric [Clapton]. I remember Eric, Carlos, Neal, and John Cippollina jamming that night on what would become 'Batuka.' Neal and Chepito were like idiot savants."

Like many other English blues players, Eric Clapton loved the Santana group. He visited Wally Heider's in late 1970 to check out and jam with the band. Neal Schon could hardly believe his eyes. When Schon later appeared with Clapton's Derek and the Dominoes at Berkeley Community Theater, Clapton invited him out for the encore. According to Herbie Herbert, "Clapton asked him to join Derek and the Dominoes. Neal said he'd already joined Santana.[14] Then Neal just said to Clapton, 'Can I play some of your solos at the show tonight?' He had such nerve."

Says Schon: "I finally joined Santana and my job was trying to keep my feet on the ground half the time, 'cause they were one of the biggest bands in the world. All of a sudden I'm outta high school, travelling the world. It was an experience I'll never forget."

Then, in February 1971, Chepito Areas suffered a brain hemorrhage just as Santana were due to travel.[15] Santana first tried Willie Bobo (who'd toured with Cal Tjader and led his own bands), on timbales for the first stop of the tour, the Soul to Soul show in Accra, Ghana. Ghana was then just entering the first flush of its independence from Britain, and the concert was a planned celebration featuring the cream of US soul and jazz, such as Roberta Flack, Les McCann & Eddie Harris, Wilson Pickett, and Ike & Tina Turner. "One of the things about that amazing trip to Africa was playing with Wilson Pickett," Schon says. "He was like God over there. James Brown was number one and Wilson was number two. The coolest thing I remember was the night before the show, [the African musicians] gave us a concert. It was so amazing; [they were] playing on logs—some of it sounded like Sly. It was all syncopated like funk. I've never heard it like that again."

---

[14] At Carlos's invitation. [15] Comments Johnny Villanueva: "Chepito was slipped some acid, doing a show with Jimi Hendrix. After he had the aneuryism, when he came back, he was a totally different person, a real prankster, just totally different, but he can still play his ass off." Adds Herbie Herbert: "Chepito had impossible chops, I swear to God; "at that moment he was the best percussionist in the world; and with all deference, that includes Tito Puente."

The gig was captured by a film crew and released in the cinemas the next year as *Soul to Soul*. Santana were shown pumping out "Jungle Strut," "Waiting," "Black Magic Woman/Gypsy Queen." Willie Bobo seemed a little out of his depth, got ill with almost the rest of the band, and was replaced for the remaining dates by Coke Escovedo.

"[Coke] came along at a time when we needed something stable," says Carlos. "He was a great musician and comes from a family of great musicians." Jorge Santana remembers Coke's influence on the music scene at the time: "At that time he was more known than his brother Pete."

"I remember Coke rehearsing at the Fillmore West with Azteca. He was an awesome player," recalls Johnny Valenzuela. "He played with Mongo Santamaria, Cal Tjader, and had his own thing going."

Neal Schon: "Willie Bobo was a really funny guy, very talented; but he wasn't Chepito, nor was Coke Escovedo, with all due respect to him. I've seen a zillion percussionists and there is no one that has the resilience and capabilities that Chepito has. A completely amazing player, he was the driver of Santana; he kept time and pushed time; he was like a box of fireworks."

Michael Shrieve met bassist Dougie Rauch, with the Voices of East Harlem, on the *Soul to Soul* trip. "I remember we got to talking about the new era of funk, like the Ohio Players, Kool and the Gang, Bernard Purdie. There was a lot of interest in a certain kind of funk-playing then.

Photo: Rudy Rodriguez

Coke Escovedo joins Santana for the rest of their 1971 European tour and further dates in the USA.

Dougie was a serious funk guy; he was very different in the way he approached the bass. He had a real mathematical mind; he was into odd time signatures done in the funk genre. He was different; he had this huge Afro, purple velvet or velour suits, purple shirts. He drove around in a Citroen with rose-colored shades, had a beautiful apartment in Nob Hill. He was one of the most different, cosmopolitan cats I ever met." Shrieve invited Rauch to join the band as a back up for David Brown, whose talent was being eroded by escalating drug use.

On the first leg of their European tour, Santana was almost involved in a riot in Milan, Italy, due to the no-show of the band's equipment and subsequent cancellation of the concert. Rolie and Carabello attempted to appease the unruly crowds. Guns were pulled on the band and a crewmember was taken hostage. Herbie Herbert finally recovered the band's truck and equipment.

Doug Rauch, bassist from the Voices of East Harlem, also joined Santana as part of their 1971 European tour.

Carlos Santana (left) and Neal Schon on stage during the 1971 European tour.

A film of Santana's European tour during 1971 (which never got to final cut and print), shot during their visits to Italy, France, and Switzerland by English filmmakers Nick Rowlands and Mike Myers, shows a band under the strain of three years of hard touring and the excess of success. With Dougie Rauch, Coke Escovedo, and the personnel team of Stan Marcum, Ron Estrada, Herbie Herbert, John Villanueva, and Barry Imhoff on board, this dynamic line-up was almost too combustible to last. Santana played two sellout shows at the Hammersmith Odeon, London, in which the band, with Coke Escovedo on timbales, blazed. "When we went to London, I went to the Stones' place, Stargroves, to negotiate the mobile for the show, talking to [Jimi Hendrix's producer] Eddie Kramer," says Herbert. "I remember Kramer was recording the show. Carlos and Neal, who'd just come out of the hospital [with the flu] in Switzerland, were being watched by Eric Clapton, Jimmy Page, George Harrison—the cream of the pop aristocracy. Every guitar player in the world was at that show. Neal was as sick as a dog but he just jumped over that shit. He just wailed. It was funny 'cause if you watched David Brown, he'd be tapping his foot in a totally different time to what he was playing."

"Carlos was real nervous the night we played Hammersmith Odeon with Clapton, Page, and Beck there," recalls Schon. "I remember Carlos was drinking Bromo-Seltzer to calm his stomach down." The shows started with the instrumental "Ballin'," a rarely played piece on which the ensemble sizzled. A particular standout from these shows is the version of "Soul Sacrifice," with a big funk, wah-wah beginning by Carlos and Schon. Carabello particularly did a fine, rapid conga solo on this outing. They were awarded a rapturous ovation, driving the crowds into a frenzy.

Not everyone was as ecstatic. "This stiff-upper-lip guy, he was the stage manager, was trying to close the curtain on the band at Hammersmith, London," says Herbert. "He wanted a curfew. Being a hippie from Berkeley, I didn't want to do it but I had no choice. I wrapped him in the curtain, gave him a haymaker, just knocked him out."

Upon their return to the states, the band began working on more material for their third album, but "things were coming unglued," according to Herbert. At a gig at Cobo Hall in Detroit, the band were administered a communal dose of acid to try to alleviate the tense mood that surrounded the members.

Herbie Herbert: "When the band was splitting up, we tried to change the spiral by dosing them with liquid Owsley. It was Gregg's first acid trip; we took the drops too, to stay on the same page. It was the most electrifying show at Cobo Hall at Detroit and Carlos was wondering what was going on. Gregg said, 'We're all tripping.' This was about two days after Carlos and the percussion section had their Mexican standoff."[16]

Neal Schon: "We used to drink from a big keg of beer; everyone got blasted [on LSD]. The music was really electric. We started to come on about half way into the performance. We took the audience on a excursion."

That summer also saw the great original Santana band with Schon, augmented by Rico Reyes and Coke Escovedo, play their swan song, closing as the Fillmore's final act on July 4, 1971—the beginning of the end of an era. Santana are also captured on the *Last Days of the Fillmore* soundtrack, with a striking version of "Incident at Neshabur" and a one-off version of "In a Silent Way," underpinned by David Brown's ominous bass rumble showing the way for the more jazz-fusion-inspired work of Santana.

---

[16] Carlos refused to tour again unless Carabello left the band, due to friction, partly over drug use.

Photo: Joan Chase

Rico Reyes and Carlos Santana

There has been some confusion over what happened to the accounting and royalty aspects of the original Fillmore triple live box set release. Allegedly, a lot of the bands involved did not receive due royalties. A film of the same name was released in 1972. It seemed to be filmed by cameramen in the grip of a quaalude vortex, with wobbly camerawork, shambolic montage cutting, and poor, muddy sound. Sloppy and uninspired, it even dampened the impact of Santana's impassioned set.

"That night at the Fillmore was the greatest musical night of my life," says Johnny Valenzuela. "The tickets were $3.50; they were sold out and we had to get a ticket outside for $12—that was unheard of at the time. Tower of Power came on; of course they were awesome. Then they were setting up for a mystery band; all I saw was this wall of amplifiers. This guy comes out in this Elvis-looking suit. Clean cut, short hair. Then they launch into 'Born on the Bayou.' It was Creedence Clearwater Revival. The crowd just went nuts. By the time Santana came on, the crowd was in frenzy. Chepito got me backstage and I remember having a drink with Carlos. I think Carlos was on such a natural high that night. I was behind the amps, behind Chepito, just watching the set."

Santana at the time did little in the way of interviews, but Ben Fong-Torres's excellent *Rolling Stone* piece, which went to print in December 1972, titled "The Resurrection of Santana," shed some light on the band's astonishing ascent towards fame and their subsequent fall. Again, it highlights the turmoil, inspired lunacy, and sheer chutzpah of that time in the music business before corporatism and bean-counting became paramount.

Photo: Joan Chase

Santana during one of many poses for the *Santana 3*
inner sleeve photo sessions.

Photo: Courtesy Neilal & Amber Schon

BATUKA

Santana 3 album cover artwork.

Mike Carabello and Gregg Rolie on their "hogs."

All photos on this spread: Joan Crase

After the phenomenal sales of the first two records, Santana pulled off a triple whammy by recording *Santana 3* in 1971. The road to recording the disc, however, was littered with bullshit, remembers Herbie Herbert. "When it was time to do the third Santana album, it's: 'Money doesn't matter; you guys have sold zillions of records.' It was also: 'You guys are destroying our infrastructure at CBS.' Our main argument was, we don't wanna record in Los Angeles; it was anathema to a hippie. Your engineers suck; so fuck you. So we were told they were building a CBS studio on Folsom Street (which used to be Coast Recorders) and you WILL record there.

"I go to the new studios, walk into Studio A; all of a sudden, I'm grabbed. 'What are you doing in here, this is Roy Halee's studio, that's for Simon & Garfunkel and Blood, Sweat & Tears!' OK, so I set up Santana's gear in Studio B. It was small, brand-spanking new, just cherry, tits to the Ritz. Johnny ['Zopi'] Villanueva and me were setting up for Santana; we met the studio manager, Roy Segal. The band showed up and they just opened the front door and Carabello rode his Harley in from the front to the back.

Michael Shrieve, left, and David Brown, right, flank Clive Davis, CEO of Columbia Records.

Neal Schon on stage

Photos: Joan Chase

"Upstairs is American Zoetrope, [Frances Ford] Coppola and George Lucas, making that film THX1138, while all this is going on. Chepito had a kleptomaniac streak; he just started and when we looked up, he'd stolen everything—light bulbs, soap, and even the pencils. After that first night at CBS, things were a mess. I'd go in next day; I see Roy Segal, who was beet red. He lunged at me. 'Motherfucker, heathen, you bastards, fuckin' ingrates, destroying my facility, everything's gone.'

"I say, 'Chepito's a freakin' klepto, man, I don't know what we can do about him.' Segal shows me feet marks on the wall, skid marks from the Harley on the linoleum, walls are scraped. 'You're gonna be so fuckin' sorry.' Grabs the phone: 'Clive, this is Roy in San Francisco; those fucking bastards have wrecked the studio.'

"Clive says, 'Put Herbie on. Hi, this is Clive Davis, how's it going, how's the recording going?'

"'Oh, it's going great.'

"'OK, give me Roy again.' Clive says to Roy, 'They are recording, they are making progress, and don't call me again.' Click! They were crazy during the third record but there was a lot of excitement also. I thought that record was a peak."

Santana 3 is an astonishing tour-de-force with a ferocious edge. "Batuka" is Neal Schon's debut proper. A Sly-influenced conga pattern by Carabello, supported by Areas's cowbells and Shrieve's crisp hi-hat, underscores a wild guitar solo that cuts and parries against the onslaught of Carlos's, Rolie's, and Brown's rhythmic thrusts. Schon's playing echoes Hendrix and leads the vanguard for the later chainsaw-playing of Pete Cosey and Reggie Lucas in Miles Davis's band. As on *Abraxas*, the first side has the feeling of a seamless suite. A short vibes passage played by Shrieve introduces "No One to Depend On," which itself owes some kudos to Willie Bobo's "Spanish Grease." A sultry Gregg Rolie song, "Taboo," allows Schon further room to flex his radical, fiery style. "Toussaint L'Ouverture" closes side one and is a Santana classic—a hot ride through some of Santana's best ensemble playing. After a dynamic opening by Carlos, the percussion section opens up for some serious grooving, over which Carabello and Areas solo on conga and timbales respectively. The tension builds again after a smoldering midsection in which Carlos's sweet guitar sting draws the piece towards its powerful conclusion—an immense finale with Rico Reyes and the band chanting "Vamonos negra, a bailar mi guaguanco," over which drop some of the hottest solos Santana ever recorded. Rolie takes the first solo turn, Schon the second, followed by Carlos; then they stoke the temperature higher by going around again. Schon's second solo is a deranged explosion, which ends in a haze of pure feedback. Carlos's burning solo takes the song to its abrupt end. Adds Mike Shrieve, "I remember we did several takes of it; it was all about the performance—the energy on that take was so high, so intense, whenever I sit in with Carlos I ask to play that one."

The album's second side had a lot of grit, too. "Guajira" stands out as a beautiful, folksy take on Afro-Cuban music. Superb vocals by Rico Reyes lend it the "sounds from the street" tag that the band enjoyed. Mario Ochoa contributes an authentic salsa-style acoustic piano. Areas's bass intro and timbales fills are a delight, with a little Chepito flugelhorn to round things out before a sweeping solo by Carlos, in which his guitar has the edge of a violin in tone and sharpness. "Guajira" really was the biggest Latin-flavored cut with its insistent cha-cha-cha beat and Spanish lyrics. It's another Santana classic.

"Everybody's Everything" thunders along on an Areas drum track and features a classic solo by Schon, stepping on the wah-wah midway through to push the solo up a few more (buenos) notches. The Gene Ammon soul-funk jazz vehicle, "Jungle Strut," gives Rolie, Carlos, and Schon a chance to again blow with passion over a boiling percussion section. Michael Shrieve brought "Jungle Strut" to the table: "I loved that Gene Ammons tune; the original had Bernard Purdie on drums." "Everything Is Coming Our Way" is a sensitive Carlos original, which benefits from a glorious Rolie Hammond B3 solo. It's a short respite before all hell breaks loose for the final track, "Para Los Rumberos," a Tito Puente tune that finishes the album in lightning style. Shrieve remembers Coke Escovedo bringing the tune in during the album's recording. It affirms and stresses the Latin roots of Santana's music, complete with razor-sharp trumpet flourishes by guest Luis Gasca.

Santana 3 rushed into the *Billboard* chart in mid-October 1971, peaked at Number 1, and stayed there for five weeks. In total, the album spent 39 weeks on the chart. "Everybody's Everything" was released as the first single, attained the Number 12 slot, and charted for 10 weeks. "No One to Depend On" was the second single, which stayed on the chart for nine weeks and reached the Number 39 position.

Carlos Santana

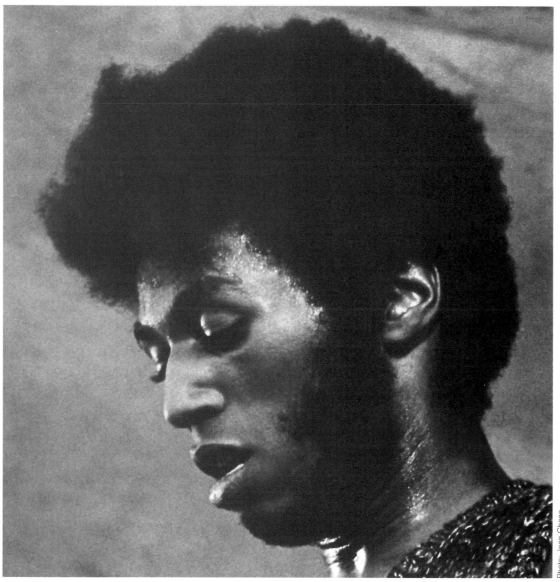

Photo: Joan Chase

David Brown

The album was wrapped in an evocative fold-out cover with the Heavy Water Light Show's projection on front. A mystical amoebic lunar landscape is towered over by entities, which look as if they are locked in spiritual combat. The inner sleeve featured a sepia-tinted group shot in which the original band stare defiantly into the camera, giving off the attitude of musical revolutionaries. "Chicks loved the band," recalls Jeff Trager. "Here was this bunch of far out, good-looking, intense, evil guys with big hair. They had the groove and they never gave it up!" In retrospect, they were less united than they looked; each band member has a different take on the recording experience.

"The third album had everything on it; I think the band jelled well," says Gregg Rolie. "When the music didn't jell, our communication wasn't there. To be 21, you've got everything, you can do anything you want, you get a little spoiled and stupid. It was too much, too soon for everybody."

"It was my first record. I had no fear," says Neal Schon. "It was pretty much one-take solos on all the record. Even 'Touissaint' was live in the studio—really great energy. The original band was a monster in its own right. Looking at it now, everyone had their choice of drugs. Had everyone not been so high, we might have weathered it. By this time these guys were fucking insane. I've been in a lot of different bands, but no one comes remotely near to being insane as these motherfuckers. But everybody had their day in court, you know."

"Playing with those guys was something else," according to David Brown in a 1987 interview at Mission Cultural Center. "It was always a good game with Santana. The third album was great for me. I wrote 'Guajira' along with Chepito José, and that was like giving back to the Latin community what they gave me: 'You gave us love and the music; here's this back.' I wrote that in Hawaii. I would do it all over again for free."

"I'm surprised the third album was as coherent as it was," says Shrieve. "It was a terrible time; a lot of dissension and cocaine around the band. It wasn't quite the bar scene in *Star Wars*, but it was wild, it wasn't pretty. It doesn't matter if it's [happening] in the Four Seasons Hotel; it's still low-rent stuff. It was too crazy. That's why it imploded."

And that's why, perhaps, as Jeff Trager notes, "'Everybody's Everything' was the first Santana single that didn't do so well." Like the band, "it was played, but it went cold pretty quick."

Santana 45 vinyl single sleeve: released France, 1972. Note the spelling mistake "No One to *Defend* On"

Courtesy: CBS Records

Michael Shrieve

Santana

Photos: Joan Chase

NO ONE TO DEPEND ON

Carlos Santana

Santana 45 vinyl single sleeve, released USA, 1972.

Carlos Santana: "We entered one of the worst periods of my life. Success was getting to be too much. We were trying to make *Santana 3*, but overindulgence in everything available to a successful rock 'n' roller was becoming a problem. I started catching my friends shooting up in the bathroom."

"The fame and where it led to, people thinking they were untouchable, kinda blew the band apart," says Michael Carabello. "When Neal came out on the road, he'd room with me. We hung out and I taught him some bad habits. Drugs were free-flow back then. Sly, Jimi, and Keith Richards influenced other drugs. I think what killed us also was we were always on the road—no breaks. I think we were lost for a while. We practically worked 365 days a year. As we became successful, our managers and road crew thought they should be rock stars also. Nobody, apart from Bill Graham, kept a level head. The drugs affected us on the road; we had X-rated people hanging around, drug dealers, and vice people. We certainly stayed awake a lot."

Courtesy: CBS Records

Santana 45 vinyl single sleeve, released France, 1972.

Cocaine and heroin were making big inroads into the Californian music scene, and an element of glamour was associated with the use of hard drugs and its network of shady, yet colorful characters, loose ladies, and sexual intrigue. The good-time high came with a steep price; rock stars at this time were starting to die from hard drug use, mostly accidentally. Jimi Hendrix, Janis Joplin, and Jim Morrison of the Doors had all died before their thirtieth year.

"We were about three weeks from going to New York and we heard Jimi had passed," says Neal Schon. "Eddie Kramer did some recording for the third record at Electric Ladyland Studios. When we were in the studio; they showed us some of Jimi's clothes and stuff. Carlos and the band weren't happy with the way things were going in the studio, so we bailed. We were really bummed by Jimi's death. The vibe of being in Electric Ladyland after Jimi dying was not cool."

"Cocaine ruined and changed the landscape of our communities," says Percy Pinckney. "I think Sly Stone was a genius, but his popularity grew too fast for him and the drugs overcame him." Drugs also overcame Coke Escovedo, one of Santana's drummers during this period.

Photo: Johnny Valenzuela

Johnny Valenzuela tries out some groovy snakeskin covered timbales.

Johnny Valenzuela: "I remember Coke rehearsing at the Fillmore West with Azteca. He was an awesome player. He played with Mongo, Cal Tjader, and had his own thing going. He became a really good friend of mine and I was really sad to hear he died. He was on the way to a gig with Tierra and he was saying he didn't feel too good. I think they thought he was just being Coke, y'know, a real character. On the way to the show, he became sicker and died of liver damage. Even early on the drug thing was pretty heavy. I used to watch musicians in my own band do so much stuff, they would be peeing blood in the bathroom.

"It was part of the scene. Everybody was doing it, but you'd start to hear David Brown or Carabello were getting busted, or Chepito. Chepito was close to me, so he was the first I saw doing that stuff first hand. I've been in dressing rooms with Luis [Gasca], Mike Shrieve, Carmelo [Garcia]; sometimes they'd look like they were eighty years old but they were only in their twenties or thirties."

Villanueva (aka "Zopi") got caught up in musician's demands for nose candy as well, according to Herbie Herbert. "Zopi had to deliver stuff to Electric Ladyland."

Photo: Joan Chase

Gregg Rolie buys a Detomaso Mangusta sports car, originally kept for Steve McQueen.

Santana 45 vinyl single sleeve, released Mexico, 1972.

Courtesy: CBS Records

Sometimes the consequences of the drug scene were merely hilarious. "I remember Gregg Rolie tried to buy a real fancy car. It was a weekend and he's in his usual street wear," relates Fred Catero. "The salesman thinks: how do I get rid of this asshole? Gregg finally asks him, 'How much is this car?' It's, say, $50,000. The salesman says, 'Sir, we'll have to do a credit check.' Gregg says, 'It's OK, I'll pay cash.' So they go into the manager's office and sit down and Gregg pulls out a wad of bills; I think it was hundreds. So the guy starts counting; he's getting up to say, fourteen thousand. Gregg asks for the bathroom and the sales guy lets go of the money. Gregg comes back from the bathroom; it's back to twelve thousand. So eventually the guy's almost counted the bills. Finally Gregg says, 'STOP! If you count another bill, I'm walking out. If you don't trust me, I'm walking.'

Gregg finally closes the deal and the guy says 'You can't take it now, the shop is closed.' Gregg says, 'You can take the window away.' They get a guy to come and cut the window out! As Gregg drives off the showroom floor, the look on the salesman's face is priceless. And y'know what? He totaled it the first month."

Another on-the-road incident was the time Herbert and Rico Reyes got into an altercation: "Herbie's got Rico Reyes in a full military, pressed against the ceiling," recalls Villanueva. "Jim Hainey, the truck driver, we gave him a pound of weed. We're upstairs at the Howard Johnson going through all these changes with these idiots; [we said] 'Fuck this, man, let's get high,' go to Hainey's room. We knock on the door. After the third time the door opens. 'Wow, man, I thought you were the fuzz!' [Hainey], he'd tried to shove the whole pound down the toilet. The room was totally flooded out. They had the whole floor of the Howard Johnson and they never lost the attitude, y'know, fighting. Victor Pantoja had a knife pulled on him by Booker T. [of Booker T. and the MGs]. He wanted to kill Victor. Victor was screaming his head off; he wants to kill someone else. It was crazy."

Herbie Herbert remembers: "If anybody tried to attack us, the band would be right there. Me and Zopi were just about to be attacked by this crazy guy at Boston College. He had a hammer in each hand; he was coming at me and John and we were just fucked. Outta nowhere comes the whole band; Carabello comes and grabs the hammers, flips them up, and they land in a folded up basketball net. Then they jumped the motherfucker. The band would often jump us, too, out of the bushes."

Shrieve adds, "I can remember this little white boy from the suburbs, sometimes thinking, 'this ain't Kansas no more,' one knife fight being stopped by Sly in the hotel; as he walked into the middle of it, he stopped it—he was a very powerful, potent person."

In 1971, the band flew to Lima, Peru, to play a show for earthquake victims. "I can remember the coke thing in Peru," says Herbert. "We had prodigious amounts. The government deported us[17] and we sent Steve Kahn and Bob Gordon to retrieve the gear—over fifty cases of gear. We had been living in this house in San Isidro for two weeks. Mason jars full of the finest cocaine, big Peruvian newspapers full of coca leaves. All this was in my suitcase—the movie I'd made, loads of stuff. One day, we had to go to customs when the gear was returned and get the stuff. It was scary as hell. We got there, drove it away, and everything was there—the cocaine, the coca leaves, everything." As Carlos put it: "Rock and roll madness at its peak."

Santana's own weak link was Alberto Gianquinto, the talented but mercurial pianist. According to one observer: "There was an event on Wood Street; all these old-time musicos [musicians] in this place jammin' one after another. Alberto strides right from the side of the stage and plays this volcanic eruption, rips the place in half, and then just splits, maybe a two-minute performance. He was a troubled spirit, fucked up, but there was room for that street presence in Santana."

"Alberto was a accomplished musician," notes Herbert. "He was playing with the James Cotton Blues Band. For a white kid from San Francisco to be playing with one of the best blues bands in the country was something else. He had greasy black hair; he lived that cool cat vibe, and [he had] heroin. Alberto really influenced David into heroin [when] he moved into the house on York Street."

David Brown's fall due to drugs had the force of tragedy, as he'd had such a promising beginning. Brown was known for his stunning good looks ("the prettiest human being, I've ever seen," claims Herbie Herbert), his easy acceptance of nearly everyone ("Other people were very racist but David was color-blind"—Herbert again) and his almost studious lack of predictability. "David had this stunning, chiseled face and he could get away with wearing all these different headscarves and bizarre stuff," says Rolie. "He would show up in new clothes, and we'd be like, 'Where's the old ones?' He'd just leave 'em in the dressing room or in the trunk of his car."

According to Herbert, Brown and Chepito Areas were "like Abbot and Costello, they were so funny together; non-stop about their sexual prowess. [In the bedroom], Chepito would take everything off except for his black socks. I guess that was to keep him grounded!"

---

[17] According to Carlos Santana, "For our own protection, we were shuffled out of the country" after "the communist students rioted against the USA."

Michael Shrieve: "David Brown was a unique guy; he was very unassuming in terms of his personality. It's like I never heard him stand up for himself or fight back. Musically, as a bassist, there was some things that was so funny we'd play together, he'd really play behind the beat; like on 'Jingo,' his foot would be beating in four—I couldn't understand how he was hearing it. The band always wanted to be THE thing. David used to hang out with Carabello; they went through their Sly Stone phase together. They tried to emulate Sly, which wasn't a good idea for anybody. They had the look, wearing wigs. It would be easy to be enamoured of Sly Stone, both in his personality and his music; off the stage he was a huge personality—he made you feel like you could do anything. Sly was happening, Miles with Bitches Brew was happening, Hendrix was happening, and when we were in New York, we were all happening together. David, being a stunning black man, lent us a lot of credibility as a multiracial unit. I miss him all the time."

David Brown's sisters Diane Black and Jan Cameron were backup singers with Sly Stone. They recalled when "We went in the studio with Sly a couple of times through this girl Dawn who was with the Brides of Funkenstein. Sly called us the Wild Bunch. This was around the time we were playing and recording with David. We went to see Sly at this club one night; he was beating the drums, he suddenly fell over backwards and he disappeared—we never saw him again that night."

Diane and Jan Brown: the Wild Bunch.

Photo: Courtesy Diane Black/Jan Cameron

"David Brown was very discreet and mysterious," says Schon. "He'd have all kinds of shit going on that nobody would know about. I met Sly Stone at Folsom Street, but everyone was messed up on cocaine, and the chances are if they hung with him, they'd be messed up even more. I think everyone had mental breakdowns, with the fatigue and aftermath of that drug. Everyone that does cocaine, everything's gonna fall apart around them eventually."

Diane, Brown's sister recalls: "We didn't know David had a drug habit. When we moved to our new house, that's when David told us he had a two-hundred-and -fifty-dollar-a-day habit. That was really shocking to us."

David Brown

Photo: Joan Chase

One day, the Santana band left the rehearsal room at the original rehearsal hall on Fillmore Street. "David was just passed out, up against the wall, really nodded out," says Herbert. "He'd been warned after a series of things, and I had to wake him up and say, 'David, you did it bad this time, we have to let you go.' I always had time for David. Set him up in whatever new apartment he was currently moving to. You can go to the darker places, or see him as a total person of beauty we went through a wonderful era with. When David was gone, it wasn't the same band. Tom Rutley! Forget about it! They found him at a Playboy club, playing with the house band."

"David was having problems; he was still in the band," says Shrieve. "So we had Dougie Rauch come in as a last resort. Dougie had great respect for David. Dougie had a large effect on Santana; had he been alive now, he'd be perfect for this age—he was very gear orientated; he'd have completely been into the whole computer thing. Dougie never really got the credit he deserved. He was an innovator who turned the bass around."

A meeting was called at Gregg Rolie's house in Mill Valley to discuss the band's escalating drug usage and to try to promote some understanding to counteract the increasingly tense group situation. The band collectively agreed things were out of control, particularly in respect to heavy cocaine use. Gregg Rolie: "I remember the meeting. The band was pretty much in agreement to try and control the drinking and drugs, except for Carlos. He wouldn't agree that his dropping acid was a drug problem and it had anything to do with any of the problems at hand. The lack of compromise was pretty much it for me."

"The original Santana band went to cocaine heaven," says Herbert. "The acid, though, just acerbated the problem. Carlos would be listening to Mahavishnu in his room, saying 'This is where we should be going.' My feeling was, 'No Carlos, this is over everybody's head; what we're doing now is right on the money. Don't go there.' Y'know: Great jazz chops? Chops belong in a butcher's shop.

"Carabello was nuts. I tried to help him out and get him to apply himself; if I had Cheppy [Chepito] there, I'd be downloading him like a program. Next thing I know he was getting arrested, naked, in a closet, with a pound of coke. Even Gregg eventually got into blow. By the time it came to *Caravanserai*, nobody was going to the studio at the same time. We were devastated at the end of the first band, all this bravado, Carlos thinking the grass is greener elsewhere, and Carabello not missing your water till the well runs dry.

"Gregg and I agreed that the early Santana really put everything on the line. Somebody had to have vision and steer things. It wasn't just the drugs, but the inmates were running the asylum. Management was higher than the band, just too high to get the job done. [Co-managers] Ron Estrada, Stan Marcum, and David Brown took themselves out of the game. There are only two types of people in the world: those that don't know and those that don't know they don't know. I know I don't know. By this time Stan is really junked out; he's managing the biggest band in the world. They had the world by the balls, but they just let their opportunity go by." Carlos admits in retrospect: "Everything was tight until we realized we were touring too much; we didn't have the management to say, 'you tour for six months and take three months and learn new music.' We were like frogs in a blender. To make yourself feel good, you take more drugs. We needed to replenish, to refuel. That's what I tell the new bands, three weeks on, three weeks at home."

Michael Shrieve: "I can see the cocaine and how we had changed; it was as if we were the lost boys. Now we've gone over to the dark side, the light has left us. I can see the distance between us and I felt bad for us, because we didn't want it to be like that. The drugs? We weren't capable of dealing with it. It was too hippie. I remember once when *Abraxas* was coming out, the first release of *Abraxas* was there to greet us at the airport, after we got back off tour, and my name wasn't on the record. I worked so hard on that; I edited the singles and we all worked real hard. Stan Marcum looks at me and says, 'Hey man, but you know you played on it.' I knew at that moment we were in two different places."

Leaving Santana, Alberto Gianquinto had a $83,000 debt to the government, which he laid at the door of a Santana accountant, who made "mistakes."

He led an increasingly rough lifestyle during periods of the seventies, getting shot and stabbed but managed to get "recovery" thru Alcoholics Anonymous. He then joined Columbus University to study a degree (French and jazz) and get away from the street life that both enticed and endangered him in the city.

"Santana was breaking up. In the middle of that, they were doing *Caravanserai*," says Jeff Trager. "I remember it was Gregg Rolie's birthday. We were at Bimbos [and] got a call from Gregg's father in Seattle. We go up there and Gregg takes us out on his brand new speedboat. Gregg's drunk, we're out in the middle of this lake, we break down, and we're stuck out there all night. That's when he played me the *Caravanserai* music."

Photo sequence: Jim McCarthy

Mike Carabello throwing it down on congas.

102

DRUMS ON FIRE

Beginning in the mid-1960s, inspired by Michael Olatunji's *Drums of Passion* and Mongo Santamaria's *Afro Blue*, drummers took to the streets to trade licks and school each other. Michael Carabello was a spectator and part of the emerging street percussion scene. "There was a lot of music going on; my grandmother would play records of Latin stuff; she lived over at Double Rock by Hunter's Point. My grandmother's was one of the first Puerto Rican families in San Francisco. After she died, my mom and I moved to Sunnydale Projects, over by the Cow Palace. Kind of funny that years later I'd play there with Santana. From there we went to live in the Mission. I got a lot of inspiration from hanging at Arcelio's house. They were like my second family."

On weekends, Carabello's dad would take him fishing at San Francisco's Municipal Pier in Aquatic Park. "I'd see these beatniks playing bongos and congas there but they weren't great players. I go over and watch them play. I was about nine or ten years old. Eventually, I went there one Sunday and it was a different bunch of people—some black cats, Cubans, and Africans playing Afro-Cuban drumming. So, I'd go fishing all the time, just to listen to these cats. One day I'd sat in and played. These guys, I found out, belonged to the Haight San Francisco Boys Club. After this I went to Polytechnic High School in the Haight Ashbury district and these guys were in my art class. Mr. Diamond would let us play congas in art class. I picked up the Afro-Cuban thing there and also from a cousin of Chepito's (this is way before I met Chepito); he was a great conga drummer. I met Carlos [Santana] in junior high school. Danny Haro was a drummer also; his family brought Carlos's family over here. His family owned the La Palma Market on 24th and Florida and they knew Carlos's father José. Everybody in the Mission went to St. Peter's Catholic Church. I went there for catechism. Carlos and I both liked to draw in high school; Carlos went to James Lick Junior High."

Mike Carabello, Santana's conga drummer, was part of the emerging "Percussion in the Parks" culture.

Photo: Joan Chase

"I think the whole Latin rock thing had a lot to do with the drumming in the parks," says conguero John Santos. "Before any of those bands happened, the drummers were hanging in the parks: Dolores Park in the Mission, Sproul Plaza on the University of California's Berkeley campus, Aquatic Park, and Precita Park; also 'Hippie Hill' in Golden Gate Park. We used to play at Marshall Banks Park in Daly City and on the top of Potrero Hill. For example, the first conga drummer that Santana had, Marcus Malone, would play there; also Carabello and Chepito.

"There was a guy called Harold who used to roadie for Santana. He had a house on Mullen Street, where they used to rehearse. The musicians would gather at the street fairs. I grew up two blocks from Mullen and I'd hang at the fair; they'd block the street off, put up a stage outside José Najera's house. Raul Rekow and I would also go to San Bruno Park to play a lot. We went to all the places. Dolores Park was the main one to hang at. Marcus Gordon, he was the first one to play the bata drums. He came from New York; he taught and it's mushroomed into a flowering scene today. Drummers like Pobaji and Babatunde Lea, they still play in the community now; they were from that first drum wave."

Johnny Valuenzuela: "We used to go to Dolores Park and Aquatic Park and all the conga players would jam. Mingo Lewis and Chepito would be out there. Mingo, I think is down in North Hollywood, working in a drumstore. Mingo was another awesome player; he was confident and he could give Chepito a run for his money. When he got off the drumset you'd have to buy brand new heads. He'd put welts in 'em, he'd hit them so hard. I worked on a bill with Dakila, Mingo's band, and Chepito's All-Stars—they were like Azteca—to promote his solo record. Chepito was a role model to me then. People would steal and take advantage of him—steal his gold records, y'know. He would cry with the success and the excess. Carmelo Garcia, who had been with Mongo Santamaria and also with Luis Gasca, also was a real happening player around that time. The young Raul Rekow, who played with us (and later joined Malo) had incredible energy and brought in other percussionists to jam with us. Leo 'Pepe' Rosales was one of them."

Photo: David Belove, Courtesy John Santos

John Santos

Dolores Park, Mission District, San Francisco.   Photo: Bob Sansoe

104

"In places like Aquatic Park and Dolores Park, the drum which was so essential to the sound had blossomed, and in the mid-1970s, Diane Feinstein [a San Francisco city supervisor] was saying you could no longer drum there," recalls Chuy Varela. "She signed the 'bongo ordinance'— she couldn't even tell the difference between a conga and a bongo.

"Street drummers were secondary victims of the crackdown. This was after the lowrider problems. Right here in Dolores Park, John Santos and Raul Rekow would play congas in the park on the weekends, and it got to be bigger and bigger; it attracted other good players. You'd have eight drummers sitting on the park benches. It was a nice acoustic vibe. The neighborhood filed a petition to stop this—again there was a clash, the mayor got involved, and the drumming got banned. The musicians fought it the best they could. Not everyone appreciated or understood the music. Raul Rekow and John Santos were cited—given fines, man!"

"It put a big damper on the scene," Santos says. "Most of the current drummers stopped going, but the community rose up in defense of the cultural statement."

Photo: Ricardo Vinos, Courtesy John Santos

John Santos

Photo: Jim McCarthy

Buddy Miles and Ron Johnson,
Live at Lincoln Festival, England, 1971.

LA FUENTE DEL RITMO / LAVA

Ron Johnson, Neal Schon, Hawaii Crater Festival, New Year, 1972.

Photo: Joan Chase

Buddy Miles

Photo: Herbert Worthington

By the end of 1971, Carlos and Buddy Miles got together to play live and record at the Hawaii Crater on New Year's Eve. The show itself, according to Neal Schon, was a complete "bosh"—a stoned, incoherent disaster. The band was made up partly of Buddy Miles's current touring band, Schon and Carlos, Hadley Caliman, Luis Gasca, Victor Pantoja, Coke Escovedo, and Greg Errico, the drummer with Sly and the Family Stone.[18] Buddy Miles's bass player, Ron Johnson, was a unique individual, spending most of his onstage time pumping out bass lines while revolving on one leg.

"Ron Johnson always had a wild look in his eye, like he was tripping on acid a lot," according to Schon. "The rehearsals were all over the place and everyone was doing drugs, nobody was very centered."

[18]

Errico grew up in the Mission district and had played with Carlos Santana at a neighbourhood pizza parlour circa 1964. He also went to school with Chris Wong. Later, he joined Freddie and the Stone Souls. "The Latin music scene wasn't really known, just the guys in the neighborhood," he says. "I was part of the musical blast, right in the middle with Sly Stone."

Willie Bobo   Buddy Miles   Victor Pantoja

Photo: Joan Chase

Columbia executives were not satisfied with the master tapes they received, and a recording of the whole thing was attempted again, live in the studio. The results are evident on *Live: Carlos Santana and Buddy Miles*, released in January 1972, complete with badly-spliced crowd cheering effects. Rolie, Areas, and Shrieve were absent, although Mike Carabello got dubbed onto the studio version. The set that made the records included roaring versions of "Marbles," a John McLaughlin piece, which segued into "Lava." Both cuts featured Schon at full frenzied flow, with a battering backbeat supplied by Errico and Buddy Miles's drumming. "Evil Ways" followed with horns and a short breather where one of Carlos's few solos springs out on the record. "Faith Interlude" has a brief, breath-of-fresh-air guitar solo from Carlos and then it's into the down and dirty funk of "Them Changes." This song had already been an R&B hit for Buddy Miles and was also featured on Hendrix's *Band of Gypsies* live recording. Carlos and Schon get down to some dual-edge funk rhythm playing and again, Schon takes center stage with a guitar solo deliriously soaked in wah-wah pedal. The second side of the record featured a jam called "Free Form Funkafide Filth." The 25-minute piece plows through various moods but is mainly notable for seriously demented playing by Schon and some parrying guitar between him and Carlos.

Ultimately, the big change for Carlos came in the form of a new musical direction represented by the band's next release. "I turned over a new musical leaf when we recorded *Caravanserai*," he says. "I was moving into the unknown. I didn't read music. I was working with advanced musicians like sax player Hadley Caliman, guitarists Neal Schon and Doug Rauch, Chepito, Mike Shrieve, Mingo Lewis, who were well into jazz."

Photo: Joan Chase

Carlos Santana and Buddy Miles

Michael Shrieve, doing the "drum thin

Photo: Joan Chase

Sleeves, Courtesy Columbia Records

Santana 45 vinyl single, released Greece, 1972.

Santana 45 vinyl single, released Germany, 1974.

Caravanserai is a turning point in Santana's music, and also marked a shift from the 1960s to the seventies. It divides many Santana listeners, especially those who loved the early band. However, there is much to enjoy here. Jazz influences abound in the presence of Pharoah Saunders, Miles Davis, and Gil Evans, while Schon, Rolie, and Areas ensure some of the early Santana flavor is evident. The album spans many tastes and again, as in *Abraxas*, flows like a suite. "Waves Within" shows Dougie Rauch's feel for outside time signatures and the current fusion of the Mahavishnu Orchestra. "Look Up to See What's Coming Down" features guitarist Doug Rodriguez,[19] wailing against a wah-wah funk wall overlaid by Rolie's Hammond B3 flourishes. "Song of the Wind" is a standout; again Carlos and Schon join forces to create an extraordinary instrumental piece on which both players stretch, full of fire and atmosphere, to an almost impossible segue where Neal takes over from Carlos, both displaying their telepathic guitar interplay. "On 'Song of the Wind,' I took the tape home and re-recorded my drum track. That's what you hear on the album. If I'd messed up, Neal and Carlos would have been mightily displeased" Shrieve says.

"All the Love of the Universe" showcases a storming Mike Shrieve drum track, as he drops jazzy fills through bar breaks and really opens up the drum kit's rhythmic base, over which Schon and Rolie wail furiously. Says Shrieve, "My playing then was really influenced by Jack DeJohnette and Tony Williams. I very much wanted to include that style of playing in there. No punch-ins on the tape; it wasn't pop music drums, it was playing over the bar lines, stuff like that." Shrieve's early interest in ambient and electronic music is apparent here in his spacy electronic sound collage of "Future Primitive" wrapped around a frantic percussion jam featuring Mingo Lewis on congas and Areas on yet another speedy timbales outing. "Stone Flower" demonstrates Carlos's and Shrieve's growing interest in Brazilian music. Says Shrieve: "'Stone Flower' was a instrumental by Antonio Carlos Jobim. I wrote the lyrics on acid. Carlos and I sang the song."

---

[19] Rodriguez also played with the Voices of East Harlem and went on to join Mandrill.

"La Fuente Del Ritmo," written by Mingo Lewis, is another frenzied jam in which the percussion interplay is inspiring. The explosive track introduces the master conguero Armando Peraza on a bubbling staccato bongo solo. The album closes with "Every Step of the Way," a piece that starts with a brooding intro savagely punctuated by guitar slashes and excellent conga and timbale licks. Building to an orgasmic musical climax, the second part has a strong Gil Evans influence orchestrated by Tom Harrell. Carlos shows an approach to his playing which is lighter, jazzier, stretching for the note. The track (and album) closes with the sound of Rolie's Hammond organ bidding a poignant farewell to the Santana band and to an era.

Shrieve remembers that "*Caravanserai* was a difficult period. The music changed and not everybody liked it. The original Santana was THE band before *Caravanserai*, there's no doubt about that. It was a hard time—a lot of drugs, mismanagement, we were very young. For Carlos and myself it was a matter of survival. I felt that because of the drugs thing, that Carlos and I felt the music would save us. I'm proud of the fact that our relationships have sustained and we've been able to put stuff behind us, as that was the most important period of our lives. I loved going to that place. It felt really good."

Herbie Herbert feels technical troubles ruined the album despite the artistic quality: "*Caravanserai* was really poorly recorded, I'm talking [back in] the vinyl times. It was too long, too much music, the levels were low. Components of that record fitted Carlos's career, like 'Song of the Wind,' half of which is Neal Schon. Neal ripped that solo on 'Everybody's Everything,' which is a real famous solo. I think things deteriorated, with all the arguments around *Caravanserai*. I wanted to be with Gregg Rolie and Neal so bad, there is no doubt then that Gregg was the boss. Anybody who thought otherwise is taking bad acid, in suppository form."

Photo: Malo Archives

Tom Harrell, during his sojourn with Malo, found time to arrange orchestration for Michael Shrieve's "Every Step of the Way" on *Caravanserai*.

Photo: Joan Chase

Gregg Rolie's Hammond B3 sound closes the *Caravanserai* album.

"There was discontentment about the direction on *Caravanserai*," Schon agrees. "It has got some interesting stuff, but for me the third album was a much stronger outing. Gregg had the moxie to make it work. When Gregg stepped out, it just fell apart. Drugs were the downfall of that great band. As things grew sour, I think the band was pissed off. By naming the band after Carlos, it could only go to Carlos."

Clive Davis, president of Columbia Records, wasn't pleased in any case, according to Shrieve. "I remember him coming to the studio. He felt we'd made a big mistake, as it didn't do as well as the first three." Carlos, however, was satisfied:

"I have to play the music that is in my heart. After I came out with *Caravanserai*, after the first three albums, some people put it down. Years later many of those people have commented how that album taught them to listen to music in a different way. It was ahead of its time, but I can't wait for people to catch up; see you later. In order to grow you have to take a chance and you have to learn from everything. I don't really care about the criticism."

Carlos Santana

Photo: Joan Chase

MANDRILL/BEAST FROM THE EAST

Hailing from the Bedford-Stuyvesant district of Brooklyn, New York, this group is one of the great Latin-funk-jazz-soul treasures of the period. They bridged the gap between the East Coast funk/Latin scene and the Santana-inspired sounds from the West Coast. The group was formed by the Panamanian Wilson Brothers, a family crew of astonishing multi-instrumentalists. The Wilson Brothers' musical background is a melting pot of culture and training, blended with the sound and heart of urban America. They have a combined talent that makes up the signature sound of the band.

Carlos is the musical foundation of the Wilson Brothers' team. He is lead singer, rhythm guitarist, and also plays flute, timbales, trombone, and alto sax. Lou is the main lyricist of Mandrill and also contributes musically. He is a master conguero/percussionist, plays trumpet, and sings lead and background vocals. Lou has always provided a focal point for the group's stage presentation.

Ric (Doc) plays sax, percussion, sings lead and background vocals, and contributes to the overall creative process, lyrically and musically. His forte, however, has always been behind the scene, anchoring the Mandrill production team, and is considered to be "the glue" that holds all of the elements of Mandrill together.

Carlos Wilson plays guitar at RFK Stadium in 1973.

Ric Wilson vocalises at RFK Stadium in 1973.

Lou Wilson on trumpet at RFK Stadiun in 1973.

Mandrill at L.A radio station to promote the *Composite Truth* album.
L to R: Fudgie Kae, Omar Mesa, Carlos Wilson, Radio DJ, Claude "Coffee" Cave, Neftali Santiago, and Ric Wilson.

The Wilson Brothers' sound is tight and flavorful. Early Mandrill formed around this unique feel during jams at mother Doris Wilson's beauty parlor on Marcy Avenue in Brooklyn, New York. Wanting to expand the band, the Wilsons added organist Claude "Coffee" Cave (keyboards, vibes, percussion, vocals). Coffee's passion was going to see Miles Davis (with Tony Williams, Wayne Shorter, Ron Carter, and Herbie Hancock) play at clubs like The Village Vanguard. Ironically, a few years later, Mandrill played with Miles Davis (Michael Henderson on bass, Keith Jarrett on keys, etc.), as special guests at the Fillmore West, May 6 through 9 in 1971. Like the Wilson Brothers, Coffee was also knocked out by Santana: "When I heard them, I thought, 'this is what was in my head.' Gregg Rolie's sound was an inspiration to every Hammond B3 player thereafter." For Coffee, Mandrill was fertile ground for all kinds of ideas. "Carlos Wilson and I did most of the string arrangements on the Mandrill albums. Ron Carter was a close family friend and he, along with one of our co-producers, Alfred Brown, helped us put together the musicians for the string sections on some of Mandrill's albums."

Rounding out the original line-up was Bundie Cenac on bass, Omar Mesa on guitar, and Charlie Padro on drums. This Mandrill band played twenty-two instruments between them. Omar later became a Shri Chinmoy disciple, joining Carlos Santana and John McLaughlin in wearing the traditional all-white outfits.

Claude "Coffee" Cave gets down on the Hammond B3 at Ernie Isley's 21st birthday party in New Jersey.

Ric and Lou Wilson playing horns at Ernie Isley's 21st birthday party in New Jersey.

By the end of 1970, Mandrill went from performing local clubs and concerts at the New World, Blue Coronet, and Brooklyn Academy of Music to signing their first major record deal with Polydor Records' president Jerry Schoenbaum.

Their first release, *Mandrill*, owed a lot to Santana and the psychedelic era. However, Mandrill's synthesis of horns and rhythm and blues, mixed with Latin/Afro/Caribbean flavors was unique at the time. The Polydor albums were mostly recorded at Electric Lady Studios in Greenwich Village, New York. Coffee Cave recalls: "Jimi Hendrix came in and said, 'I've been hearing great things about your band. When I get back, we should jam.' Unfortunately, he never came back."

Mandrill Is, released in 1972, introduced Fudgie Kae Solomon on bass. Fudgie's bass style is fundamental to the Mandrill sound. Before the year was out, Mandrill would go through one more line-up change.

Neftali Santiago, drummer and vocalist from Spanish Harlem, was introduced just before the band recorded *Composite Truth*. Santiago had already been playing songs by Mandrill, Santana, and Buddy Miles when he joined the group, and had the perfect mix of rhythms the band was looking for. Neftali remembers that, "Mandrill really reflected the East Coast street culture and the mood of the people. Like Santana, we are a people's band. College radio played the *Composite Truth* album around the clock. Block parties would play Mandrill records in their entirety, and all over New York, Philadelphia, and Washington, D.C., bands would regularly play Mandrill music in clubs. As a live entity, the band went from 'Mandrill,' our theme song that revealed a deep pulsating feel of Afro/Cuban rawness, to a rock/bush feel like 'Hang Loose,' to 'Hagalo' and 'Cohelo,' in a total Latino clave vibe, to the monster funk grooves like 'Ape Is High,' 'Mango Meat,' and 'Fencewalk.' As Carlos Santana remarked about the original Santana band, 'They had a lot of gears.'"

Mandrill at Tower Records, Los Angeles to promote *Composite Truth*.
Back row: Neftali Santiago, Claude "Coffee" Cave.
Front row: Omar Mesa, Carlos Wilson, Ric and Lou Wilson.

Neftali Santiago playing drums in San Diego, 1973.

"When I was auditioning for Mandrill, they really needed a heavy funk thing on *Composite Truth*. Tiki Flowood, drummer (from Funkadelic) was the king of syncopation around then. He passed away just before we were going to record an album, called *Kiki Versus Neftali*."

Composite Truth, *Just Outside of Town*, and *Mandrilland* became rare groove classics. Dougie Rodriguez on guitar was a strong contributor to the *Mandrilland* feel. He arrived after Santana's *Caravanserai* recording. Rodriguez was a friend of Santana bassist Dougie Rauch and was also his fellow band member in the Voices of East Harlem. At the end of 1974, Santiago, Solomon, and Rodriguez left the band for artistic reasons.

In 1976–77, United Artists released two albums, *Beast from the East* and *Solid*. During this period, Wilfredo Wilson, the fourth brother, joined Mandrill, and added his magic on vocals as well as bass guitar and percussion. This union gave birth to songs like "Solid," "Tee Vee," "Wind on Horseback," and "Peck Ya Neck." Mandrill recruited Tommy Trujillo on lead guitar, Andre Locke on drums, and Brian Allsop performed bass on selected tracks.

Arista Records (headed by Clive Davis) released four Mandrill albums in 1978: *We Are One*, *The Greatest*, *New Worlds*, and *Getting in the Mood*. This ensemble created songs like "Funky Monkey," "Ali Bombaye," "Too Late," and "Can You Get It."

In 1982, a small record label called Montage (subsidiary of Capitol Records) released the Mandrill album *Energize*. "Put Your Money Where the Funk Is" was about to drop as a single when the record company folded unexpectedly. Today, the Wilson Brothers remain the driving force behind Mandrill, strongly supported by long-time band member Neftali Santiago and a new generation of players. They are still touring the U.S. and internationally.

Claude "Coffee" Cave, wails on Hammond B3 at Ernie Isley's 21st birthday party.

Neftali Santiago, RFK, 1973

Neftali has a story regarding Harvey Mason and the *Headhunters* record by Herbie Hancock. "Harvey told me at the Roxy club in 1978 that he based his drum lick on 'Chameleon' on my drum part on 'Fencewalk.' His brother was playing trumpet in the Mandrill band. He came backstage and after some ribbing, he admitted that the 'Fencewalk' beat was on the same syncopation."

All photos: Courtesy Mandrill Collection

ENTRANCE TO PARADISE

Bill Attwood

Malo were taking the Santana banner and getting ready to run with it. After the move by Santana to a less commercial stance with *Caravanserai*, Malo's sound was even more authentically Latin-based. The horns gave it a salsa-fried charge, but again, this was totally original, San Francisco-Latin music that existed solely on its own terms. Consequently, Malo's success was due to "a mixture of talent and persistence," according to manager Doug Tracy. "Jorge, for example, really came into his own as a composer. He was a fabulous player live, an excellent rhythm player also."

Forrest Buchtel

Tom Poole, Bill Attwood, Forrest Buchtel

Photos: Rudy Rodriguez

"They [Malo] were well respected for their musicianship," Michael Shrieve agrees. "The band was real good. Jorge was on guitar. I think it was difficult being Carlos's brother but I always felt he held his own really well. To us it didn't matter how famous anyone was.

"Around the time that Santana was really taking off, one of the most satisfying things about the whole scene was the music was really vital. We were aspiring to play more than just rock and roll like the other Bay Area bands. We were really into Miles and Bitches Brew, and we would jam a lot in the clubs. All the musicians in the Bay Area would hang out; this was between 1969 and 1971. Luis Gasca had this scene at Andre's on Broadway—kinda Latin jazz-fusion. Herbie Hancock would be there. Larry Graham played at this other club on Sundays [The Orphanage], a really funky scene. So there was the Latin thing, the funk and the jazz thing all going on. [Tower of Power drummer] David Garibaldi and Carabello were living at my house in Mill Valley. The Pointer Sisters would come over to jam; it was great fun. Greg Errico was around; in retrospect we were doing classic stuff, as it turns out now, and we were all friends. Carmelo Garcia[20] seemed really professional, to me, as a young kid. These guys seemed older, more experienced. Carmelo was a wild player with a wonderful spirit and energy. He had a broad personality. It was just a thrilling time. Chepito would walk into a club like a king—again the broad personality. He was so exciting. Whenever he got on the bandstand, the whole place lit up; it was a noticeable difference."

Johnny Valenzuela remembers the commune-like atmosphere that prevailed in those days. "Originally, I was with Soul Sacrifice with Raul Rekow—we went to the same school, Balboa High School in San Francisco. I brought Raul Rekow [Santana's longtime and current conga drummer] to his first band practice with Soul Sacrifice. After that Arcelio saw us at the Nite Life and really enjoyed Raul's playing. He walked up to the stage, said, 'I want you' to Raul, and about a month later, Raul was gone. Carlos Badia was the conguero after him. We were all mingling and jammin' around the city at such happening spots as the Nite Life, the Ghetto on Mission Street, the Matrix, Mr G's, the

Raul Rekow, seen here playing congas with Soul Sauce at Balboa High School, San Francisco.

Raul Rekow on stage with Sapo.

Photos: Courtesy Johnny Valenzuela

---

[20]   An extroverted timbalero who played with Luis Gasca. Entertainment promoter Jim Cassell, head of the Berkeley Agency, notes: "Carmelo Garcia was on a lot of those Mongo records. He was a real good-looking black guy, but got extremely spaced out on vast amounts of cocaine. He would get into these real long intense timbale solos."

Yellow Brick Road. I remember Chepito in those days; he'd come to the club where we'd be playing, I was about 17, he'd drive up in this long white 1969 El Dorado, big beautiful car, always pretty girls with him—he had such a great impact on the Latin percussionists in town. I'm thinking, that's what I want to be like. This is before his Rolls Royce! Leather, suede, and diamonds. He was my mentor. Wow, he was awesome, although he's kinda four-feet-something, he was a giant. Everyone wanted to play like him, including me. His playing would dazzle people in the audience. Soul Sacrifice used to play at the Ghetto on Mission Street and at the Nite Life. Soul Sacrifice was getting popular and we were playing Santana in the clubs. Chepito would bring other Santana members along to jam, Gregg Rolie, Neal Schon, and Carabello. When they weren't working, they would come and sit in and play their own music.

"Later on, along with Malo, we were rehearsing Dakila[21] at David [Rubinson]'s back rooms at night, on 1588 Market Street, right across from the Fillmore building. Directly above us were Bill Graham's offices. We could hear Bill screaming and yelling at someone on the phone, directly over us. Man, that guy knew how to slam down a phone. I was hanging out with some of the other acts David was lookin' after—Tower of Power, Cold Blood, the Pointer Sisters, Herbie Hancock, as well as Malo. Before things broke with the Pointers and Malo, we were so broke we would all share loaves of bread, some mayo, and bologna to make sandwiches to keep going. I met Clive Davis at David Rubinson's office, and Dakila got signed to Epic. Clive was a giant in the music business."[22]

Dakila with Johnny Valenzuela, seen here third from left

[21] Dakila was a mostly Filipino band that included Johnny Valenzuela; they recorded two albums for Epic Records.

[22] Clive Davis produced Santana's *Supernatural* in 2000.

David Rubinson had already had a first stab at producing an initial Santana album in Los Angeles (after they were signed to Columbia for $25,000, along with Chicago, Laura Nyro, Johnny and Edgar Winter—all unknown outside their respective locales). "After David delivers the album, it was rejected," says Herbie Herbert. "He lost face and control right there. A street band like Santana, you give them an inch and they take two miles. The bloom was off the rose: 'We don't wanna make another album with this dingbat.' They saw through David's talent or lack thereof."

Rubinson did have an astute sense of other people's talent, however, and his attention turned to Malo. Says Chris Wong: "I think Rubinson approached Blue Thumb records at that time, whose release roster included Hugh Masekela, Dave Mason, and Luis Gasca. David went ahead and secured a deal with Warner Bros. (Rubinson had a production deal with the band and the Warner Bros. deal was through his company). I think the band got an initial $25,000 advance from Warner Bros. I remember at the time the Pointer Sisters really envied us 'cause we had a deal. We were impressed by David—he had the big office and he already had Taj Mahal, Herbie Hancock; he tried to get Dakila going too."

Fred Catero and David Rubinson

"David Rubinson was a dynamic individual with unbounded energy. He could instill enthusiasm in the labels and promoters and he would take the ball and run with it," says Doug Tracy. "He would be in the office at six in the morning to New York doing deals. I always respected his hustle. He was a force to be reckoned with. He worked a lot with Funky Jack Leighton at Funky Features over on Haight-Ashbury. When he moved into the Market Street address, he had a sign up: 'Everythin' I Do, Gonna Be Funky From Now On!' He was always trying to get soul. He produced everybody: Malo, Tower, Pointer Sisters, Moby Grape, HooDoo Rhythm Devils, Elvin Bishop, Cold Blood, and Herbie Hancock. He was one of the forces in the Bay Area scene."

Arcelio Garcia, Jr.

Fred Catero, who engineered all four of Malo's Warner albums, recalls David Rubinson's style: "David was so hot when he came out here, he was like a wolf in a chicken coop that's never been invaded by wolves. His philosophy was, if a band wasn't well known or new to bring in some heavy hitters. He did it with Herbie Hancock and he did it with Malo. He had a very overbearing style, too; that's the reason he and Herbie Hancock parted company."

Arcelio Garcia, Jr. and Leo Rosales

Photos: Malo Archives

Arcelio Garcia recalls Rubinson's early influence: "Boy! David, he really loved the band. He came in, but he wanted personnel changes. We had already started recording the album before the Warner Bros. deal; the negotiations took a long time." (Rubinson was acting as negotiator plus taking a ten-percent manager's commission, according to Garcia.) "David was opening the doors and Chris was walking in behind him, so he was worth it." Garcia also asserts the album took a while to nail. "The album was in the can and then it came out on New Year's, 1972. That's when all the personnel changes came about, during that time of recording and working up the band."

Richard Bean played timbales and sax in the group. He would play a significant part in the band's initial success, but was one victim of the personnel changes made by Rubinson as the recording progressed. "David Rubinson, I can't say I liked him," says Bean. "He'd say, 'If you're gonna be the baddest, you got to get the baddest.' He destroyed a sound we had built together. We were rehearsing down on Market at Rubinson's offices and then we're having all these meetings. First one to go was David Guzman. Richard Spremich replaced him. Carlos Gomez went and Abel [Zarate] came in. Richard Kermode came when Ismael [Versoza] went. I got inducted into playing timbales—Arcelio got a set from his mom's restaurant. So suddenly I'm playing timbales; I was just learning to play them. I was still playing timbales just before the first album.

"We'd done 'Suavecito,' doing the final mixes at Funky Features in the Haight. I thought something was up, so finally I heard I was out of the band. I felt cheated that I didn't tour with that band after 'Suavecito' came out. They waited for enough time to get my vocals on the album. David Rubinson was very underhanded and manipulative. They did "American Bandstand" without me; it kinda hurt and, sort of like the first Milli Vanilli, they just lip-synched it."

Hoping to create magic on the self-titled Malo's debut, Rubinson drafted Coke Escovedo on timbales and Victor Pantoja on congas. ("Both Coke and Victor brought an earthy Cubano feel to the rhythms on the six album cuts," says Garcia.) Believing the recording needed "a punchy horn section," Garcia adds, Rubinson summoned Luis Gasca, with his high-octane trompeta style, to augment Roy Murray on trumpet and trombone.

"Gasca had an impressive musical pedigree. One of his first gigs as a teenager was with Beto Villa's big band out of Texas," says Chuy Varela. After graduating from both the New England Music School and Berklee School of Music, he had played with Woody Herman, Cal Tjader, Count Basie, and Mongo Santamaria, as well as with his own jazz ensembles.

"He got a contract with Atlantic Records; he was called the Little Giant," Varela says. "He also got into the fusion thing happening in Texas with Little Joe y La Familia. [Leader] Joe Hernandez was very brass oriented, [doing] polkas with hip arrangements. Luis was like a gypsy; and he came here to San Francisco to play with Joe Henderson, the saxophonist. When he got with Malo, he really connected with Chicanos." Gasca also appeared at Woodstock with Janis Joplin's Kozmic Blues Band, and he brought to the Malo session keyboardist Richard Kermode from her outfit. Kermode's beautiful son montuno riffs graced the first two Malo albums; his haunting vamping can be heard to great effect on the cut "Café" on Malo's debut album.[22]

Abel Zarate credits Richard Kermode with a push towards jazzier voicings. "Richard would push me towards jazz; he was getting me to listen to Freddie Hubbard and Antonio Carlos Jobim. Richard had an apartment in North Beach with Luis Gasca. He had this big, airy room with no furniture except this beautiful grand piano, where he'd rehearse during the Malo first album; he'd turn me onto lots of chords and styles. Luis was a character; he didn't pull any punches."

---

[23] On the second album, Kermode was to give the band one of their truly transcendent moments with his stunning piano solo on "Oye Mama." Kermode also went on to play with Santana on the albums *Welcome* and *Lotus*.

Zarate's guitar playing had developed from playing in Motown garage bands. He was aware of Arcelio in the Malibus early on. "I was in a rival band at the time called the Righteous Ones [with Richard Bean]. We did [songs by] the Miracles, the Temptations; we did a Battle of the Bands with Malibus at California Hall at Polk and Eddy. That segued into a love of blues, Butterfield, Bloomfield, as well as Gabor Szabo, Chico Hamilton, Willie Bobo.

"I actually met Carlos when I was fourteen years old. Before the Santana Blues Band, we auditioned for the same band—the Righteous Ones. I walked in and the drummer was my cousin Leo Bell. I was really scared, and there was Carlos, sitting on the floor playing the blues. [The Righteous Ones] were doing a lot of Motown, and they chose me because of the fact that Carlos wouldn't be around for too long, as he had his own vision.

"One of the first bassists I played with was Gus Rodriguez, who grew up with Carlos. I was checking out the Fillmore, the Avalon Ballroom. I got my own thing going called the Naked Lunch, which had Roy Murray and Richard Spremich. We were playing at the Family Dog at the beach; we were opening shows a lot— we opened for Creedence Clearwater at the Fillmore—but we never recorded as a band. Naked Lunch was already playing at the Fillmore. Chris Wong approached me—he liked my songwriting and playing; there was an upcoming project involving Jorge Santana. Jorge and I went to school together. The original Malibus had a lot of weak players; it wasn't going to work in the studio. So the original band consisted of half Malo and half Naked Lunch"

"Carlos's path and mine had crossed many times in our careers. I saw Carlos doing the Al Kooper[24] thing, but then I saw him at the Avalon Ballroom with Santana; I'd never heard anybody playing like that! Carlos had a lot of charisma on stage. He's such a soulful player. It gave me inspiration; this guy's washing dishes at Tick Tock's, and here he is up there doing it. It made it feel achievable." Chris Wong originally invited Zarate to join the band. "I already knew Jorge from Mission High School; I'd sit in with his band," Zarate says. "Then I ended up getting a call from Arcelio. They were rehearsing down at David Rubinson's studio; I think they wanted to hire me more on my songwriting, as they already had Jorge. Jorge is a good guitar player. We traded off a lot on the first album. I was in the band for about six months before we started the album. So things started to happen fast. Pablo and I worked up the tunes in terms of the arrangements, and I had a lot of input on that record. "Peace," for example, had a lot of [the group's] Chicago influence and a real Gabor Szabo feel in the middle.

Abel Zarate with the Righteous Ones.

Abel Zarate wailing on stage with Malo.

---

[24] Carlos was invited onstage and played a solo on the track "Sonny Boy Williamson," which appeared on the album *The Live Adventures of Mike Bloomfield and Al Kooper* in 1969.

"It was great watching Coke in the studio, I'd never seen a timbales player play like that. He'd listen to it, say, 'OK, let it rip,' and there it was, just one take! Chepito played more, like, rock, but Coke was playing the real shit. A lot was done live, with very little overdubs.

"David was a tough producer to work with. I kinda had butted heads with David; for example, he didn't want the middle jazzy section in 'Peace.' I said, 'We've been up all night doing this,' but it got worked out. Fred Catero was pretty cool—a low-key guy. Jorge and I always got along but when it got to the Malo thing, there was some friction. I think he wanted to make his mark; he probably had second thoughts about a second guitar in the band."

Pablo Tellez also remembers Rubinson's approach to reshuffling the band. "When the decision was made to get new musicians, David Rubinson already knew what he wanted. He got Luis, who also knew Richard Kermode. For me, they were too much. I think Richard was about five years older than me. I wasn't awakened to that scene they were in, but slowly I saw the drinking, the drugs, the womanizing; all the stuff that they were already experienced in. But Rubinson knew what he could get out of them. The album was very well put together. Arcelio's input was very strong and original. What happened was we needed to get the album out by a deadline; in order to do that, we let the music breathe by just releasing six longer pieces. I believe it was very well put together, the best!"

Abel Zarate

Photo: Rudy Rodriguez

SPANISH GYPSY/LITTLE GIANT

"Luis Gasca was the man," according to Chuy Varela. "Luis came out of those early Tijuana orchestras in Texas; they were pachuco orchestras, and the guy that gave Luis his break was Beto Villa. He had a big band, and Luis enrolled in school in North Texas and learned to play jazz and landed a gig with Woody Herman. He was the featured trumpeter and got a contract with Atlantic Records."

Gasca had the little-known but superb *For Those Who Chant* album, featuring the original Santana band with eleven different percussionists including Coke Escovedo, Chepito Areas, Carmelo Garcia, Lenny White, and Mike Shrieve on some heavy jams. The group rehearsed at Andre's, the club with whom Luis had a residency, and apparently recorded at Columbia Studios on Santana's studio time. The album, released on Blue Thumb, is, in its way, a classic. Jazz meets Latin rock in the four sprawling tracks, notably "Street Dude," "La Raza," "Spanish Gypsy," and "Little Mama." The record is a meld of Bitches Brew meets Santana. On "Little Mama," Carlos and Neal Schon exchange some interesting guitar flurries. Joe Henderson offers thoughtful tenor sax throughout, and "Spanish Gypsy" has an amazing jam session, in which ten different percussionists get down while Carmelo Garcia and Victor Pantoja go back to Africa with a free-for-all chanting session.

"I was on that *For Those Who Chant* album. The sessions were very disorganized," says Abel Zarate. "Me, Pablo, and Jorge were down in the studio. We were really green, really naïve. There's Lenny White, Stanley Clark, all these great players. I actually did a couple of pieces on there; I was sitting right next to Neal, but I didn't get credited or paid for the session.

"That was a renaissance period. Luis was a great mentor—he was seasoned; he taught me and Pablo about space. I used to jam with Luis and Michael Shrieve at Andre's. We used to take the music out into the ozone."

Photo: Rudy Rodriguez

Luis Gasca in the studio

124

Jeff Trager recalls, "I was at those sessions and I used to see a lot of those guys at Andre's on Broadway. Everybody would go and jam; you'd see Neal and Carlos there, Herbie Hancock would be there, just ten or twenty people in the audience. Luis had Hadley [Caliman], Gregg Rolie, Rick Stevens from Tower of Power down there, man. All those guys jammed there. There was no door charge on the weekends. They'd play at Bimbo's for five dollars a head. It was the greatest."

"Andre's was an after-hours joint," remembers Abel Sanchez. "Musicians would show up after playing the other clubs, jamming from 2:30 'til 6:00 in the morning. Luis burned a lot of people, but musically he was great. He'd always be saying, 'Watch the lip, man! Watch the lip!'"

Unfortunately, *For Those Who Chant* didn't sell. "It wasn't more than jams, with nothing really to play on radio," says Trager. "Maybe it did thirty-five thousand copies." According to Bill Perasso: "I think the Luis Gasca releases [on the Fantasy label] sold more locally. You had to know the guys who had the jukeboxes."

Gasca was notorious for his antics as much as for his music. He once faked his own death, insists Jorge Bermudez. "Some drug dealers were after him. A friend of mine saw him at an airport; he goes, 'Hey Luis!' 'No man, it's Johnny Spade, that's my name now.' Can you believe that?!"

Photo: Rudy Rodriguez

At Luis Gasca's *For Those Who Chant* sessions

Jorge Santana   Pablo Tellez   Leo Rosales   Abel Zarate

Malo: a mixture of the streets and sophisticated horn arrangements with a tinge of Latin soul.

All photos this spread: Rudy Rodriguez

SUAVECITO

Jorge Santana

Pablo Tellez

Malo was recorded and mixed at Pacific Recording Studios, down the peninsula from San Francisco in San Mateo, where Santana also had recorded their debut. Recalls engineer Fred Catero: "Malo were much more Spanish than Carlos. You could hear a lot more roots. One nice thing about recording Malo was they were no trouble. After Santana and doing *Abraxas* and dealing with David Brown and his whole drug thing, Malo seemed manageable. Jorge, to me, always seemed more integrated into the band. He seemed to me to be like his father, José; Jorge wasn't the focus, it was the whole band."

Consequently, each band member contributed something distinctive to the overall sound. Pablo Tellez in particular deserves a greater reputation; his playing on the first four Warner-released Malo albums reveals a flurry of rhythmic originality. As well as being a central writer and rhythmic pivot in the group, he also had a very distinctive bass style, both propulsive and melodious, pushing and surging the rhythm section in a constant meld of Latin/funk invention. If, most prominently, Larry Graham from Sly Stone's band took kudos for his evolvement of the original 'finger poppin' and slap style, Tellez, along with Dougie Rauch (in Voices of East Harlem and Santana) and Francis Rocco Prestio in Tower of Power also took the instrument to another level, redefining the textures and possibilities of the bass.

"Pana," a simple song about hanging with friends, written by Arcelio Garcia and Abel Zarate, kicked off Malo's eponymous first album. Zarate's clean jazzy stylings are evident here, and the way he and Jorge Santana combine their distinct but complementary guitar styles sets the tone for the album. The band gets down to some serious grooving—Luis Gasca opens up the pressure, with Coke Escovedo providing a hot one-take timbales solo to heat the stew up even further, seasoned by Richard Kermode's solid keys. It's a great example of a band getting off in the studio.

"Just Say Goodbye," a song brought by Luis Gasca (also recorded on his *Born to Love You* album on Fantasy) shows a more reflective side of the sound (Garcia remembers: "Luis was cosmically inclined, everythin' related to the cosmos."). Zarate and Jorge stir a superb wah-wah into a cauldron of sound that amounts to a frothing rhythm gumbo, with Richard Spremich flailing his drumsticks and Victor Pantoja laying down a furious funky conga pattern. The intensity builds until topped by the hot sauce of a chant-like vocal until the track ends in a serene and lyrical coda which has Jorge weaving sweet guitar runs around the vocal harmonies.

"Café," the third cut, keeps up the pressure starting with a "trick" opening that cuts to a hot cha-cha with Pantoja laying down a tumbao under a unison guitar and horn riff. Coke drops tasty timbales fills throughout Garcia's impassioned vocals, and Kermode provides the song's calypso-like, steel-pan-flavored piano part. The cut features some truly beautiful guitar wailings by Jorge and Zarate, again nearly wearing out their wah-wah pedal—a superb performance caught by Rubinson and engineer Fred Catero's finely-crafted production. The song closes with a cheeky nod to Santana's "Guarija" before its dramatic end.

Photo: Malo Archives

Richard Kermode

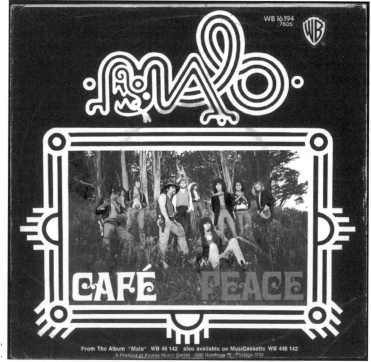

Malo 45 vinyl single release,
Germany, 1972.

Courtesy: Warner Bros. Picture: Etienne Houben

"Nena" came around from a chance incident: Arcelio Garcia seeing a little girl crying on the street and, attempting to cheer her up, she started to laugh. He brought the simple melody to the rehearsal room; Tellez worked on a bass line that would provide the pulse for Garcia's effective lyrics and melody. The tune shows off Tellez's propulsive bass to great effect alongside Coke's great timbales work. The heat doesn't let up as the band goes through their paces on the fourth cut, which allows the band room to solo, with Kermode providing an outrageous three-note vamp, until the tune goes up a notch with Zarate and Jorge's unison guitar parts and a particularly joyous timbales roll from Escovedo. Every Latin-rock junkie has his or her moments, and that is one of mine. "Nena" belts home to a double-time climax. "Suavecito" follows: a romantic, mid-tempo pop song that bears the hallmarks of Richard Bean's songwriting style; a sweet, commercial, but essentially Latin, approach.[25] "Richard Bean came up with the original idea for the song 'Suavecito,' but it needed Pablo and myself to get it to the stage where David Rubinson would record it. We added a bridge, different chord changes, before we brought it to the studio," attests Abel Zarate. Bean would later team up with Jorge to co-write, sing lead vocals, and play guitar on Jorge Santana's first solo album, *Jorge Santana*, released by Tomato Records in 1978.

The last cut on the album, "Peace," which grew out of a jam in the studio, sports a speaker-popping production in which Tellez and Spremich lay down a heavy, almost oppressive groove. Garcia's lyrics don't compromise either: "Jesus rules the nation, battles for the population/They hung God, nailed Him on the cross." Garcia displays his Mission-Christian background and his best Puerto Rican-James Brown chops in a series of screams that lead to a Spanish-influenced soprano sax break from Roy Murray. The influence of Abel Zarate and Luis Gasca can be felt in a section that encompasses Latin lyricism, Gasca's Miles-Davisesque trumpet flavorings, and a gentle swing backdrop from the ensemble. A stirring soprano from Roy Murray leads to a section of Jorge's and Zarate's guitar meditations, which evolve into a raga-style guitar piece before stepping on the obligatory wah-wah to bring the band thundering back for the main ostinato, closing this superb first studio effort on a triumphant and exploratory note.

Courtesy: Warner Bros.

Malo's first album

[25] Heard to further effect on his Sapo album on such cuts as "Been Had," "Can't Make It," and "Sapo's Montuno."

"To me, Abel Zarate and Neal Schon were the prodigies of that era," Chris Wong recalls. "I think Abel, if he'd been white, woulda gone a lot further. I've got tapes of Abel and Jorge at the Heliport, just wailing; they were on fire."

"Suavecito" provided the band a Top 20 US hit, which charted almost immediately. David Rubinson had trimmed the album's version from 6:36 minutes to a more radio-friendly 3:25. It was a matter of two weeks before the single and album hit it big. First "Nena" was released as the "A" side hit before "Suavecito" was flipped as the single and went through the roof. Brian Rohan attests, "'Suavecito' was a wonderful song; Rubinson wanted to put that out in November, but we waited till January, and it became an enormous hit. That is a signature song. Everybody knows it."

"When I was with Elektra, I heard Malo straight away on the single 'Suavecito,'" says Jeff Trager. "We were in the same office as Warner Bros. Bill Perasso, at Warner Bros., the branch manager, was responsible for breaking 'Suavecito,' for making that a big hit. San Francisco was where it broke; then the rest of the country can jump on that. [Perasso] did the same thing with Tower of Power with 'You're Still a Young Man.' He created such a buzz that somebody had to step up to the plate and hit a home run!"

The album itself, released at the start of 1972, won favor with disc jockeys and many critics, remaining in the US Top 20 for a number of weeks. Rubinson maintained that the album shifted 7000 copies in its first week in the Bay area alone. Malo also embarked on a two-week tour with Quicksilver Messenger Service, taking in dates in New Haven, Staten Island, Atlanta, New Orleans, and Florida.

"Suavecito" was partly born of Abel Zarate's mastery of jazz chords and progressions; he and Pablo Tellez had worked up the tune from Richard Spremich's initial melodies written in high school math class. "It was a nice song but it wasn't what I wanted. At the time, Carlos had that bad shit out from the third album, y'know, like 'Batuka,' 'No One to Depend On.' I think I was more into the hard stuff," Zarate says.

For Jorge Santana, it seemed the right tune to break on radio. "I couldn't imagine any other song being as friendly to the audience. It had a light sound: congas, guitar, keys, a real calypso feel; also the ending has a great feel to it." As producer Gregg Landau points out, the song became a lover's anthem. "Chicanos were into slow dancing, and ballads were really big."

Richard Kermode and Abel Zarate on stage with Malo.

Jorge Santana

Photos: Rudy Rodriguez

130

Warner execs threw an unveiling party to herald and boost the young band's success before the press and radio corps. The album and single were receiving heavy airplay, and Warner pulled out the stops to ensure maximum coverage. The first junket was held at the North Beach Revival club on January 10. The band delivered a blistering set. The north wall of Tower Records in the city was emblazoned with a full-scale mural of the stunning album artwork.

The legend behind this distinctive and eye-catching cover is that David Rubinson saw it on a calendar while chowing down at the Roosevelt Tamale Parlor on 24th Street. Jesús Helguera, a Mexican artist who produced commercial art during the 1930s, had rendered a romantic and evocative painting picturing an Aztec warrior holding his princess in a smoldering embrace that somehow complements the intensity and the inherent nobility of the music contained within the record. Apparently Helguera was in the hospital at that time, and the artwork royalties paid the cost of his operation. Alongside the first three Santana album covers (by Lee Conklin, Abdul Mati Klarwein, and the Heavy Water Light Show), it freeze-frames a time and shows the interconnection between art and music of the Bay area at that time.

Rubinson and manager Wong also made sure the album was well served with some additional publicity. The album's serpent-style logotype of the Malo name, by John and Barbara Casado, was sent to label executives on embossed flour tortillas, many arriving at their destinations in an advanced state of molecular decay. Malo also embarked on a two-week tour with Quicksilver Messenger Service, taking in dates in New Haven, Staten Island, Atlanta, and New Orleans.

Photo: Rudy Rodriguez

Chris Wong and Doug Tracy handle affairs at the Malo office.

Courtesy Malo Archives

Malo's future road manager, Doug Tracy, was a student at San Francisco State College in 1972 when Malo began their first tour. "Some friends were going to University of California at Davis, up by Sacramento. We were all hanging out at the Fillmore. My friends, they would come down with a band called Group E. They had a fellow called Dickie Peterson and his brother Jerry. They combined with another Sacramento band called the Oxford Circle. They started out as a eight-piece blues band but then we all went down to Monterey and saw Jimi Hendrix; we thought 'This is different, let's try this.' So they dropped down to just a three-piece. I think we were the first band to bring Marshall amps over from England. It went to a power trio and that was Blue Cheer. We did that for a while, and then Bill Graham's organization introduced me to David Rubinson, and then I got with Tower of Power.

"They were a fabulous bunch of people. They were playing clubs in Oakland, in the East Bay. The *East Bay Grease* album was out around then. They were having trouble because none of them were 21 years old, and the alcohol-control beverage people were bustin' 'em. I got them a bunch of fake IDs, which solved that problem. We did some live performances on KSAN radio station and caught David's attention, and got a record deal on Fillmore Records at first. We did some wonderful shows and some great road trips with Santana. We did shows with Aretha Franklin and also Creedence Clearwater.

"Tower had some things happen early on. Rick Stevens would sing the ballads, 'Sparkling in the Sand,' that sort of thing. We had another singer called Rufus; he was more of a Wilson Pickett-type vocalist on *East Bay Grease*; he sang most of the leads on there. Rufus had a drug-induced ego problem and left the band abruptly. Rick kinda stepped into his shoes and he became quite a showman. He was very shy, but on stage he came into his own. When I first met him he claimed to be involved with the Black Panthers. He did have some drug difficulties, as did most of the band actually; it was a source of friction for me and really caused me to leave their immediate circle. After I left, I heard that Rick got involved in a bad drug deal down in San José; there were some weapons involved and he shot a couple of people, and then he was up for multiple homicide."[26]

Malo existed at a time before the current pigeon-holing and categorization of music forms, and so an array of acts opened for them, such as Fleetwood Mac, Long John Baldry, Black Oak Arkansas, J. Geils, America, Pink Floyd (Garcia maintains their drummer Nick Mason has still got a turquoise ring he gave him). During this period, Tracy went to see Malo at Rubinson's urging. "The band was doing some strange bills, with everyone from Savoy Brown and John Mayall to Deep Purple and Humble Pie, even a show up in Montana with Helen Reddy—no shit! Stuff so completely different from Malo. Tina Turner was about the closest." Malo and Quicksilver Messenger Service seemed a better pairing, however the slanted personalities of the bandleaders ensured further on-the-road drama.

Photo: Rudy Rodriguez

Doug Tracy, tour and road manager for Malo

---

[26] At the time of writing, Stevens remains in San Quentin prison.

Dino Valente, the self-styled leader of Quicksilver had a predilection for the Peruvian Marching Powder, which exaggerated certain less-appealing aspects of his character. After one such backstage fracas, Francisco Aguabella administered a resounding open-hand palm slap, which chastened Dino, at least momentarily.

"My recollection of the Quicksilver tour is that we were up in Canada, doing shows in Calgary and Edmonton," says Tracy. "We had separate dressing rooms and the band were drinking backstage. Things came to a head because of the egos between Arcelio and Dino Valente; there was this groupie going back and forth stoking the situation. Arcelio got a little pushed outta shape and it turned into a confrontation. Quicksilver went on and did their show. We had to get Arcelio outside, as he was out of control—then it continued on at the hotel; the Quicksilver people were trying to find Arcelio, you know, bangin' on doors. I was feeding Arcelio more booze to try and get him to pass out before he found them. Dino, he was a real punk, a kind of a cowboy. [As the tour went on] we did a show in Central Park and we tried to keep the bands separate."

After this, Malo was whisked back to the Bay Area to play Winterland on February 4 and 5, before doing an opening slot at the Whiskey A-Go-Go in Los Angeles. Later, Warner Bros. threw a press bash in LA before this gig on February 14. Malo was one of the first Latin bands to play Carnegie Hall, supported by Pure Prairie League, on April 12, 1972. They also appeared at the Schaeffer Music Festival, which was staged at New York's Central Park on August 7, 1972.

"Suavecito," so different from the other material on the album, ended up being both a blessing and a curse. "'Suavecito' enabled us to tour, but we didn't follow it up with another song like that," says Jorge. "There was always the problem of borrowing money to finish the tour, but it put another home-grown band on the scene."

Pablo Tellez took a while to assimilate the initial surge of success. "For Jorge and I, kinda at first it didn't register; I think the only one at first that knew all this was Arcelio—he really enjoyed the glamour and he understood what that meant. After a while, you're driving and listening to the radio and you think, 'Wow! That's me!'"

Tower of Power with original vocalist Rick Stevens (far right).

Photo: Courtesy Tower of Power

Francisco Aquabella: Don't mess with Mr A.

Photo: Malo Archives

ABEL ZARATE

Abel Zarate left Malo just before their second recording. "I was in the band for a couple of years. It was a roller coaster ride, man. Missing so many dates led to me leave." His contributions did continue on the second album, however; he co-wrote "Latin Bugaloo" and "Momotombo," and worked on horn arrangements with Tom Harrell, also on "Momotombo."

After Malo, Zarate went on to play with Neal Schon, Luis Gasca, James Mingo Lewis (on his *Flight Never Ending* solo project), with Richard Bean in Sapo, and the bands Suave and Wizard and many other Bay area musicians. "I owe a lot to the Escovedo family. Coke Escovedo took me under his wing. I'm on the *Comin' at Ya* album. We had a hit with 'I Wouldn't Change a Thing,' a song penned by Johnny Bristol.

"I was with Coke for about two years. Coke was a great player but with more vision he could have done better. We played with Earth, Wind and Fire, Parliament and Funkadelic. Towards the end of the Coke thing I was playing with several different bands, Sapo and Mingo Lewis. Mingo's stuff was very progressive. Also I was with Michael Carabello and Attitude; they had David Brown on bass, Angel Orozco from El Chicano on drums, and singer Erroll Knowles. We did some demos at the Automatt and they sounded great.[27]

"I got to know David Brown when I was in Coke's band. He was really different to Chepito and Michael. In those years, those guys were brutal to each other. Michael was a gangster; he was really protective of me but you didn't mess with Michael in those days. He was definitely not a shy guy. But he's real mellow now. David was into martial arts; he was real fit and he was so gentle. I think he had a real fragile spirit. He tried to get me into Hiroshima, the Japanese fusion jazz band. David spoke Japanese and was well respected in Japan. David played with them for a while. He was a beautiful person.

---

27 Attitude had one single released on Armstrong Records called "Pretty Little Girl" with Knowles, Abel, Carabello, and Brown. Says Zarate: "Errol Knowles was a good singer; he was one of Coke's singers in Azteca but I think he's doing time now. Erroll Knowles was in Azteca and the second version of Sapo; Erroll was the reason I got to play with Willie Bobo. I heard he'd fallen in with the wrong people and he's in prison for armed robbery. To me, he was such a loving guy, very street smart; I found it hard to believe."

Photo: Malo Archives

Abel Zarate

Photo: Courtesy Diane Black

David Brown: respected in Japan

Photo: Christopher Wong

Abel Zarate in the Malo first album heyday.

"Then I left Coke to go play with Willie Bobo. He was very New York, a real hard leader. Errol Knowles got them to fly me down to LA for the gig. Michael flew down to LA with me for my audition with Willie Bobo. My introduction to LA was Victor Pantoja picking us up at the airport. It was a rainy night. We're zooming down Sunset Boulevard. I'm in the front seat with the guitar between my legs. We got into a fairly brutal accident; so we're on Sunset Boulevard, the police are coming, and we're getting the beer out of the car and hiding it in the bushes. I got the gig with Willie.

"Willie Bobo was like a father figure, but he was also a brutal band leader. Willie didn't like to rehearse a lot. He thought it got in the way of spontaneity. He would give you the chart, play it through once, and then onstage he'd call the songs off spontaneously. Willie was very connected in LA. All the heavies would come and see him. Sometimes, Willie and I would be screaming at each other backstage; he'd be like, 'Get your ass on stage motherfucker!' Afterwards, Willie would say, 'I wanted to get you mad, so you played your ass off!'"

Photo: Rudy Rodriguez

Arcelio Garcia, Jr. dances the Latin Bugaloo along with a passionate senorita.

LATIN BUGALOO

The second album from Malo, appropriately entitled *Dos*, was a dark, dense, tough collection of music. In many ways it is less accommodating and less radio-friendly than the first album. It's a uncompromising record, filled with a primal percussive spirit which takes the Afro-Cubanisms further; and the drums, unbelievably, are allowed even freer reign. Where the first album still retains vestiges of their R&B roots, Malo's second recording is charged with a savage intensity and moments that take the listener back to the music's African heritage. The album in many ways does not follow the commercial pulse forged by the first record.

Promo shot around the Malo debut album release: Leo Rosales, Pablo Tellez, Arcelio Garcia, Jr., and Jorge Santana.

Photo: Rudy Rodriguez

Francisco Aguabella's conga playing bridges the gap between Cuba, Africa, and North America. He has a deep knowledge of the religious aspects of Santeria. Music was in Aguabella's blood from an early age. He was born in Matanzas, Cuba—a port city to which many Africans arrived with the slave trade, which lasted until 1888. To this day, Matanzas is heavily populated with Cubans of African origin. Here these Africans from Yoruba, Calabar, and other locations developed the style of drumming that became known as rumba—a pattern that forms the basis of much Cuban music, Latin jazz, and salsa. Spanish culture introduced guitar, song, and other harmonic elements to an explosive cultural hybrid that gave the world danzón, guajira, guaracha, cha-cha, and the mambo. Perhaps the most pervasively popular Cuban style to influence the Latin American music scene is son (incorporating son montuno). Other rhythms include Mozambique and songo, and have merged into the newer forms of timba and onda nueva.

Jorge Bermudez: "Francisco was like the Thunder God. He was very terse on that *Dos* album; when he soloed, he played ahead of the time, then behind the time, then resolved in time. If you listened to him while you supported, you were in trouble. Fred Catero said, 'Just don't listen to him.'"

"We had all kinda drummers. Jorge Bermudez was a friend of Raul Rekow. Rick Quintanal, he was a mellow player, kinda laid back. But Francisco would kick him on to play up on top of the rhythms," says Tellez. "There was always this conflict between the two styles. Francisco and I had the same basics of salsa; we would always play on top of the time, so the drummer had no choice but to go with what we were doing."

Photo: Rudy Rodriguez

Jorge Santana and Francisco Aguabella pile on the pressure live.

Photo: Jorge Bermudez

Jorge Bermudez appeared on conga and percussion during the Malo *Dos* sessions.

Bermudez, who played congas on some tracks, briefly followed Rekow into the chair. "My brother Ron had known Chepito's family back in Nicaragua. He was super sweet to Leo [Rosales] and I, 'cause of the Nicaraguan thing. He brought us to an *Abraxas* session. For Leo and I it was like going to Asgard.[28] They had the chicks, the clothes. They were real rock stars. The story goes, Chepito was dosed with acid before a show and he changed from then on. Leo's dad passed around that time; he had made it clear to us it was OK to party, but also respect the art."

Leo Rosales's hard-edged timbales style would play an integral part in the Malo sound. His approach developed from his initial use of the conventional drum kit, which he'd started playing at the age of nine. He played in another high school group around the Mission called Soul Sauce; his uncle, Edgar Rosales, had played conga with Cal Tjader, and Leo's band was named for a Tjader album. By the time of *Dos*, he'd also performed with the Escovedo Brothers. "When Santana came out, I was about fourteen years old. I'd heard rumors about them, you know—percussion with rock and roll. It changed my whole concept of playing. I was at junior high; we'd have drum-offs—kinda drum battles. After Santana came out, it influenced the whole Bay Area thing. Blues Image was a band around at that time with a Santana flavor.

"I met Chepito Areas at a neighborhood party and we became friends. I appreciated what he was doing and tried to imitate his style. He would put me on the guest list at Winterland. I would be flattered to be compared to him; his style was so unique, his rhythmic patterns, his stick control, his flair; he wasn't Cuban or Puerto Rican, but he was the first guy to bring timbales to rock. He wasn't really playing salsa. There's never been anybody like him. Like Mike Carabello's conga playing—again, totally different. Carabello had this style that was all his own; he was this young guy who took those rhythms and adapted his own form. The way he played guaganco, mambo, or cha-cha-cha, or 6/8s that he'd got from the street, with David Brown playing these simple powerful bass lines."

---

[28] Home of the Viking gods.

Leo Rosales plays timbales with Malo.

Photos: Rudy Rodriguez

The opener on this outstanding record, "Momotombo" has the band hitting the ground at full speed with a razor-sharp horn arrangement courtesy of Tom Harrell and Abel Zarate. From the outset, the band maintains a no-holds-barred mode. Leo Rosales and Francisco Aguabella immediately come into their own with a rock-hard onslaught over Richard Spremich's drums. Jorge Santana drops in some flavorsome funk chords to spice up the mix. The arrangement twists and turns at every corner, and an awesome timbales roll from Leo Rosales sets up further massed horn magic. A mini-bolero sets up the ensuing sequence. From then on, Tom Poole and Bill Atwood, on trumpet and trombone respectively, trade soaring horn licks before Jorge slides in with a piercing, distorted guitar figure, vamping around the main melody line, the drums bringing the horns back for a tumultuous and joyous end to this knockout opening cut.

"Momotombo" paves the way for "Oye Mama." This cut shows this edition of Malo at its Latinate best. The cut smokes like crazy, with Rosales and Tellez displaying an almost telepathic rhythmic interlock alongside Aguabella, Bobby Ramirez on drums, and Bermudez on congas. Richard Kermode introduces the track with two piano flourishes before the band settle into an aggressively controlled, horn-driven steamer. The unison horns tear it up to bring on a scorching hot trompeta solo by Forrest Buchtel. This brings Richards Kermode to the fore to plough a New York salsa-style intro which ripples and cascades through some seriously beautiful Latin changes—a pure masterpiece of soulful delicacy. The band fall out to let the drummers through in the first of the three main percussion breaks on the album featuring a sharp staccato bongo solo courtesy of Rosales, underscored by Kermode's hypno-piano figure. Aguabella lays down the conga over a massed percussion assault while the drummers play a triplet pattern to bring the tune to its logical conclusion.

Richard Kermode plays keyboards with Malo onstage.

Richard Kermode at the apartment he shared with Luis Gasca.

Photos: Rudy Rodriguez

Tom Poole plays trumpet backstage
before a Malo gig.

Jorge Santana and Leo Rosales.

Photos: Rudy Rodriguez

"Forrest Buchtel just overdubbed that solo on 'Oye Mama' in about one," says Bermudez. "Richard Kermode was a beautiful soul. He sat with Leo and I, and played all kinds of stuff, explaining clave and accents. He lived next door to Leo at the party house on 1216 Naples. Pete Escovedo also mentored us: he also taught us how to get the girls while onstage."

"I'm for Real" provides a temporary respite heralded by a lyrical violin intro by Jorge and Carlos's father José Santana. Arcelio Garcia sings a quasi-biblical, Genesis-inspired couplet about the "dawn of time, before the waters came." This changes into a more uptempo beat, against which the band keep changing the musical template, the music moving back and forth with Garcia declaiming "I'm for real" (as a lover), until the song hits a driving cowbell riff and some passionate tenor sax blowing by Hadley Caliman, backed by Rosales's big beat.

The music on the second side of this intriguing record segues through the next three tracks in an essentially uncompromising, superb suite of music. The music on this second side appears to straddle both the heaviest and darkest, and the lighter, more romantic side of Malo's music, with an adventurous disregard for convention in tandem with an even more authentic Afro-Cuban base.

"Midnight Thoughts" starts the ball rolling with a horn arrangement, courtesy of Pablo Tellez, that has an Asian sensibility. This moody atmospheric piece is cut by Tellez's and Jorge's guitar signature, which opens the piece to a yearning flute excursion by Hadley Caliman. A samba-based shuffle leads to a beautiful trumpet counterfoil by Tom Poole, which allows the band to push the envelope musically. The piece segues into "Hela," giving way to an awesome attack on congas and drums. Jorge's guitar and Rosales's metallic timbales slice through the intro; the piece gathers breakneck speed with an Arcelio vocal and horn unison riff that hits you between the ears. Jorge screeches into the picture again with an orgasmic, spluttering guitar part with heavy use of sustain and wah-wah, which comes to a cliff-hanging stop. Bermudez's congas completely break down the music to its African heritage, with Aguabella summoning up the forces of primal Africa, live in the studio. This is one of the most naked and edge-of-the-world sequences for a band to attempt, during what essentially was a release aimed at the record-buying public. A glorious full-band, live chant of "Hela, hela" backs Pete Garcia smashing a wooden plank on the studio floor. The chant and cracking of wood becomes almost overwhelming until the sound begins to fade and Raul Rekow's congas precede the ominous push of the monster final cut, "Latin Bugaloo."

The superb horns (again arranged by Abel Zarate and Tom Harrell) break into a mix of Latin-based rock, big band, and funk, with Arcelio exhorting everyone "to dance and get outta here," in one of his most uninhibited vocal performances. The band roars back, Pablo Tellez drives them even harder, bringing this suite to a close with an almighty scream from Arcelio before the funk-driven finish.

Leo Rosales remembers: "Man, that was a tough album. I wrote 'Oye Mama' with Arcelio, and there was 'Hela' with Francisco doing his African chanting. We had been playing together for a year and a half and the band was real tight. So we went in the studio with a lot of confidence. I remember sitting down with Forrest Buchtel and humming the horn lines, and he was just playing them back to me. The solo by Richard Kermode was a one-take. I said to Forrest, 'I want a bullfighter kinda feel at the beginning.' That's where that high register trumpet stuff came from. Those were the days."

"When Leo and Francisco came into the band, I felt the material was more structured, but also the rhythms and horn lines were heavier," says Jorge. "I don't remember doing any more than four takes on any one song or on the overdubs. The energy was so aggressive and we were very consistent." Adds Pablo Tellez: "In some ways, the best players we had were right there. It was such a powerful, high, rhythmically knowledgeable outfit; the combination was such a united entity, technically and spiritually. The album was pretty rushed, but it involved the least rehearsal we had." And according to Garcia, the pressure of touring forced the band to perform the minute tape rolled: "We were on the road so much, when we started, we laid 'Momotombo,' 'Latin Bugaloo,' and 'Hela' live in the studio.

Richard Kermode practices cowbell before a Malo gig.

Photo: Rudy Rodriguez

Malo *Dos* album cover.

Photo: Courtesy Warner Brothers Records

The album, with the Malo logo immediately recognizable, was jacketed with an embossed logo on a stark, brown card foldout sleeve—a style that hinted at the "roots" music within. It managed to be at once elegant and primitive. The production, again helmed by Fred Catero, had a strong visceral feel with a harder but beautifully balanced studio sound.

"It was quite a different record," says Doug Tracy. "Part of the problem was the cover; they came up with a brown bag-type thing, and what I wanted was a brand on the cover, kinda gleaming, burnt in. We blamed the packaging [for the lack of sales], but I don't think that was the problem. The record company didn't get behind that second record very much, but I guess that's a common complaint. David [Rubinson] tried real hard. He wanted another home run; he would go and kick Warner Bros. in the pants and maybe they didn't know how to work this album. Part of the enigma of the first album was, 'Suavecito' was a hit; but really, that's not what the band was about, and there wasn't a 'Suavecito' on the *Dos* album. The album was very Afro-Latin.

"Fred Catero was great to be around, he was one of my favorite people of all time. I'd see him as much as I could, mostly in the studio. He was the president of NARAS[29] in the Bay area. I'd worked with Fred in the studio with Blue Cheer. How he got on with David Rubinson for so long is beyond me. I'm sure that David traded on Fred's talents tremendously. An extremely talented guy, Catero Sound was always one of the high points of the San Franciscan music scene. That last *Ascension* album, Fred was the man. He made that work for us."

---

[29] National Association of Recording Arts and Science, administrator of the Grammy awards.

Photo: Rudy Rodriguez

Tom Harrell and Tom Poole: Malo horns onstage.

Tom Poole, who went on to play with Boz Scaggs, came into Malo after the first album. "One of the great trumpet players called me up to do the gig, Tom Harrell, right at the end of 1971. I was about 23 years old; I didn't fuckin' know what was going to happen. I had done the *Last Days at the Fillmore* gig with Boz Scaggs. I got the gig to do the Malo tune 'Pana' in the studio. We were told we could invite as many of our friends as possible. So there are thirty-five or forty people in the studio. Rubinson and Catero were there with their hair down to their ass. They overdubbed Bill Graham's voice and the Fillmore crowd.

"That was a great band and I had a lotta fun! I remember our first gig was the Ghetto Club in the Mission. Some guy hit Arcelio's wife and Arcelio's onstage saying 'I get off at two and I'm gonna kick your ass, you sonufabitch!' I'm thinking, 'What kinda band's this—I've gotta fight to stay or to leave?'

"The first album's out and they're ready to go on the road. I remember Arcelio getting hit by eight cops on that Quicksilver tour. Chris Wong as a kid had this '57 Chevy and he's manager of Malo. He told me he's got a new Mercedes coupe and a house in Marin but he's got no money. Right. I'm thinking, 'sure Chris!'

"Tom Harrell leaves the band and then they got Bill Atwood [from Cold Blood]. Bill can play—a real be-bop player. We called Bill 'Crusty'— every once in a while he would be a bit scabby, y'know. He was always destroying rental cars and stuff. Bill would teach me a lot of dirty things. Bill was a real prankster. The first thing we did was short-sheeting Jorge and Pablo's beds. We used to get a kick outta that, because the road can get crazy and boring. We called Chris 'Hold Wong' or 'Wimpy Wong' cause all he did was eat hamburgers.

"We were on the road, in the Howard Johnson hotel. Nightlights by the bed, remember that? We go to a gas station and get fireworks; we get firebombs, rockets, cherry bombs, crackers, etc. Atwood looks around, starts putting these down his pants. When we're in the car, Atwood's like 'We got the power.' Chris Wong was in Room 517—how's that for memory—Bill borrowed a screwdriver, we mixed up ketchup, water, etc., left it in a container over the door. We short-sheeted his bed, sewed up one of the sleeves of his jacket. Remember the light bulbs? Atwood would insert the firecracker into the bedside light, real careful.

Arcelio Garcia partying with Raul Rekow after a Malo show.

Photos: Rudy Rodriguez

144

Chris Wong after a night of cherry bombing, short-sheeting, etc.,—the trials of Malo's manager.

Photos: Rudy Rodriguez

Mike Heathman, Malo's trombonist.

"So Chris is heading back to his room; BLAM!! The door is off its hinges, we're laughing our asses off; our ears are against the wall now. All of a sudden we hear this, 'OH FUCK, WHAT THE FUCK IS GOING ON??' We could hear the ketchup and gloop hitting its mark. We could hear Doug having a good belly laugh, he's having a good time with this one. Next he's trying to get into bed, 'WHAT THE FUCK!!' Wimpy Wong calls the manager up: 'What kinda place is this?' I was laughing so hard I couldn't breathe.

"Bill used to teach me Charlie Parker, Dizzy Gillespie tunes, and Miles Davis tunes. Another time we were doing this coliseum somewhere. Richard Spremich was the 'rock star' of the band; he'd be checking the audience, let everyone know he was there. So Atwood ties a tampon to Richard's back belt loop. There were some cute women around, you know. Richard's on his way to the stage, sees these two girls, 'How you doing?' Starts to walk onstage. These women start howling. He figures he's being real cool. Walks back to the dressing room, someone says, 'What's that on the back of your pants?' He walks back to the dressing room but he can't see anything. He was spittin' blood mad!

"Mike Heathman [a trombonist] was also with us. I can remember the time after *Dos*, [something] to do with the band royalties. I think Jorge wanted to split everything up equally but Rubinson had other plans. Bill, not known for his tact, said, 'Fuck you, David! Fuck this shit!' He just walked out. Raul left and so did Richard Kermode. Richard Kermode and I played together for a while; we were that close to getting a deal with Creed Taylor, doing fusion in seven, nine, eleven, and thirteen time. I was also in a band with David Brown [of Boz Scaggs, not Santana] and I played with Gregg Allman down south."

"Malo was like a dream come true. We were so electric, before we got on stage people could feel the vibe. Backstage we'd chant together with cowbells and stuff; it was religious, we'd hang together. You don't get that feeling often. I get it now with Etta James, but that Malo band was real special."

Leo Rosales recalls: "The band dissolved because of royalty points. After the first album, Arcelio, Jorge, and Pablo were making the royalties off the first album. We felt we had a great crew; we knocked people dead every night. Pablo was a master of disaster all the way. We got to the second album and we felt that the reason the first album was kicking ass is because of the way we're playing together now. We were so hot! We were playing the Whisky a Go Go, Long Beach Arena, Don Kirshner, 'American Bandstand' with Dick Clark. We did the National Coliseum with Buddy Miles, 'Rollin' on the River' with Kenny Rogers when he had the First Edition—that's 'cause 'Suavecito' crossed over.

"Anyway, we're writing all these new songs and the band is jumping. All of a sudden management comes in and says how the points were going to be sorted out before we started recording the record, how it was all going to be distributed. So we were all sitting at David Rubinson's office on Market Street, across from the Fillmore Auditorium, when Chris Wong and David told everybody what they were going to do—after we had promoted the first album: 'These guys are gonna get this much and the rest of the team is gonna get this much.' It's like, some guys are gonna get twelve points and then the horns and rhythm section, who are making this thing jump, we're gonna give you two or three points. The horn players put their trumpets in their cases, shut their cases and said, 'Fuck you and bye-bye!' The band dissolved on that day.

Photo: Rudy Rodriguez

"Fuck You and Bye Bye." David Rubinson attempts to sort out Malo points in a tense band meeting at his offices on Market Street.

"I didn't go. I made a couple of enemies with the guys who were going 'cause they wanted me to leave with them, but hey, I'm seventeen and a half; it didn't seem to me to be a good move right then. After a month on the road, I was getting a check for, let's say, $600 dollars. So we were supposed to be recording the second record; that was tough. They had a deadline with Warner Bros. to get the album out. So when the band quit, they had to start hiring people. I was sad that Raul was gone, as we had gone to school together and then Francisco came in. It was like living with the King of Conga Drums. He's very stern, doesn't do drugs. He fit in perfect. It wasn't really what I'd call a heavy-drugs band—nothing like what was happening with the first Santana band; not even close. They had a lot more popularity than we did, and I guess the casualties were greater. We partied a bit; I was one of the worst offenders. We got a new crew of players, like Tony Smith, Ron DeMasi, the other horns, and the band was jumping again, and they got back on track. I got a little disillusioned, left the group at eighteen-and-a-half, and got married and stuff."

Top: Leo Rosales fires it up onstage with Malo.

Center: Abel Zarate and Leo Rosales onstage with Malo.

Bottom: Leo Rosales, Richard Spremich, and Arcelio Garcia, Jr, onstage with Malo.

Photos: Rudy Rodriguez

Photo: Rudy Rodriguez

Azteca live at Cinco de Mayo show in San Diego, 1973.

Photo: Joan Chase

Azteca group shot: Back row: Tom Harrell, Jim Vincent, Paul Jackson, Pete Escovedo, Lenny White III, Mel Martin, Bob Ferriera, Jules Rowell.

Center: Wendy Haas, Victor Pantoja, Coke Escovedo.

Front row: Rico Reyes, Errol Knowles, Flip Nunez, George Di Quattro, George Muribus.

NON PACEM

Azteca, a sixteen-piece band formed by brothers Pete and Thomas "Coke" Escovedo, was tipped to be the next big thing to break out from the Latin rock movement. "Azteca were to be the Latin-rock supergroup," says Jeff Trager, who brought Elektra recording company executives to see them play. The Oakland-based band consisted of bandleader Coke on timbales, Pete on percussion and vocals, Wendy Haas on vocals, Victor Pantoja on congas, and Paul Jackson on bass, among some of the cream of San Francisco-based musicians. "They took the sound in another direction," says Pete Gallegos. "They had real sophisticated arrangements; Pete and Coke were on the cutting edge. They were flamboyant characters. They'd always have a timbales battle at the end of their shows."

As did the members of Santana and Malo, the Escovedos learned music before they could talk. Their father had emigrated from Mexico to West Oakland, and took the family to the tardeadas at places like Sweet's Ballroom downtown. "My dad was a frustrated singer," says Pete. "All these big bands would come to town; my brother Coke and I would listen. At the beginning I was self-taught. My younger brother Coke started playing and we formed the Escovedo Brothers; it started as a cojunto band with trumpets and the rhythm section. I played with Carlos Federico around town, and I was listening to a lot of jazz. There was a New York timbales player [who] lived near me called Joe Ross[30] who really was into the Cuban and Puerto Rican stuff, like Tito Rodriguez, Noro Morales, and Machito. We had a Latin-jazz sextet in the early sixties. Then Coke got the call from Santana and he went with them."[31]

Victor Pantoja also brought a Caribbean flavor to the Chicano band. Born in Puerto Rico and raised in New York, he started playing at age eight. "My first band was with my sister," he remembers. One of his main influences was the Cuban rumba style of Carlos "Patato" Valdes. Pantoja played bongo and conga with Orquesta Cachao in Puerto Rico, then went on to play with Tito Rodriguez, Tito Puente, Machito, and "loads of others. I was with the Harry James Orchestra. When I was about fifteen I played with Herbie Mann. We went to Europe; when I got back, I played with Jimmy Smith. I knew Luis Gasca from the Stan Kenton days. I came out to California, playing with Wes Montogomery. I had also met Willie Bobo; we were from the

Coke Escovedo plays timbales on the road with Santana, Europe, 1971.

Mike Shrieve plays drums with Santana on the road, Europe, 1971.

Photos: Joan Chase

---

[30] The father of Gibby Ross, who played with Malo.

[31] Pete joined Santana on tour after *Santana 3*.

same barrio. We used to play at a place called Count Basie's." After a slow start, Azteca agreed to a promising deal with CBS. Pete Escovedo recalls: "When we formed Azteca in about 1970, it took us a while, but we signed with CBS. We did a showcase at [San Francisco's] Kabuki Theater for the labels. Clive Davis brought us over to London to play at the convention, along with Weather Report and Earth, Wind and Fire; we were the big signings that year."

According to Trager, Jac Holzman of Elektra wanted to sign Azteca. "He made them the biggest offer in the history of the company. He'd signed the Doors and Judy Collins, [but] the Escovedos signed with Clive Davis on Columbia because [Columbia] had the mystique—they'd done it with Santana."

Azteca's first single release, "Ain't Got No Special Woman," from the first album, simply titled *Azteca*, suggests Davis tried to capitalize on the popularity of the Santana sound by adding Mike Shrieve and Neal Schon to the line-up. Schon in particular turns in a scorching guitar solo over the rhythm section of bass man "Headhunter" Jackson and Lenny White on drums. Schon pushed the band into overdrive as Coke's timbales spur him onward. Otherwise, the album has the soul and R&B flavors that Coke Escovedo favored. Azteca's second album, *Pyramid of the Moon*, again features a impassioned Schon stand out, "Whatcha Gonna Do?" Schon builds his guitar solo with economy and tension to make this a Latin-rock classic.

Neal Schon: "Luis Gasca would say to me, 'You've got eyes to play.' I played with Azteca; again, it was a very drug-induced band and I wasn't digging it—I wanted to get away from that. That's the reason that band went down so fast; also, too many members to go on the road. To me, the drug thing started to get an evil tang to it—one day it's cocaine, the next everybody's speedballing and everyone's nodding out. I've seen so much of that, so many people die, it's a very scary scene."

Abel Sanchez reinforces Neal's view. "Everybody thought cocaine was the best thing since mom's apple pie; it was glamorous and it was everywhere. In those days, nobody realized the impact of the drug scene. It got real gnarly to be around later on."

Coke Escovedo with personalized timbales at Cinco de Mayo, San Diego, 1973. Lenny White on drums in background.

Photo: Rudy Rodriguez

Azteca 45 single release, Holland, 1972.

Photo: Courtesy Columbia Records

Photo: Johnny Valenzuela

Wendy Haas and Errol Knowles vocalists onstage with Azteca Jack Murphy Stadium, 1973.

Photo: Courtesy Etienne Houben

Coke Escovedo (far left) with Santana in Germany 1971.

Jack Leavitt, one of the first promoters to get involved in Latin music, produced the first outdoor show with Azteca in 1972. The co-founder (with Gary Perkins) of Avalon Attractions[32] remembers that "Santana's band had broken up and Coke Escovedo was managing Azteca. I paid those guys the deposit, half up front. Coke signed the contract. The day of the show, Coke's telling me, 'You didn't pay the first half.' I hated doing business with that motherfucker! I paid 'em the second half. He wanted to take me to the Musicians' Union court. I put my shit on the table… you know, 'I'll see you cocksuckers in court!' I never heard another word outta them. Coke was a fuckin' lunatic!"

"It was the first show done at the Jack Murphy Stadium in San Diego. This was after the Chicago Cubs played the San Diego Padres in baseball. After Altamont, no one wanted to book hippie gigs. Boz Scaggs was also on the bill. Mike Shrieve was on drums and Neal Schon was also playing with Azteca.

"Azteca played to a crowd of forty-eight thousand that day. There was a good buzz about it. In the old days, it wasn't so much of a business; the guys would come down on Tuesday to do a gig on Saturday, if they could still stand up."

Herbie Herbert was at the sound-mixing board for that show, working with equipment he'd taken from Santana to settle payment of a debt. He was so broke he was sleeping on Leavitt's sofa. The same craziness that had toppled Santana surrounded Azteca like an unshakeable hangover.

"Just before a show at Bimbo's, Coke Escovedo says, 'Herbie, you want a one-on-one, some coke? I did it and I was frozen solid, like a woolly mammoth. I couldn't do my job. At first you think it helps you, but this shit was really bad. So, by early 1973, I quit; it wasn't even $35 a gram, [but] that was the last time I got high on blow."

Azteca received limited airplay; the band was doomed to a brief career. "The easy answer to why the Latin-rock scene wasn't bigger? That's real easy: they didn't play it on the radio," Leavitt says. "Even today, I think there's only one rock station that plays rock en español—the rest play mariachi, banda, norteña, real accordion music, old style. They've been playing it all these years. Santana weren't really perceived as Latin, and they crossed over to the white market."

---

[32] Not to be confused with the Avalon Ballroom, founded by Chet Helms.

Bill Perasso agrees. "The music wasn't that easy to sell; sure, it sold to inner-city folks, real hip people. Santana was played a lot by Tom Donahue on KSAN. We really believed in 'Suavecito.' We had the two strong black stations that would support this music as well; there was KDIA in Oakland, and KSOL where Sly deejayed in San Francisco. They'd sometimes keep records on heavy rotation because white radio would pick stuff up. They did the same with Tower of Power, the first album, the single 'Sparkling in the Sand'; they played it to death on KYA." Jeff Trager is more critical. "Azteca wanted a bundle [to sign with Elektra] but they weren't worth it. You know why? It had been done. Santana did it, and they just didn't hit the Santana peak. Just like Graham Central Station wasn't Sly and The Family Stone. Azteca sold like maybe a hundred thousand units—maybe. Columbia spent a lot of money. You spend that, you gotta have a hundred thousand units on the street; you have to, because Clive Davis said you better." Even Herbert admits: "With Azteca, we didn't come anywhere near the glory of the first Santana."

"I think the musicianship was real good," Pete Escovedo insists. "I think the band was ahead of its time. It broke up when Coke left. He got a deal with Mercury.[33] He wanted to do a more soul thing. So I started playing timbales again. [When] Victor Pantoja got sick, I brought my daughter Sheila in. After a trip to South America, I gave the Azteca thing up and did two records with Sheila, with Billy Cobham producing. I went with Santana later for three years; I did the *Inner Secrets*, *Oneness*, and the *Moonflower* albums."

Pantoja, for his part, was simply worn out; a response symbolic of the times. "I don't have real good memories of Azteca," he says. "I got in a real hole, moneywise and stuff. It lasted about just two years. I had to do all the bookings. After Azteca, I came up to Los Angeles; I was going to hang up my drums."

---

[33] Releasing three solo records, Coke, followed up with *Coming at Ya* and *Disco Fantasy*.

Victor Pantoja, conga veteran, with Azteca.

Photo: Johnny Valenzuela

Pete and Sheila Escovedo pose for their *Happy Together* album release.

Photo: Phil Bray; Courtesy Pete Escovedo

Pete Escovedo plays timbales at the Jack Murphy Stadium, 1973. Behind him, Michael Shrieve guests on drums.

Photo: Johnny Valenzuela

Photo: Rudy Rodriguez

Malo in transition, after recording their *Dos* album.

DANCE TO MY MAMBO

Malo went onto record their third album, *Evolution*, with the notable additions of Ron DeMasi on keyboards and Tony Smith on drums. Both of these musicians were extremely intense players, bringing yet another dimension to the Malo sound. "Richard Kermode had gone off with Carlos Santana to do the *Welcome* album," says Arcelio Garcia. "We found Ron DeMasi out at a gig in Fremont. Dave Rubinson brought Ron Smith in [on trumpet], and we also saw Tony Smith playing at the Nite Life; I seen [him] doing all this Tower of Power stuff and singing. Man, he was hot! Last time I saw Tony he was coming down Fifth Avenue in New York; he was already about six feet and three inches, but he was on skates with five inch wheels—he looked about seven foot high.

Ron DeMasi, the astonishing keyboardist who joined Malo for the *Evolution* sessions.

Tony Smith (previously with The Loading Zone) was a virtuoso funkmeister on the drum kit.

Photos: Rudy Rodriguez

"Tony Smith was a great funk drummer; he had been with the Loading Zone (with Dougie Rauch). We also got Steve Sherard playing trombone around that time. I remember when [conguero] Francisco Aguabella came down; [he was] real conservative. He sat down for three days, listened to what we were doing, smoking his pipe, and then sat down again and knew everything back to front. *Evolution* had a lot of soul funk influences, but there was also my direction on 'Merengue' and 'Dance to My Mambo.' I felt Jorge's influence was more on those Chicago horn-style tunes."

Jorge Santana: "It was between Al Zulaica and Ron DeMasi for the keyboards slot. I think we also auditioned [pianist] Carlos Federico[34] around then. He was more a traditional Latin player; however, when Ron DeMasi got on that organ, he just blew us away. Before Tony Smith, we had Ricky Quintanal, who was a very free-spirited player. Everybody knew Tony around the Bay Area. I think he came from the Mother Lode [band]; he was hanging out with Dougie Rauch, they were doing real fusion-type music."

Evolution is a mixed bag. On the one hand there is a strong influence exerted by Smith, the incoming drummer and vocalist, but Arcelio Garcia's influence also is felt strongly on the more Latin tunes such as "Merengue" and "Dance to my Mambo." The album starts with "Moving Away," a horn-driven funk-rock piece echoing Garcia's comment about the Chicago influence entering the Malo sound. Tony Smith's vocal is confident, but the material isn't strong enough for an album opener. Tony Smith does a whirling dervish funk dance around his drum kit in a masterpiece of syncopated control until he bows out and rejoins the band proper, all the while supported by DeMasi's clavinet and Pablo Tellez's funky bass inventions. All in all: a fairly undistinguished opener, apart from Jorge's and Smith's solo pieces.

"I Don't Know," penned by Sonny Henry, writer of "Evil Ways" and other Willie Bobo cuts, is the second piece. A gentle Fender Rhodes intro heralds a strict clave tumbao over which Arcelio and Tony Smith sing in unison. The song has a plaintive feel, and melody that descends into ambient atmospherics by guitar and piano, glued together by Smith's light hi-hat beat. "All for You," written by DeMasi, Tellez, and Jorge is another plaintive ballad piece with muted horn backing. Smith addresses the song to a "dream little child," while Garcia sings, "it seems I've been a thousand places and I've seen a thousand faces," with a sense of real world weariness. The excellent harmony vocals lend to this an almost 5th Dimension feel, and show another aspect of Malo's reach.

Album cover art for Malo's 1973 release, *Evolution*.

Photo: Courtesy Warner Brothers Records

---

34   Both Zulaica and Federico ended up on the album.

A melodic roll on the cowbells by the timbales player announces the arrival of "Merengue," a fast, furious groove slammed along by Smith's solid drums and Francisco Aguabella's rolling conga pattern. Jorge plays the plaintive guitar refrain with a sound similar to [that of] brother Carlos's on "Guarija" from Santana's third album, hinting at the brothers' Mexican mariachi roots.

"Dance to My Mambo" is exactly what it says—a call to the dancers driven by Aguabella's rimmed timbales. Garcia's rough, tenor vocal blends perfectly with Tellez's vocal to form an instantaneous melody. Fine horn playing lends this song a sense of urgency. Staccato horn lines kick in to set the tune up for a joyous trumpet solo by Forrest Buchtel, ably supported by Tellez's stunning hypno-bass playing, which is really locked with Aguabella's conga and overdubbed cowbell. Unison chant vocals complement a first rate, tight-as-hell ensemble piece.

"Entrance to Paradise" is a beautiful, lyrical Jorge Santana guitar-led piece. Garcia remembers Jorge's initial resistance to including it on the album, even though the band had included the song in their live set as early as 1971. "Jorge didn't want to do it at first, but I like that song a lot. Carlos had done 'Samba Pa Ti,' [as Jorge] didn't want to do it 'cause he thought it sounded like Carlos; but to me, it's my favorite on that album." The tune opens with lyrical Jorge guitar, using feedback to introduce a complex piece of many changes. The song reverts to a straight-ahead tumbao with manic organ from DeMasi, who really lays down the funk. Backed by Jorge's repetitive funkisms on guitar and Tellez's hypnotic bass figure in a more Latin style, in this section the music manages to be both in the funk groove and the Latin one simultaneously.

The album closes with a Malo tour-de-force: "Street Man," a slab of Mission-style fusion funk that shows perfectly how this band both assimilated the various contemporary and roots sources of their own music, and also how they reflect several different strands of early 1970s American music in the process. Starting in 2/4 time and overlaid with DeMasi's swirling organ playing, "Street Man" is a perfect vehicle for Garcia's passionate gruff vocals, and also has a certain street-poetry quality with lines such as, "Hustles from day-to-day/is the way that he exists/Street Man's got an answer for the things that he has missed. /His momma had to raise him/working in the shops/Street Man made his own way by pulling out the stops." The band cook like crazy as the horns set up the song's middle section; DeMasi, on madly funky organ, piles on the pressure until the band go into total melt down, backed by Tellez's exhilarating bass and Jorge's funk slashes on guitar. Smith kicks the band in the ass further to let DeMasi fly. Tellez goes into overdrive, pumping the rhythm section as DeMasi dives into the final section of his solo. A superb example of a band getting it on, full-tilt, and a great ending to perhaps an uneven third album.

Jorge Santana has fond memories of "Street Man." "Musically, that song has the edge, such energy—the band was so syncopated in a fusion way. We had so much potential musically there. It is really hip drumming, really reaching for the edge. Arcelio has the clave in his heart but also he's got that Wilson Pickett soul man thing; so in one musician you've got two great outlets. So, I can see those different influences. 'I Don't Know' was an attempt to get a radio-friendly song. Really though, the album didn't go so well in terms of sales."

Doug Tracy: "I loved that album primarily because of Tony Smith and Francisco. It was an extension of more roots-oriented music. Tony was one of my favorite musicians of all time, as a drummer, a singer and as an individual. He was a real sweet guy; no ego. He could really sing, and sometimes that really helped with harmonies; he really helped Arcelio out. He went on to play with Jan Hammer and Jeff Beck and other people.

"Francisco was really respected. He had a lot of mischievous parts to his character. He was like a mentor to Raul Rico and Leo Rosales. He was a very funny man but he'd talk a lot. When we went out he'd have us in stitches, you know, ordering: 'A rrrrummm and a Cok-a.' Just the way he'd put it, really crazy! Francisco was a master musician and he had a good influence on the band. We were all in awe of him. Guys like Poole, Buchtel, and Atwood were crazy; you'd think they were the kids as opposed to Pablo and Jorge for example.

Malo appear on American Bandstand, 1973.

Photo: Rudy Rodriguez

"Arcelio was always a loose cannon, so you never knew what was going to happen. They did that 'Sesame Street' show, too; Ron Smith arranged those. The first song is 'Welcome' with Jorge translating from Spanish. Joe Reposo wrote those songs and we cut them in a day. 'Show Me How You Feel' was another tune. It showed another side of the band."

"At that time, the band was experiencing all these internal changes, but we were able to adapt and absorb these, so we were always changing; every album has a totally different feel," says Tellez. Garcia's hard-living and hard-drinking lifestyle seems to have caught up with him around then; as he remembers: "I came off the road and I was in a club with my cousin and I just passed out. My face and eyeballs were all yellow; I ended up in the hospital being treated for cirrhosis of the liver, and then I got hepatitis off of somebody's glass. I lost a lot of weight in about three weeks; I thought I was gonna die. They told me if I didn't take care of myself, I was never gonna sing again. It took me a long time to get back to the music business—almost three years."

Chris Wong also recalls; "Arcelio and Richard were two different kinds of performers but things were getting outta hand some times, I remember one time we were playing with Iggy and the Stooges at the Whiskey, Arcelio was drinking and really stoned, he's sloshing his drink all around, you know, slurring his voice, I think the performances weren't so good at that time.

"I feel that a lot of outside influences destroyed the first Malo band— youth, people wanting better hotels, bigger rooms, shit about limos. I think some people felt they were treated as sidemen. One of the things that got me going, too, was the drugs. Again, a lot of the time it was out-side influences. I remember seeing guys snorting coke on the plane; I'd be so mad, but what can you do? Dino Valente, these guys, they were all doing it then; the scene was awash with cocaine. We were getting sick and tired of getting new personnel, particularly teaching horn guys the breaks. When we got veterans in, they'd be brainwashing some of the guys, you know, like, 'You don't have to do this or that!' [Saxophonist] Hadley Caliman, for example, Luis Gasca, Snooky Flowers (a respected jazz sax-ophonist, who'd been in Janis Joplin's band with Luis Gasca), etc. These guys were older; they'd been in the game a lot longer.

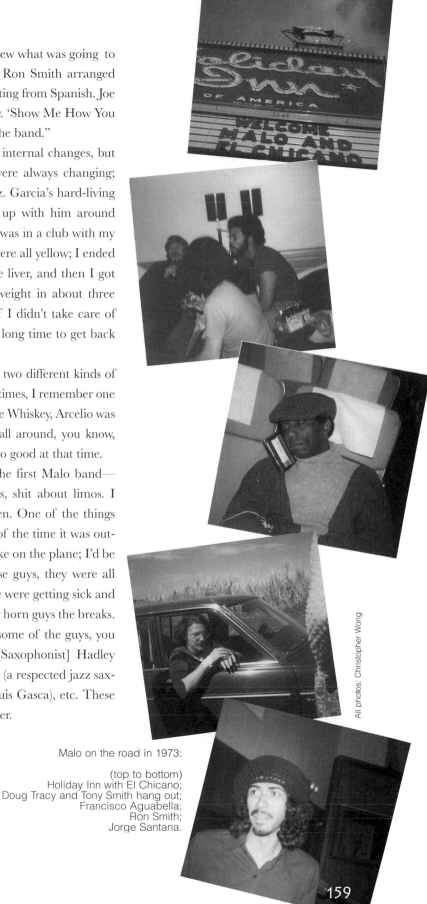

All photos: Christopher Wong

Malo on the road in 1973:

(top to bottom)
Holiday Inn with El Chicano;
Doug Tracy and Tony Smith hang out;
Francisco Aguabella;
Ron Smith;
Jorge Santana.

159

Ron Smith, trumpeter on the record, landed up in trouble, too, according to Doug Tracy, who wrote to a judge to supply a character reference: "he got involved in an ugly scene around a smack bust and was facing some serious jail time. I hope everything worked out for him." Smith has seemingly disappeared, not being heard of for years.

"David Rubinson, to me, was a typical New York personality: very loud, boisterous, egotistical, confident; when you're making that kind of money, it's easy to get that way. I found myself, in a strange way, getting like it too. I got the big desk—it can start to overtake you. You could get really paranoid about whose sayin' what to whom. Especially when they started pulling away from me. I mean, in the end of it, I got a phone call from Jorge, saying, 'Well, you know, we're at the attorney's office and we're gonna leave you.'"

Photo: Rudy Rodriguez

David Rubinson at Funky Features.

Malo Archives

MEMO FROM
JOSEPH B. SMITH

David

I'm sure that the true facts lie somewhere between their version & yours —

It's obvious to me that Malo is a high priority item with our entire organization & rest our case

WARNER BROS. RECORDS INC., 4000 WARNER BLVD., BURBANK, CALIF. 91505

Memo from Joe Smith, head honcho at Warner Brother Records to David Rubinson.

Malo Unjades the Record Biz Stalwart
by David Rubinson

In a tiny Chicano night club, overlooking beautiful San Bruno's railroad yards. Not far from a million mediocre Daly City fantasies—a new band. They spelled night with a "te" on the sign over the door. Two crossed champagne glasses etched in pink neon. The-flash-Nite-flash-Life-flash. Two bucks at the door. Fifty cents for girls.

The guitar player killed me. The singer killed me. The bass player really killed me. The other guys didn't. Oh Cisco. Oh Pancho. Here we go again. Hoho Hoho.

Malo Archives

David Rubinson's self-penned piece on his discovery of Mal

160

MUSICMAKER: ABEL & THE PROPHETS

Of the pre-Santana bands, Abel & The Prophets broadened the spectrum of musical references by bringing a soul-funk edge to Latin rock. "I went to Woodrow Wilson, a black school, so I grew up on the soul-James Brown thing. We got the name Abel & The Prophets from the book by Kahlil Gibhran. We started playing at high school rallies." A number of local bands were experimenting with the soul-Latin fusion as well. "Gregg Errico had a band at Jefferson High, I think called the Fascinations. Chepito was playing trumpet at the Nite Life with the Aliens. Limbo was another Latin rock band. There was a band called Christian Black—they were pumping out a mix of bugaloo, soul, and Latin. Luis Gordon got Crackin' fired up in San Francisco; they were in the Brothers Johnson bag, a great funk band. "All the bands would go to get outfits at the Town Squire, a clothes shop; they'd sell ten of everything, gold coats or velvet collars. Gregg Rolie's band, William Penn and His Pals, were into the Paul Revere look. We battled against them at California Hall and Long Shoreman's Hall. They had a dead-on Paul Revere and the Raiders sound. The Mission bands were pretty competitive; they would try and kick your ass!

limbo

Limbo Productions, San Francisco

Ivan Gomez, Management
Sallie H. Rush, Publicity

Photo: Christopher Wong

Limbo, one of the Mission district bands that didn't break out!!

"Bob Ramos was involved with Santana, and then he came to manage us when we signed to Fantasy Records in 1970. We got on the charts through [black radio stations] KDIA and KSOL and a DJ named 'Skin and Bones' Bob Jones. We had a local hit called 'Musicmaker' from our album *Please World*. When I came out with the first album on Fantasy, with a name like Sanchez, people were writing, 'Where's the Latin thing?' We did better in Europe than here.

"We were on a roll but our heads got big real quick. We started telling Fantasy how to run their company. We made three BIG mistakes. We didn't really have any business sense; we turned down a European tour with Creedence Clearwater. We wanted to make thousands like Santana. We told them, 'Fuck that, we ain't going!'

"Mistake number two, we played the Fillmore and Bill Graham wanted to manage us but we had Don Wehr (he had the music store). Don told us, we don't need Bill Graham, and we're going to be bigger than him. Mistake number three, hey! Ain't those two mistakes big enough?

"We ended up playing as the house band at the Orphanage, [which also booked] Buddy Miles, Sly, Larry Graham with Graham Central Station. It was real hip; it was on two levels, upstairs it had pillows at the front, and little coffee tables a foot high. It held about a thousand people. It was a dynamite club."

Photo: Abel Sanchez

Abel Sanchez (third from the left) with the Prophets.

Photo: Abel Sanchez

Abel Sanchez (standing in front) with the Prophets.

Photo: Rudy Rodriguez

Arcelio Garcia, Jr.

LOVE WILL SURVIVE

Photo: Rudy Rodriguez

Pablo Tellez plays
acoustic guitar.

Wong's observations were prophetic. Malo was starting to tour less and at smaller venues, primarily due to lack of airplay. One notable gig was their appearance at New York's Shea Stadium with the Fania All-Stars. "That's the one where we got panned by the Fania people for years," according to Doug Tracy. "We were doing the show in July '73. Celia Cruz and all these great acts were playing. The baseball people were playing the next day, so they wanted to keep the people off the field. The Fania crew was filming the show for a movie. The most important thing they impressed on us was: no people on the infield; they didn't want to ruin the field and it would cost a ton of money, the baseball team wouldn't be able to use it.

Photo: Malo Archives

Benny Lazardo,
Roadie with Malo.

Photo: Rudy Rodriguez

Chris Wong and Doug Tracy in the Malo office.

"We were scheduled to go on at ten at night, so it was close to the end. Last thing I told Arcelio was, 'Don't yell and have the people come down out of the stands.' I'm in the dugouts with my wife and we're getting towards the fever pitch of the set, and sure enough, Arcelio starts, 'Hey, come on down!' Suddenly it's raining people onto the infield; they're all over the place. Well, they stopped the concert, yanked Malo off the stage; they had to clear the field. It took an hour and a half to get it sorted out, and some of the last acts didn't get to play. The Latin press was all over us for doing it. I was runnin' around, trying to get the second part of our payment, but we never got paid, we never got in the film. We didn't get anything out of it except a lot of bad vibes from the New Yorkers. Arcelio being the type of person he is wants to get the people excited, and if I tell him no, he's still gonna do it.

"The shows that stood out to me were where something strange happened. We did a press party one time for Warner Bros. at Tompkins Park in New York City, probably one of the roughest areas in Manhattan. Nobody was going to go down there and see us. Somehow they staged it, with just a little bitty band stage there to play on. Us, like idiots, we played this wonderful set for all these homeless and derelict people. I think this was to promote one of the albums. Chris [Wong] and I also managed a band called Max from LA. We took them on the road with Malo; I think we did six dates, about twenty-five people on the road. We did Wichita Falls, Amarillo, San Antonio—all these off-the-wall places. After the third show the promoter disappeared; we never saw him again. So what we did was take this entourage of people, this circus roadshow, and continued onto Waco, Abilene, and Laredo, and pretty much put on the show ourselves—did the radio interviews, then we go deal with the sound and lights people. We never could find the promoter. We took a bath but it was a great gig."

Photo: Rudy Rodriguez

Photos: Christopher Wong

Doug Tracy in Malo group meeting.

Top: Doug Tracy in bed.
Center: Francisco Aguabella in the air.
Bottom: Tom Poole tries a self-induced face-lift!

In the run-up to their fourth album, *Ascension*, in 1974, some major players bowed out of the Malo story. After parting ways with Chris Wong, Jorge, and Pablo Tellez decided to make a break from producer David Rubinson. Around the same time, Arcelio Garcia, their mainstay and leader from the beginning, also left the band. "Arcelio, he was really pugnacious to begin with, but drinking was not helping matters," Doug Tracy recalls.

"Around the time of going in the studio for *Ascension*, business was very uncomfortable," Jorge says. "Chris Wong was gone and Pablo and I didn't want David Rubinson to represent us. We were seeking managers in Los Angeles. I think David's ego was blown. We were full of uncertainties about the business. We went to the studio and requested for David not to be there, and we ended up doing the album with Fred Catero."

Willie "G" Garcia, Arcelio's replacement, appears only on Malo's fourth album. Willie G was one of three great East Los Angeles singers who fronted Thee Midniters, (the others were Li'l Ray Jimenez and Cannibal, from Cannibal and the Headhunters) a band well loved on their home patch during 1964 to 1970. Their ode to cruising along one of East LA's most popular spots, "Whittier Boulevard," was a very successful instrumental and preceded their first album, *Thee Midniters*, which sold very well. Cannibal and the Headhunters also later that year had a hit with "Whittier Boulevard," which reached No 30; they also managed to open for the Beatles on their 1965 tour. Eddie Torres, who managed them, set up Whittier Records and recorded three further albums by the group with material largely co-composed by Willie G: these were *Love Special Delivery*, *Thee Midniters Unlimited*, and *Giants*. The band also released a single entitled "Chicano Power" in 1969 (a recent Latin-rock compilation from Soul Jazz records in London, England bears the same name). Failure to break out of the East LA scene and to obtain major label interest led to the band folding in 1970. After this, Willie G got together with Li'l Ray Jiminez to front the band God's Children, who had a Top 5 recording in New Orleans with "Hey, Does Somebody Care."

George Rodriguez was a photographer who, with his brother Rudy, was documenting the early Chicano bands. "We both took pictures at the Whisky a Go Go and I think Rudy definitely introduced Willie G to Malo," he says. "Willie G's a real story in himself. He's a born-again Christian; he's a preacher now and I think he's making a comeback as a singer. He's very good. Thee Midniters had bad managers; they could have been like another Los Lobos. I don't know why they didn't get out past Los Angeles."

Chris Wong in the Malo offices.

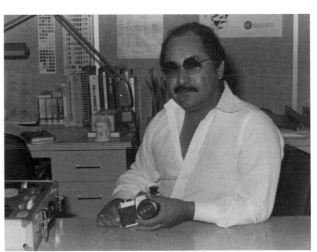

Rudy Rodriguez, excellent photographer of the Latin-rock scene.

Photo: Rudy Rodriguez

Photo: Malo Archives

167

Pablo Tellez and Willie G hit it off right away. "He was a great singer, a real sweet voice," says Tellez. Willie stayed with the band for a year, touring extensively and opening for the Temptations and Tower of Power. However, he maintained a part-time status, often returning home to Los Angeles after rehearsal—setup that annoyed Doug Tracy. "He was a very good singer and an interesting front man, but he was impossible to work with," Tracy insists, "What really killed it for me was, we were supposed to be doing this show [for] these two debutantes, two twin girls, of the John Deere family. They were paying us a lot of money. It was at the Stanford Court hotel; they gave us a suite and everything. Willie G starts calling from LA, trying to hold us up, you know: 'I need more money, I can't make it.' Willie just wouldn't go on the road. He had his own little fan club down there, in LA. So Tony Smith came to the rescue. It worked out OK. But we didn't have the proper number of musicians, so the union wasn't very happy. I found Willie G very standoffish, and he seemed hesitant to do the Malo thing. He was like a session man all the way down the line."

Despite the shaky situation, *Ascension*, the last Malo recording for Warner Bros., is an improvement over their previous release—Tracy calls it "excellent, maybe the best of the bunch, with the exception of the first one." Although missing Arcelio Garcia's strong input, Willie G more than acquits himself vocally and the disc has some strong commercial material and excellent playing. The album exhibits strong influences from Stevie Wonder, Herbie Hancock's synthesized and clavinet funk from the Headhunter and Thrust sessions, and the incredible multi-vocal layering of Marvin Gaye on "What's Going On," "Let's Get It On," and "Trouble Man."

Photo: Rudy Rodriguez

Willie "G" Garcia, renowned East L.A. vocalist, who joined Malo for the *Ascension* album.

Photo: Rudy Rodriguez

Jorge Santana takes a break during the recording of the *Ascension* album.

"I remember Jorge, Ron DeMasi, and me—we had a real open, unique understanding to working out the songs," says Tellez. "Ron DeMasi was a real spiritually open guy, he was such a unique player. On *Ascension*, I was more awakening to a loose playing style, putting all these styles together."

"Offerings," a tune that harks back to the band's early Fillmore dates, opens the album with an angelic choral vocal sound rising over the ominous Latin shuffle. The music builds into an onslaught of percussion aided by Nick Mendez's timbales and bongos and DeMasi simmering on organ in the background. Jorge opens proceedings with a heavily distorted guitar, with Tony Smith chopping away at the rhythm on splash cymbals, then cutting through the beat with his dexterous hi-hat work. All the while, Tellez lays down an ominous bass figure.

"A La Escuela," written by Aguabella, is next. Opening with Francisco chanting in Spanish, urging children to read and go to school, it's followed by an uplifting, positive tune featuring Tellez's jaunty bass. Jorge and the horn section open the joyous feel even further with massed vocals lifting the tune to another level. Jorge cuts in with a wah-wah-driven solo, while Aguabella displays his hard-hands conga playing.

"Everlasting Night" again sports the pretty melody of Jorge's guitar and some "up" vocal harmonies in keeping with the album's title (all the tracks have an aspiring, transcendental feel). The song imperceptibly picks up tempo and the lyric, "Looking around for something you need/when all the time it's been there right next to you," was not only pertinent then, but a timeless piece of advice.

"Latin Woman" shows the heavy Stevie Wonder and soul influences on the album. It's a randy, late-night lope, with Willie G testifying to the mystery of Latin womanhood. Jorge's heavily distorted guitar mutates into pure electronica at the end. "Chevere" storms out to close *Ascension*'s first side, a straight-ahead cut that shows this edition of Malo at its Latinate best. Led by a guiro-driven beat with creamy vocals, the band locks into place as Jorge hits the first of a series of piercing guitar runs that builds while the horns cook the music higher and hotter; an excellent dance vehicle.

Photo: Rudy Rodriguez

Steve Sherard, playing trombone with Malo.

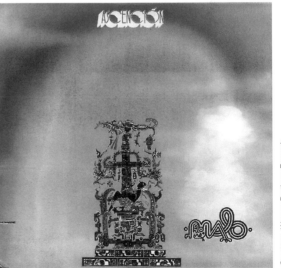

Courtesy: Warner Brothers Records

Ascension album cover art.

169

"Love Will Survive" has Jorge playing an intricate, double-tracked guitar melody over DeMasi's jubilant organ sound. "Tiempo de Recordar" opens with a slinky acoustic guitar lead shimmering over Tellez's inventive bass. A marvelous vibes solo by Ron DeMasi and a seriously grooving rhythm section offer several minutes of sheer magic until Jorge's acoustic double-tracked guitars brings this hypnotic performance to a close. "Close to Me" is a dreamy, romantic piece written by DeMasi with lyrical guitar and some soaring vocals by Willie G.

The final track, "No Matter," is a jewel in the Malo crown. If ever a track distilled Jorge Santana's talents, it is this one. As the sun set on the group's Warner recording era, "No Matter" is a fitting coda and a suitably reflective piece to close this first part of Malo's career. DeMasi and the horn section open this unusual and enigmatic song with a funk-driven, Tower of Power-influenced riff. Massed vocals carry the lyric, "There's a way/coming to stay," which manages to be both optimistic and reflective at the same time. Willie G exhorts, "Love to see you fly/don't stay behind." A muted trumpet solo by Mike Fugate ushers in a horn refrain, which sets the scene for Jorge's superb guitar solo. This is his finest recorded hour, and the solo trips through many changes—at turns optimistic and sad, laughing and crying. Recorded in one fiery take, it equals anything in the other Santana's recorded canon. Descending in a wah-wah-pulsed cascade of notes, Jorge pulls the solo out of free-fall to chop chords through DeMasi's organ swells. The vocals return with the spiritually uplifting lyric, "Look, there's something happening above/I know that something is love." Jorge's playing almost dissolves into pure feedback. Anyone who loves this art form and Latin-style guitar playing is directed to this cut—it's the real dope!

Jorge Santana live on stage with Malo.

All photos: Courtesy Jorge Santana

Photo: Joan Chase

Jorge Santana still gets chills when he listens to it. "I think it was so strong with a positive message," he says. "The style of arrangement really helped the solo. At one point, it went so high the guitar was ringing like a bell. What it did for me was it made me very strong. After we had listened to it at Wally Heider's, I went out to my car and listened to it, and I didn't like it. I came back to the studio and told Ron DeMasi and Pablo I wanted to do it again. My feeling was I hadn't been in tune with doing a take. Pablo told me I needed to listen to it again. The fact is I listened one more time and I realized that, even at that age, everybody has the ability to express themselves. The reason 'No Matter' was important was for me to go onstage and not be frightened to play the instrument spontaneously. To me the track ends that era of that whole band in a high, emotional way." In the words of Pablo Tellez, *Ascension* was "the last breath of the first Malo."

Malo 1974 lineup: Back row: Francisco Aguabella, Steve Sherard, Mike Fugate, Ron DeMasi.
                      Center row: Tony Smith, Jorge Santana, Pablo Tellez.
                      Front row: Wille G, Ron Smith.

Photo: Rudy Rodriguez

Photo: Rudy Rodriguez

Jorge Santana

MOVING AWAY

One of Doug Tracy's favorite memories is the way Malo took command of the stage at the beginning of a concert: "I would introduce the band. They'd start with a pinpoint of light on Francisco's hands. He'd start on 'Momotombo,' with that really hard conga thing going. I'd get the lights synchronized so that when the horns hit in, the lights would hit the horn section; then it would be, 'Ladies and gentlemen, from San Francisco, please welcome... Malo!' Then the whole lights rig would hit! People's jaws would drop at the sheer naked power of the band."

Photo: Julio Sanchez

Leo Rosales and Pablo Tellez at
S.I.R rehearsal studios, 1973.

Photo: Rudy Rodriguez.

Photos: Rudy Rodriguez

Malo horn section in full flight:
(L to R) Steve Sherard, Tom Poole, Ron Smith.

Pablo Tellez

Their flair for showmanship masked the underlying trouble eating away at the band's stability. By 1974, their relationship with Rubinson was nearly finished. With Chris Wong gone, the band searched for new management. "We hooked up with this guy in LA," says Tracy. "He was handling Jo Jo Gunne but he didn't do anything for us but take our money and put it into a movie called 'Carwash.' Now he's a big Hollywood producer. We went and spoke to War's manager, but we didn't like their vibe at all. He was just David Rubinson all over again; a transplanted New Yorker in LA, you know, glomming the kids. I think Jorge felt that, too. We were a bit directionless."

Malo toured for about six months after the release of *Ascension*. "Then Pablo and myself went back to David Rubinson to confirm the money for a next record," Jorge says. "This was with a whole new lineup; we were sketching out new songs. The songs were initially done on cassette; Pablo and I were rehearsing, trying to keep costs down. This was going to be the fifth official Malo album on Warner Bros. We had musicians from the Mission who were unknown—Butch Haines on congas was one. I think how it got resolved was that David said there were no funds there for the album.

"After this attempt I went and stayed at Carlos's home in Mill Valley. Carlos was always away touring. I was there for about two years; I just played guitar, ate, and slept in all that time. In that period, I played with the Fania All-Stars on 'El Raton.' We did a few dates: Miami, Shea Stadium, New York; we also went to Zaire to play at that fight with George Foreman and Muhammed Ali—that had James Brown playing there also—the Rumble in the Jungle, but I don't think Fania really features in the documentary [*When We Were Kings*]. We had a thirteen-piece orchestra. I have recordings of Cheo Feliciano, Johnny Pacheco on the plane just getting drunk, raising hell, and playing their instruments."

As with Santana, the general drug scene of the 1970s—when everything from marijuana to heroin was as available as a martini at a cocktail party—was taking its toll. Heavy drinking and drug use had ousted Arcelio Garcia; now his successor was in trouble as well. "I'd gotten pretty squirrelly and was pretty out of it on drugs," says Willie "G" Garcia today. "I feel privileged to have been a part of Malo; I was sorry to see it dissolve. Whether my personality or my addictions had anything to do with it, I'm not sure; but if I did, I really apologize for any contribution I made negatively."

174

"Drugs were appropriating good people; you'd see them getting into speed or heroin," says Pete Gallegos. "Same thing with coke but crack really turned it for the coke scene; it strung out tons of people. It wasn't recreational use any more."

Chuy Varela: "Everybody got so fucked up, y'know; that's the way you'd see people after awhile. My homeboy was real fucked up. It all became a bit harder. Chepito is the perfect example of what happened toward that waning time, how it went down. Society was changing towards a more hard time. I went in the army; I needed to get out of the scene. It was the army or jail. Some people got strung out and burnt out. Also, the FBI blew apart these movements; they infiltrated all these movements using divisiveness, heroin, etc. I think Carlos getting into the spiritual thing would make you question your level of partying."

Pablo Tellez's wife, Dora, remembers the effect of then-common culture on the bassist's playing: "I met Pablo when we were real young. I was there through that whole scene; at first everyone was like innocent kids. I remember one day, I actually introduced two groups of friends to each other to buy drugs, and I took this package home to sell it for them. I put it on the top of the closet. Eventually [Pablo and I thought], 'Let's try this [package].' It looked like cocaine but it was China white heroin. I don't think people realized how destructive heroin was around then; the hangovers from the hippie, flower-power scene. When Pablo went through the drug thing, it diminished his creativity. It took a big chunk out of him. We both hit rock bottom."

Pablo Tellez gets his Afro hair cut while Rudy Rodriguez and Bill Graham look on.

Photo: Rudy Rodriguez

Adds Tellez himself: "I look back and I think I don't know what hit me. I went from the Nite Life to Malo and then Santana; it all happened so fast. I got into a lot of trouble with my weaknesses in the area of drugs. [After leaving Malo] I had a band for a while called Searching, but that didn't happen. Before the Searching band I was with Eddie Palmieri, the salsa piano player from New York, but he kinda scared me a lot. His lifestyle, the drug scene, I mean, I was bad, too. I didn't feel comfortable even though the music was great. I was with him for a year and a half. From there I went on to get more into the drug scene, really messing up. Playing in salsa clubs at night. Five, six nights a week, I got so deep into the drug scene that I really didn't have any feeling for the music. I was just playing it from my head but my heart was not into it. My playing was just to get my next fix.

"My use of drugs continued until one day when I was alone at home. I heard this voice that said that I had no life. It was like I'd been asleep and my reality hit me. How did I get here, why did I do this? I became so sorrowful I began to weep, and I went and hid in the bathroom, 'cause I didn't want my wife to see me like that. So, I looked into the mirror and I could see two of me. There was one on the outside plus the one on the inside of me. I spoke to myself. I said, 'Yes, Pablo, you are dying.' I started to feel this tremendous feeling of power that came all over me. As that happened I began to say these words that I never would have said before. It was something like 'Satan, you are destroying me, killing me and my family—no more!' As I said that, I knew that he had no more hold over my life.

"My wife saw me and as I held her in my arms, telling her how sorry I was for all the hurt, I had a vision of a face of a man, a bald man with a beard. This turned out to be the pastor of the church where my wife and kids went. This man came to the house later that morning and we prayed. My insides opened up when I prayed for forgiveness from Jesus; as I prayed, a peace came over me. From that time on I knew things had really changed; I was born again in Jesus Christ. The conclusion is that I thank God that I came through it and I can use my experiences for the glory of God.' One by one, each member of Malo was about to break loose to be reborn.

Salvation

Malo appear live at LA's
Whisky a Go Go, 1974.
(Note the posters for Donald
Byrd's hit jazz-funk crossover,
Street Lady.)

Photo: Rudy Rodriguez

ATTORNEY TO THE STARS

Photos: Courtesy Joel Selvin Archives

Carlos Santana
and Brian Rohan

Bill Graham

Entertainment attorney Brian Rohan was part of the San Francisco music and political scene at the beginning, in the pre-hippie, pre-Latin-rock era. Fellow attorney Glen Miskel, a contemporary of Rohan, has dozens of stories about the maverick lawyer who represented David Rubinson and Malo, as well as Journey, Aerosmith, the Cars, and Boston. "Brian is pretty notorious in his own right. He operates out of the trunk of his car. His history is marvelous and he originally used to practice at the famous address, 819 Eddy Street, near City Hall. He started out with Vincent Hallinan, another legendary lawyer, who went to jail fighting for liberal causes in the thirties and forties."

In 2003, Rohan offered an overview of the city's transformation. "Here's the deal: let's start in 1960: I was paying $95 for an apartment up on Seventh and Judah Street. It was 30 cents for a gallon of gas. At that time I was very straight; I was into booze but no coke or a little pot. There was no music scene in San Francisco; it consisted of Fantasy Records, run by two brothers. They had Dave Brubeck on the label. Creedence were the Golliwogs then; I think they were with them, too. Jimmy Lyons started the Monterey Jazz Festival and Ralph Gleason was writing for the Chronicle; he was very influential in validating the music when it happened. Herb Caen was also important—a gossip columnist in San Francisco. Caen was a true bohemian. He'd lived in Paris and he hung with the musicians in the bars. Joel Selvin and Bill Thompson were copywriters then.

"FM radio was starting to come in, and there was this fucking cultural void. Three networks but no computers, no music, but it was active politically. The Free Speech Movement was going on, the sit-ins on Van Ness where we tried to integrate the auto dealerships; the cops were arresting hundreds of people. We were cutting our teeth on these cases, coming out of the Republican Eisenhower years. The Irish people were living out in the Mission, and then the Latinos started to move in. There was one old Irish judge, Thomas Fitzpatrick; it was a joint for the joint—he was a real prick!

"Then along comes Bill Graham, a real New York Jew. He was a hard-assed businessman. Then there was Ken Kesey, a wrestler, an ex-football player, a novelist; and he had this psychedelic bus. Chet Helms was this guy from Texas, which had a good underground scene; they had a lot of pot down there. If they caught you, they'd walk on your fingers. Janis Joplin came up; the Sir Douglas Quintet came up. There were a few hippies coming in but I was just doing personal injury cases, just garbage. Kesey got busted and I represented him. I went from being an ambulance chaser to being on the front page of the newspaper and on TV. This was just before the Trips Festival at Longshoremen's Hall in January 1966. Kesey's entourage was like a giant school of fish that followed him around. If you had four dollars worth of food they'd eat it; if you had five thousand dollars worth they could eat that in one night. They'd take your cars, everything, but they were a true hippie communal thing.

"Matthew Katz had come around then and he says to me, 'There's gonna be a big music scene here in this city and I'm gonna run it!' Katz, this New Yorker, had amazing taste. He found Jefferson Airplane, It's a Beautiful Day, Moby Grape. His lawsuits go on for over thirty years; ask Glen Miskel. There was a guy around then who used to insult just about everybody and that was Bill Graham. He and Kesey had a famous falling out at the Trips Festival, when Ken [who was wearing an astronaut outfit] busted his space helmet over Bill's head. [Radio personality Tom] Donahue had his record label, Autumn Records; the Beau Brummels were on there. Sly Stone was producing stuff; 'Do the Swim' was a big hit. Sly was also putting the Great Society through its paces. There were a lot of singles labels—Aladdin, Art Le Beau's labels, R&B, and shit. They knew the business but they didn't know what the scene was about. They were these voracious thieves that would knife-in on everybody. They were cartoon characters but they were connected down here.

"I did the Grateful Dead contract, which was the first big San Francisco music deal with Joe Smith at Warner Bros. I was the hippie lawyer. My persona was as one of the street guys. Bill Graham had dove in with the Fillmore. Chet Helms had started the Fillmore and then the Avalon Ballroom. Along with this, Cesar Chavez was raising Latin consciousness, the Panthers were forming, the Longshoremen were active; San Francisco has always been a strong labor city. The cops would abuse the shit out of the hippies. They had some real perverted guys on the police force. All these factors were going on.

"I had started to talk Bill into doing the record label with Santana. We wanted to do two labels, one with Atlantic [Fillmore Records], and one with Warner Bros. [San Francisco Records], and play them off against each other. On one label we had Aum. We had Tower of Power, Cold Blood; the Pointer Sisters were gonna be on there. I had a huge run-in with [producer] Jerry Wexler over the Fillmore Records label. Jerry Wexler is a muthafucking asshole, a prick of pricks. He gives you his entire jive-ass New York bullshit. I also thought he was a shitty producer.

"Ahmet Ertegun [head of Atlantic Records] came to see Santana. Ahmet just didn't get Santana. Clive [Davis] sees them, signs them; they have the biggest selling first album of all time. *Abraxas* comes out, does even better; same with the third record. I get a call from Ahmet, he says, 'Do you remember what I told you about that Santana gig? I didn't mean it.' That guy had stored that thing in his head for three years.

"Bill Graham loved Latin music but I think he didn't like a lot of the San Francisco musicians. He respected Carlos a lot and he was a great friend with Tito Puente; he came out of that Bronx Latin scene at Roseland. Bill was a hell of a dancer!"

Rohan was notorious in his own right, says Miskel. "There's a story that Brian punched David Geffen out at the Polo Lounge because of some slight." "When I punched David Geffen," according to Rohan, "it set up a principle; lack of size is no defense anymore. These little midgets used to get away with everything. Guys like Irving Azoff [a management mogul], are like looking at a really bad piece of meat." Rohan also struck a blow for Santana. "They had so much success so fast. There was so much money coming in; there was a lot of stuff with tax shelters going on. Herb Resner was a disbarred lawyer who got in with Santana; he and his son [an astrologer named 'Dr. Stars'] were looting the band. Bill called me up about a record deal going down with Carlos and the band. Bill asked me to get a better deal. So, I flew to New York. I said to them, 'You fucked them the last time; you're not gonna fuck them again. We're not going to sign this unless we get a better deal.' So, we got a huge royalty increase; let's put it this way, my fee was two million, two hundred thousand dollars more than the other guy got."

Dougie Rauch and Neal Schon at Columbia Studios, Folsom Street, during sessions for the Attitude recordings, 197

Neal Schon at the Attitude sessions, 1971. (Greg Errico and Dougie Rauch in the background.)

ATTITUDE AND MORE

Michael Carabello and Neal Schon started up the Attitude band after the split in the original Santana.
Pictured: Carabello at the recordings, Columbia Studios, 1971.

In 1972, after the release of *Caravanserai*, the original Santana lineup were all busy with solo projects. Carlos and Shrieve ploughed the fusion-era furrow by delving deeper into the jazz area with the follow up album *Welcome*; the title track was a treatment of John Coltrane's piece. Selections by Shrieve and Carlos of Coltrane's later spiritually-inspired music are echoed in the guitarist's religious search.

Carlos Santana: "My parents only taught me the basic things about spirituality. As a teenager you want a first-hand encounter with the Creator. You want to know if the Creator is Santa Claus, a product made to sell products, or is God really God. Sri Chimnoy was a spiritual education; I learned a lot of discipline from 1972 until the 1980s. I got involved with him through Larry Coryell and John McLaughlin. At that time a lot of people were disillusioned with Christianity, and we wanted to get better, not bitter; and my wife and I got a spiritual education."

All photos on this spread: Jim Marshall

Neal Schon, Dougie Rauch, Michael Carabello, and Greg Errico, 1971.

After the release of *Santana 3*, the Santana collective was showing definite signs of fatigue. "We were very tired around the third album; we were worked into the ground," says Carabello.

"I felt burnt out, so I'd just ride around on my Harley," Greg Errico says. He had left full-time work in Sly Stone's band and hooked up with Neal Schon and Carabello to spend most Saturday nights at Andre's, the after-hours club run by Luis Gasca, where the hip musical cream of San Francisco would hang at "hellacious jams." He and Schon then joined Sly's bassist, Larry Graham, in his newly-formed Graham Central Station during its first six months. Graham however, tried to reign in Schon's crazed wah-wah excursions to four-bar solo guitar breaks, which didn't suit the expansive teenager, so that incarnation folded soon after.

Greg Errico: "Right around then, Mike Carabello had started this project at Columbia Studios with most of the Santana members. It was a band called Attitude, with Chepito, Wendy Haas, Dougie Rauch, Neal Schon, and Carabello, and myself; if we would have followed through, it could have been successful. It was a screaming band. Chepito was an unbeliev-able person; he was a shining light in the party. It was party time then and not very focused. So Attitude dissolved. But years later, I was doing a lot of production in LA and picked up the unfinished tracks from around '72; we put it out under the name of Giants. I got to say, however, the business side of that was a bit dark."

"Attitude didn't last long," says Neal Schon. "It was a wish band that Greg Errico and Carabello really wanted to happen. They shopped it to Columbia but no big bites came back. It was very funky, but it wasn't Santana, more like Sly. I was learning to play funk, but it got boring. I was studying funk guitar with Freddie Stone. The funk stuff I really liked was on the Betty Davis album. She was a very interesting person but we haven't seen her in years. Carabello drove her nuts."

Before she married jazz trumpeter Miles Davis, she was Betty Mabry, "a beautiful, striking, unbelievable Afro-American woman," says Michael Shrieve. "She really influenced Miles to change direction. He was pissing off the jazzers by playing the Fillmore, which we loved." At the time of her album, Errico's first production, she was dating Michael Carabello. "Carabello brought her to Wally Heider's and she asked me to do her record," Errico says. "We used to rehearse the album tracks during the day at Andre's. She was like the female version of George Clinton, ten years before her time."

Photo: Rudy Rodriguez

Luis Gasca, the "little giant."

Photo: Mel Dixon

Betty Davis, real name Betty Mabry.
Recently separated from Miles Davis, she hit up against the Santana/Sly Stone Mission scene. Dated Mike Carabello and recorded her *Betty Davis* record with Gregg Errico producing.

Photo: Mel Dixon

Betty Davis, a Kelis; thirty years ahead of her time

"Betty really influenced Miles to change direction," says Shrieve. "Jimi's women, too. They were always around the Fifth Avenue hotel when we were in town. They were ultra cool, ultra hip, ultra beautiful. The way they dressed, there was a whole scene around them. It was great hanging around with Greg Errico, Sly's drummer. It really felt like we were some bad motherfuckers."

"Betty Davis's record, *Betty Davis*, was a blast," confirms Neal Schon. I heard it again recently and it sounds great." Originally released on the Just Sunshine record label, it's out now on CD and well worth a listen. Apart from Neal Schon it includes the Escovedos, Dougie Rauch with Greg Errico on drums, blowing on some down-and-dirty, primal-rock funk under Betty Davis's original full-on, raw vocal style on cuts like "Anti-Love Song" and "Game Is My Middle Name." Betty Davis was a Kelis or a Melkie Jean; years ahead of her time.

Shrieve was busy with his new group, Automatic Man, staging their first gigs at the Boarding House in San Francisco. The Mission district had given him an entré into an energetic culture and artistic style, but eventually, the scene had begun to crush his identity as well. At this point he began to rethink even his personal mode of expression; he was, after all, from the suburbs. "Santana were a lot of things but we were very cool," he says. "[But] I wanted to get away from all that way of being. Growing up from the age of sixteen, being around brothers, and then getting in Santana, I couldn't believe the way I sounded. I've got this recording I did for Standard Oil about drums, in which I'm saying, 'You approach the cymbal; when you go up, you don't be downshifting.' Also we were at the Montreux Jazz Festival with Santana and the phrase that all the jazz guys were using then was, 'That's what she said.' I changed the way I talked at twenty-three, so I didn't sound like a Latin black guy. Oh boy, I'd turned into this kinda cool thing, but I wanted a life beyond music, even though music is my life."

Automatic Man was another expression of independence. "I tried to put together a band that was funk based with rock and roll," he says. "Bayete [Todd Cochran] was an extremely gifted keyboard protégé from the Bay Area that people like Herbie Hancock were speaking of. He was a young guy that had high expectations but wanted to do something different than jazz. He did brilliant solos on clavinet with sustained distortion; Pat Thrall on guitar was brilliant. We went through several bass players: David Rice, then Doni Harvey—he had the Jimi Hendrix vibe. He was more like a guitar player. We rehearsed every day at my house; we really wanted to turn the music scene around."

183

Then Shrieve moved lock, stock, and drum kit to Kensington, London, England to record the debut Automatic Man album at Island Records' Basing Street studios under a deal with record company president Chris Blackwell. The Automatic Man album was a hip concept, with Island investing heavily in the group. The musicians, all from California, attempted a big, soul-rock sound. Bayete brought a classically-trained sensibility to his synthesized sound. Doni Harvey, looking much like Jimi Hendrix in furs and feathers, nailed down a firm bass foundation. Pat Thrall brought space-age guitar fireworks to the band. They recorded with Keith Harwood and Chris Kimsey, two engineers associated with the Rolling Stones. "With Automatic Man, we wanted an English engineer. We wanted to record at Olympic Studios [where the Rolling Stones recorded] with Chris Kimsey, who was busy with the Stones. He recommended Keith Harwood to do the record, so the band moved to London."

Automatic Man managed one gig at London's Marquee club. The music was awesomely powerful. You could tell this band were ON! In the small confines of the Marquee, the music literally bounced off the back walls. Jerome Rinsom (from the Detroit Spinners) played bass for most of the gig, with Doni Harvey, strangely, showing up near encore time to engage the crowd with his Hendrix visuals. Shrieve played with ferocious intensity, wielding a pair of drumsticks the size of baseball bats and using early Impakt electronic percussion pads—a forerunner of the later dominance of electronic drums in the music business.

Automatic Man, formed by Mike Shrieve after leaving Santana during the *Borboletta* recordings. (L to R) Mike Shrieve, Todd "Bayete" Cochran, Pat Thrall, and Doni Harvey.

Photo: Courtesy Mike Shrieve

The album's premiere enjoyed a big push in England with the release of "My Pearl," the debut single—a rocked-up, funky, whimsical slab of psychedelia with a very commercial hook.

"It was an exciting time in London, but I think in the end, we were just too full of ourselves and we got in the way of ourselves. I think everyone had high expectations of us. Whatever Island Records invested they didn't make back because of later problems. I don't think we ever really shined in a live setting," Shrieve says.

"We returned to the US and did a big gig at Winterland, San Francisco. It was our homecoming and we were to turn things around. I begged with the guys to just play on if there were equipment problems. The gig turned out to be a disaster, there were problems onstage, people on their knees trying to fix gear; it was very disappointing. I had a meeting with Bill Graham after that; I asked him what he thought of the group, honestly, and he said, 'It's not going to happen.' The band wanted to go to LA; I didn't want to go there, so they moved—it really felt like they were against me. This is after me supporting them for years, buying them equipment, rehearsing at my house. They did that second album *Visitors* down in LA. I had a meeting with Chris Blackwell, who was very understanding. It was not a good ending to several years hard work."

"I think Automatic Man cost Michael a lot of money," says Herbie Herbert. "I thought I could've made that band happen. Then out of the blue they got this manager, Lou Casabianca. I said 'This project is officially over.' Mike Shrieve says, 'For you?' I said, 'No, for everyone.' Nobody's heard of Casabianca since. He was the death knell."

Photo: Debbie Feingold Courtesy Mike Shrieve

Photo: Dan Weaks Courtesy Mike Shrieve

Mike Shrieve poses for his *In Suspect Terrain* album release.

During his stay in England, Shrieve also got together with Stomu Yamashta, the avant-garde Japanese percussionist, and Steve Winwood (post Traffic and Blind Faith) to play and record the *Go* project. Two studio albums, *Go* and *Go Too*, ensued with a double album, *Live in Paris*, released on Island Records. Their show at London's Albert Hall was a mindblower—a multimedia special featuring extensive laser lighting. Guitarists Pat Thrall, Al DiMeola, and Roxy Music's Phil Manzanera supplied some of the fireworks, with Rosko Gee from Traffic on bass and Klaus Schulze's synthesizer work supplying an airy, spacious feel.

Michael Shrieve also recorded a solo album, *Blessings in Disguise*, in 1974. The recording was turned down by Columbia (in Columbia's opinion, it was 'too ethnic and too electronic'). The raw tapes show Shrieve at a very interesting stage of drum development on Sly-styled tunes such as "Your Smile," which shows his approach to bop-funk playing. The album features Bayete, Wendy Haas, Kevin Shrieve, Dr. Patrick Gleeson, and Michael Henderson, who also contributes vocals. There's a heavy soul influence on the record, as well as Shrieve's experimental side on such cuts as "Mantra" and "Belle Isle."

Shrieve moved to New York, and during that time flew down to Nassau to record an entire album's worth of drum parts for Mick Jagger. Eventually he ended up on one track, "Lonely at the Top," when Jagger re-recorded the album that was released as *She's the Boss*. Shrieve then took another stab at forming a group, this one called Novo Combo. Novo Combo released two records—*Novo Combo* and *Animation Generation*—on Polydor.

"I moved to New York because I loved jazz. The Novo Combo thing was similar to the Automatic Man thing. We were a great live band; very popular in New York, but again, personality problems. In retrospect, I was just going for the wrong thing. I should have learned from Automatic Man about bands. I can see now I wanted to prove myself outside of Santana, in terms of public acceptance."

Gregg Rolie was ready to quit the music business entirely when he got a call from Schon and Herbert about their newest project. For fun, Schon had been playing around with a jam band concept that he called the Golden Gate Rhythm Section. "It was kinda like the Grateful Dead on steroids," he says. It was also the foundation of a band called Journey, which brought Rolie and Schon back together and went on to become CBS's mega-seller stadium band. However, people who really loved Gregg and Neal's Santana-era playing are directed to their first two Journey releases: *Of a Lifetime* and *Look Into the Future*. The latter's second side shows their instrumental skills to the maximum. From the slow burn of the album's title track, which builds into a Neal guitar crescendo, it segues into "Midnite Dreamer," another knockout punch before all hell breaks loose on "I'm Gonna Leave You." All of these pieces are driven by Aynsley Dunbar's propulsive, polyrhythmic bass-drum technique. Journey's first album has more examples of torrid Gregg and Neal psychedelia on cuts such as "Topaz," with its fine bluesy intro; "Kohoutek," a monster serving of nightmarish riffs by Schon and Rolie, and the large sweep of the "Of a Lifetime" intro track, which deals lyrically with Gregg's feelings about Carlos and the demise of the original Santana band. "At that time in the business, I felt it was more the 'me, me' theory going on," he says. "I want to be a star, but the band thing was disappearing, and it was a real change."

José "Chepito" Areas also obtained a solo deal, and in 1974, he released a self-named album on Columbia. This endeavor was a marked move away from the fusion that Santana were playing and a return to a more Latin-rock and salsa-influenced music. It's a classic of the time; the tracks "Guarafeo," "Funky Folsom," "Guaguanco in Japan," "Cerra Negro," and "Buscande La Gente" show off Chepito's inimitable take on Latin music. Santana members Richard Kermode, Neal Schon, Dougie Rauch, and Greg Errico join a great selection of hot, West Coast musicians, Malo personnel, and lesser known Mission players such as conga players Ritchie Giraldez, Willie Colon, guitarists Ricardo Montalban and Carmelito Velez, José Medrano on drums, Tony Juncal on bass, Tony Smith, singer and drummer who went to Malo (who wrote and opens the second side with "Morning Star"), Tom Coster from Santana on keyboards, and Tito Garcia on lead vocals.

Photo: Joan Chase

Jose "Chepito" Areas; this picture was used for his 1974 solo album release.

Carabello, Chepito Areas, Richard Kermode, and Dougie Rauch all had a hand in the short-lived Cobra band. Little is known of their music, but apparently drugs were again a major factor in the demise of this outfit. The band played a badly publicized and poorly attended gig at California Hall in San Francisco.

David Brown returned to Santana in 1974 for the *Borboletta* and *Amigos* albums. *Amigos* particularly shows his increased fluency as a bassist, with a cheeky nod to Larry Graham on "See the Light," and his dyno-funk bass on "Let Me." He also pinned down the bajo on "Gitano" and "Dance Sister Dance." He could also be found playing with Mike Carabello and Abel Zarate in the Attitude band after the *Amigos* sessions. Jan Cameron opines, "He was seriously studying bass charts, jazz, and stuff. He wanted to study with Chuck Rainey, who was a favorite. He had a band out of LA for a while called Bad Baby, but I don't think he was motivated to go back out on the road."

After Santana and the Attitude projects, Michael Carabello moved to New York and stayed with Michael Shrieve. "I played with Irene Cara, the Jim Carroll Band, with George Benson, the Rolling Stones. I called it being the 'Fix-it doctor,' adding or overdubbing percussion over other player's mistakes in the studio. Keith Richard was hanging out with Jim Carroll, so I got to play on *Tattoo You*. I was at Juilliard for a while, studying while I was playing with the Stones. I did some stuff with [timbalero] Nicky Marrero earlier and also played with Tito Puente. There are still tracking tapes around somewhere of some recordings Chepito and I did with Jimi Hendrix, with Buddy Miles on drums and Billy Cox on bass. We did that session in New York with Hendrix but not at Electric Ladyland. Later on, Miles Davis added some stuff to the tracks. Chepito and me were asked to join Jimi's band at an earlier stage." There were plenty of opportunities, but individually none of the musicians matched the success of the Santana band. It was, says Carabello, "a difficult situation."

Carlos Santana with David Brown, live onstage in 1975.

Photo: Diane Black

HERBIE HERBERT / EL JÉFE

"Herbie started out as the road manager of Santana, working really hard. He was sharp even then. He then went on to become on of the most powerful people in the record business," recalls Jeff Trager.

Glen Miskel met Herbert in 1974, while Miskel was still at law school and Herbert was setting up Primo Productions after the demise of the original Santana. Primo Productions was predecessor to the Nocturne company, now one of the largest music production companies in the world.

"It was a wild time," says Miskel. "Lou Bramy was Herbie's partner; they put together Journey. Aynsley Dunbar was a client of mine; he came from playing with Zappa, Bowie, and Jeff Beck among others. He went onto do the drum seat in Journey."

After Santana's demise, Gregg Rolie had moved to Seattle, Washington, to start a restaurant with his father. His transition to a new rock band, Journey, was aided considerably by Herbert's growing skills as a manager.

"Neal and Herbie called me, initially to play with Golden Gate Rhythm Section. Herbie was with Lou Bramy and Journey started though that connection." Herbert was to manage the group even after Rolie's departure in 1980, and to transform them into one of CBS's major sellers, achieving sales in excess of 50 million albums worldwide.

Herbert's lasting contribution to the music business was to advocate for musicians' rights and economic control of their own product; and Journey's success reflected his savvy.

"Herbie was a real student of the music business," says Rolie. "Promoters would fuck the bands, reselling tickets, the works; Herbie was very hip to it, got his own counters in there. He got involved in sound and lights, our own trucks. He was the best manager. You could learn exactly what he knew, if you paid attention. He'd have meetings, letting you in on what was happening."

Photo: Pat Johnson Courtesy Jim Welch

Herbie Herbert plays guitar as his alter ego Sy Klopps.

The first Journey records sold reasonably well. The debut Journey did in excess of 150,000 units. *Look Into the Future* sold a healthy 250,000-plus. *Next*, however only did a "paltry" 100,000, so Columbia started the warning wheels turning; CBS wanted to drop the group.[35] "Herbie went to cut a deal with CBS for Journey in New York at Black Rock. He'd walk down the street with a tie, shirt, coat, and papaya shorts from Hawaii. They were looking at him thinking, 'What the hell is this?'" Rolie says.

Despite his iconoclasm, Herbert not only renegotiated Journey's royalty rate, but agreed to Roy Thomas Baker coming in as producer, and brought in a new singer. The *Infinity* album was the result. "His restructuring of Journey's contract was one of the greatest coups ever," notes Trager. "His royalty rate was unheard of. He took them from here to Mars, man! He was a like a barracuda."

Herbert, taking no chances, booked the band on a coast-to-coast US tour at major venues, backed by top promoters. Instead of relying on CBS, who seemed to doubt the band's ability to sell or incur a hit, Herbert developed his own merchandising opportunities and worked the band from the street up ("Journey made millions off of merchandise—the T-shirts, for example," according to Trager. "Herbie had innovative ideas.")

Further innovations included the band's ability to detach from record company dependence by supplying their own lighting, transportation, sound, and other technical needs under the banner of Nocturne, the company that had morphed from Herbert's Primo Productions. Nocturne upped the ante by putting together a complex multimedia setup, combining a huge stage with a state-of-the art speaker system plus giant TV screens, which allowed the entire audience to participate fully in the "front row" experience. It became the benchmark for the music concert business; and with Journey's never-ending touring, resulted in a triple-platinum album even without a hit single. The band took home a net of at least 70 percent of gross touring dollars. The publishing side was taken care of by Weed High and Nightmare Publishing, two other Herbert-run businesses.

Herbert continues to represent artists' interests today. "The Moby Grape situation is another thing that Herbie dealt with," Miskel says. "They were a great band from the late sixties. Bob Mosley and Skip

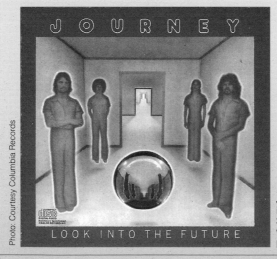

Photo: Courtesy Columbia Records

Look Into the Future, Journey's second release in 1975 displayed Rolie and Schon blowing out the wires with some deep ensemble playing.

[35] Trager remembers, "We'd listen to the new Journey stuff and we'd say, 'That's not a hit.' Johnny Villanueva would say, 'Yeah it is!' I'd say, 'Johnny, you've been smoking that shit too much!'"

Spence, two of the band [members], were both struck with mental illness around their peak. Some of the band approached Herbie in the early nineties. Their albums had been repackaged and the musicians had no rights or royalties.

"Herbie was outraged. He approached me in 1993 to try and bring some redress. From '93 to '98, Herbie paid me to reverse the situation. In '95, we succeeded in setting aside their settlement and brought a little justice to the table.

"Herbie also started working on an Internet company called music.com. His vision was to create a music company to sell direct downloads. Herbie wanted the musicians to share in the income generated, in effect by making them partners; it was ahead of its time." (Unfortunately, due to unresolved copyright legislation, the idea didn't come to fruition.)

After hanging up his manager's hat in 1993, Herbert's road took another turn with the Sy Klopps project. "In my mind the most incredible thing Herbie has done relates to the time his mother died," Miskel continues. "This pushed him in the direction of playing the guitar. He stared playing; next thing he was playing guitar and singing. Then he was gigging; soon after, he was out opening for major bands as the Sy Klopps Blues Band. The name has some mystical significance but he'll deny he's Sy Klopps.

"He opened at the Oakland Coliseum for Lynyrd Skynyrd and ZZ Top. It's an amazing accomplishment to reinvent a portion of yourself as a musician. We were sitting in his office on Third Street a few years ago; the conversation turned to early rock bands. We started talking about a band called Lynn County from Iowa. Herbie nonchalantly says, 'I'm on their album cover,' and sure enough, there he was on the cover. He had a copy on the wall in his office.

"Stories abound, like one from Don Fox. He's like the Bill Graham of New Orleans. Fox booked Journey tours for the entire country; he and Herbie were real good friends. Herbie's a large guy and he loves food. They went to a restaurant in the French Quarter, reportedly ordered one of everything of the menu, and managed to eat most of it. Herbie got to his room and collapsed onto the bed. Out of the corner of his eye, he spied chocolate mints and consumed them too!" Shades of *Monty Python's Meaning of Life*.

Gregg Rolie, onstage with Journey, shown here playing harp as well as keyboards.

Photos: Courtesy Gregg Rolie

Photo: Norman Seef Courtesy Jorge Santana

Jorge Santana Band promo shot for his 1st solo release on Tomato Records.

CANTINA

Photo: Courtesy Jorge Santana

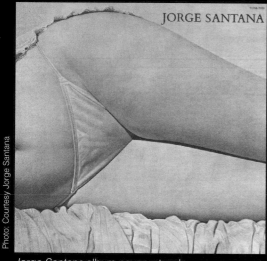

JORGE SANTANA

Jorge Santana album cover artwork

One constant in the Malo story is that the band was never constant. Apart from Arcelio, Jorge, and Pablo, the group went through significant changes in personnel due to the usual clashes having to do with money, egos, and their youthful temperaments. "By New Year's 1974, the Malo and the Latin-rock thing felt kinda done to me. It felt like the end of an era," says Doug Tracy.

Jorge Santana went on from Malo to get a deal with the New York-based Tomato Records for his new Jorge Santana Band, thanks to his manager, Sandy Newman. "We recorded in New York with Tony Bongiovi," Jorge says. "We went to the studio after we had been rehearsing for a whole year. Jerry Marshall was the drummer; he's mentioned on the sleeve but he's not on the record. When we got to New York the producer said, 'Why don't you set up and try out the songs?' Next day Tony called me and said, 'We love the music but the drummer, we need to change.' We're setting up and Tony says, 'I have the perfect drummer for you! No more than two takes of anything on the album.' Richard Crooks, that was the drummer. We did tour a lot to promote that first album," says Jorge. "We did a lot of showcases at night clubs, a lot around Florida and upstate New York. As far as I heard, we had sold up to 75,000 copies of the first album. 'Love the Way,' a commercial cut on the record, was getting good airplay, and we still toured for another two years with John Thompson on bass, Jay McKinnon on vocals, Yogi Newman on percussion, Roger Reid on drums, and Kincaid Miller on keys.

"The second album, *Three Mile Island*, was recorded in 1979 in New Orleans. We were staying at Allen Toussaint's house out on the Bayou. Toussaint told me that Tomato had gone bankrupt, so we did the rest [of the album] at Allen's on his studio time. That's why he has those songs on there; that was the trade-off. I remember having to borrow $2500 off Carlos just to get the band back home. We didn't even finish the horn stuff I wanted to do."

Jorge later put together another version of the band with Richard Bean, who also co-wrote much of the music. "We had another four-piece band called Jet; really a rock sound that took people for a loop," Bean says. "Again, people were expecting a Latin thing but it was a big rock sound. We did one performance at Lincoln Park; it was a big crowd. We started doing 'Suavecito.' The biggest Latino dudes came onstage holding up this gigantic Mexican flag. The bouncers couldn't move them. It was like the national anthem to them. I had tears in my eyes. It was one of the best moments in my life."

After leaving Malo, Richard and his brother Joe Bean auditioned players for a new group they were forming called Sapo. The personnel included conguero Raul Rekow and bassist José Simon (presently working as a well-known comedian). "We auditioned loads of players; we had a fourteen-piece band at first," Bean says. "I had songs like 'I Can't Make It,' which was ready for the second Malo album, and I started writing a lot of new material. We got Raul from Malo, after another one of Rubinson's meetings. [We had] Phil Scoma, our guitar player before Oscar Estrella, who was a happening guitar player! Kincaid Miller, our keyboardist was hanging out with Neal Schon around then. He's playing with Pablo Cruise now."

Photos: Courtesy Jorge Santana

TOP
Richard Bean

CENTER
Richard Bean and Jorge Santana

BOTTOM
Richard Bean and Jorge Santana on tour.

Richard Bean plays timbales with Sapo.

Raul Rekow plays congas with Sapo.

Photos: Johnny Valenzuela

Bell Records signed Sapo in 1974. "They were having a lot of internal turmoil," Bean continues. "Their whole staff flew out to see us. We did a showcase just for them at the Hawaiian Gardens in San José. They were knocked out. The original producer was going to be Allen Toussaint, but he was busy with Dr. John; John Simon produced it, he'd done Blood, Sweat & Tears. We originally did it as a four-track and overdubbed it like crazy"

"I Can't Make It," from the debut album, was a lowrider street anthem, particularly around 24th and Mission in San Francisco, around First and White streets in San José, and at Sunday parking lot hangouts throughout the Bay Area. Other standout cuts were "Ritmo Del Corazon," "Been Had," and "Sapo's Montuno." With Fred Catero at the engineering helm, it was a great example of Latin-fused rock and jazz, but didn't get the radio play it deserved. The band went on to open for salsa stars Ray Barretto and Tito Puente, and stayed together till 1977 when Rekow left to join Santana. In 1980, with "disco taking over everything," Bean formed Wizards with Abel Zarate. "We had Gabriel Del Rosario on bass, Ben Reyes on keys, and Raul on drums, [but] it was hard to get bookings then. We weren't doing Sapo or Malo stuff."

Doug Tracy managed several other Bay Area bands, including Frisco Nickel and David & The Four Skins, before getting together with Arcelio Garcia to work a band called Zorro. "They were doing some of the material which surfaced on the black album [*Malo V*]. They were doing some Earth, Wind & Fire kinda stuff; y'know, disco-type material. They were all really young kids. They had a timbalero—he was funny kid, like a Latin Groucho Marx; I can't remember his name though! I don't think any of 'em were 21 years old. Arcelio was on his second or third wife then, so it was a bit of a struggle. Most of my input was trying to push a demo, which we did at Funky Jack's down in LA."

In fact, most of the band members were residents of the government housing projects on Army Street, says Gregg Landau, who spent a stint as Zorro's guitarist: "Johnny Watson, Nerio de Gratia, a full vocal section. We toured Canada with Wilson Pickett and with Tierra. Zorro lasted about two years; the whole disco thing was kicking in, or the serious salsa, so Latin-rock started to phase out."

Photos: Malo Archives, Courtesy Traq Records

In 1975, Garcia took a hiatus from the music business to move to New York. "I wanted to study Latin music, and where better to study?" he points out. But his enthusiasm for fronting a band didn't stay quiet for long. "I started up Malo again in New York. I was back with a vengeance. Traq Records put out the album, simply titled *Malo V*. I was touring; we were doing gigs at the Village Gate in New York, also in Chicago and Philadelphia. I had a whole other band in place, with guys like Carlos Rivera on guitar."

Malo V, released in 1981, has both influences of the New York salsa scene plus fringes of disco stylings (such as the use of synthesizer drums). The album sports a fairly stark cover—just the Malo logo stamped in gold on black. The recording opens with synthesizer drums competing with Charlie Torres's timbales fills and a galloping conga pattern by Ruben Rosa on "Lady I Love." Dick Mesa of Tipica '73 floods the outro with smoky sax playing. "I Found You Out" is a storming number, written by Arcelio, that jogs at a mid-tempo pace. It features excellent rippling piano work from Eddie Martinez, and is perhaps most reminiscent of the older Malo material. Carlos Rivera supplies the requisite guitar work, complete with piercing upper-register riffing at the solo's end. "Good Tasting Stuff" launches with the sounds of a rowdy party taking place in the studio as the "revelers" chant the song's title. Again, the use of synthesizer drums dates this piece to the early eighties. Intricate vocal work intertwines with the horns to bring this song to its conclusion. "It's a Lovely Day" opens side two. A relaxed tune, it drifts in a summery haze, reminding one of "Groovin'" by the Young Rascals.

TOP
Malo V album cover artwork.

CENTER
Arcelio Garcia, Jr. with the New York version of Malo.

BOTTOM
Remember these?
Cassette copy of the *Malo V* release.

"Cantina" is classic Latin-fusion, a dark, subterranean monster. Buried on the middle of the second side, this killer instrumental cut is a scorchingly intense, brooding mini-masterpiece. Featuring a superb piano solo by the late, great Jorge Dalto backed by a completely rocking percussion section, "Cantina" was written by Malo's then-keyboardist José Gallegos. It breaks into a furious Brazilian-style roller coaster ride with additional percussion by Porthinio and the famous Latin bandleader Machito. With wide-open production values, the track segues through some heavy changes before crashing to a halt under a slamming final piano chord. The last song, "Young Man," is a cautionary note from Arcelio to the young street dweller about the potential pitfalls of drug use. Driven by staccato bongo work and sterling piano, this cut drives along with that same disco-style underpinning. *Malo V* was not a financial success for Garcia. He stayed in New York until 1984, when he decided to return to the West Coast.

Arcelio Garcia, Jr onstage with Malo.
(In the background, Charlie Torres on timbales.)

Ruben Rosa on congas.

Steve Longo on guitar.

ARMANDO PERAZA / HANDS OF AFRICA

During the original Santana band breakup, percussion was needed for the *Caravanserai* album sessions. James Mingo Lewis (who had been picked up in New York during the 1971 US tour), was still on hand, as was Chepito.

Mingo was responsible for penning the furious montuno-driven track "La Fuente Del Ritmo." Mingo supplies the piano figure underpinning the piece that introduced Armando Peraza's entry to the ranks of Santana and Latin-rock history. Armando's startling, staccato reverb-laden bongo solo erupts out of the speakers on the song's outro. Carlos Santana described Armando at the time as "the Miles Davis of the congas." His conga patterns, played in a "revolving" style, had an open, almost abstract edge to them. His rhythms, whilst retaining the Afro-Cuban basis, also added notes and tones from within the drums themselves.

Armando Peraza is one of the great Afro-Cuban master drummers—a link between African drum lore, via slavery, to the musical foment of Cuba. Early details of Peraza are hazy, due to his birth documents being destroyed in a blaze. He was born in Havana, Cuba on May 30, 1924. In Cuba, the style of playing and the percussion sound was heightened by heating the drum skins with kerosene lamps. Peraza played hard-core rumba and abacua with bands like El Bolero de Tata. This involved call-and-response drumming to the dancers' movements. He met and befriended the young Mongo Santamaria also; Mongo was playing with Conjunto Matamoros, and Armando was developing his technique with Conjunto Kubavana.

Armando Peraza,
Cuban master conga drummer.

Photo: Courtesy Josephine Peraza

Their paths crossed again when Armando left Cuba to substitute for the ailing Mongo in the Black Diamonds group in Mexico. He picked up work along the way with Celia Cruz, playing alongside Carlos "Patato" Valdes—another hot-shot Cuban conga player.

However, Armando had been in at the beginnings of the US Latin-crossover scene. He and Mongo managed to play in New York City with the mighty bandleader Machito; and watching was the jazz saxophone nemesis Charlie Parker, who immediately got him to record with him, laying conga riffs over the powerhouse drums of Buddy Rich. Problems with immigration for black persons meant he left for Mexico to get the relevant papers and then returned to the USA. He ran a dance revue (the Afro Cubans) at the Cable Car Village Club in San Francisco, and decided to settle there. Marlon Brando and other conga-loving hipsters would show up to dig the hot Latin sounds. But San Francisco has not always enjoyed its liberal tag—the city had segregated musicians' unions for white, black, and latinos when Peraza first arrived.

A stint and plenty of recordings with George Shearing followed. Shearing, a British-born, blind jazz pianist who refused to deal with the color issue stated, he 'simply couldn't see it!!' Here, Armando replaced another great Cuban conguero Candido.

There was plenty of work in the pre-Santana days, too; gigs abounded at clubs like El Matador, the Say When, the Black Hawk, Jimbo's Bop City, and countless others. Willie Bobo was on the scene, too, and the two recorded with both Shearing and Mongo, who cut many sides for the Berkeley-based Fantasy label. After this he went on to play with Cal Tjader, another hip vibes player, who carved a niche in the 'cool school' of Latin jazz. There isn't enough space here to convey Tjader's influence on the Latin-rock wave, but his many influential albums permeate the music of the emerging sounds of Santana, Malo, the Latin Bloods, and others.

Armando also played on the soundtrack to the *Che* film, which explored (in a Hollywood style) Guevara's and Fidel Castro's revolutionary lives. The music, composed by Lalo Schifrin, also features Cuban friend and supreme conga master Francisco Aguabella. He also recorded his own *Wild Thing* album in 1968, featuring a young Chick Corea, which bridged the gap between the earlier SF jazz inflections and the later raw sound of Santana.

"Chepito" Areas and Mingo Lewis recommended him to Carlos Santana in 1972, and the next wave of his illustrious career was set. He played with Santana for eighteen years, finally leaving, because of problems with diabetes.

Peraza, a true original, was approached to join Azteca, but Santana intervened. Joining them for the radical musical departure of *Caravanserai* saw him work through the *Welcome* and *Borboletta* sessions. This was followed by the live *Lotus* recordings in Japan, and after Mike Shrieve's departure, the seventies-style gloss of *Amigos*, *Inner Secrets*, and *Marathon*. Further on, into the eighties and nineties with *Zebop*, *Beyond Appearances*, and *Spirits Dancing*, there is no let-up in his fiery intensity. Honored at many musical tribute nights and at least two "Armando Peraza" days in San Francisco, Armando is a living testament to staying on top of the times and staying on top of drum time.

Armando Peraza rehearses with Santana at S.I.R. rehearsals, San Francisco, 1973.

Photo: Julio Sanchez

"The Chronological History of Salsa" at the Victoria Theater, Mission district, S.F., featuring Armando Peraza with the Orquesta Tipica Cienfuegos, Jan 20, 1980.

(L to R)
John Santos, Rick Rangel, Gary Flores (trumpet), Harold Muñíz, José Flores, Armando Peraza.

Photo: Courtesy John Santos

Photo: Courtesy Arcelio Garcia

Arcelio Garcia, Jr. returning to San Francisco, in front of the Golden Gate Bridge.

COAST TO COAST

Photo: Courtesy Dr. Gonzalez

Dr. Bernie Gonzalez
(The Rock and Roll Dentist)

Bernie Gonzalez grew up in the Mission district—his father owned a neighborhood shoe store—and knew Garcia from the old 24th Street days. Gonzalez was attending dental school in 1984, but he'd never abandoned his interest in music. For the previous ten years, he'd been active in the community-produced 24th Street Fair in the Mission (a massive event with about 250,000 in attendance each year), and had become friendly with local musicians. "I was working with a local band featuring John Watson, who did some work on Malo *Dos*. He kept mentioning he knew Arcelio. I hadn't heard of him in a long time. I was walking up 24th Street and I bumped into Arcelio; he was hangin' out. He had a cassette with some tunes. He told me he was putting the band together back here. He asked me to manage them; I was like, 'Oh God!' I started to ask him, 'Is Jorge Santana in the band; Is Leo Rosales in the band?' Arcelio says, 'No, they are not in the band; I've got a new Malo band in New York!'"

Photo: Courtesy Arcelio Garcia

Arcelio Garcia, Jr. plays guiro.

Photo: Courtesy Malo Archives

Arcelio Garcia, Jr., Randy Bachman (photographer), and Dr. Bernie Gonzalez.

At about that time, Gonzalez was introduced to club owner Ron Sansoe, who was familiar with Garcia. "I met Arcelio through his brother Pete," Sansoe says. "Pete brought him to my bar. To tell you the truth, I wasn't a fan of Malo then. Pete always used to tell me about 'Suavecito,' but that wasn't a favorite of mine. When I met Arcelio, I thought he was a real nice guy, very charismatic. We started to talk about doing the shows and we end up going to Bill Graham's office. Bill listened, but he passed on it. Bernie Gonzalez, Pete Garcia, and I decided to get together to do the show.

"Pete and I went out to Long Island to hear the band. Arcelio takes us back to his pad and cooks this huge Puerto Rican-style dinner. Arcelio's a great cook! We headed down to the rehearsal studio and they fuckin' blew us away! He just came in and he had all these people lined up; it was well put together. He just walked through the whole show in an hour—boom, boom, boom—one song after another: 'Latin Bugaloo,' 'Momotombo,' 'Nena,' and more. Pete and I stayed out there for four days.

"The band had that New York flavor. Some of the personalities were cool, a lot less kicked back than the West Coast vibe. Arcelio had some great players. Two guitarists, Steve Longo, did most of the leads. Gary Maggio was the other. To me, the percussion section didn't have that same feel from the original players. Ruben was actually a good conga player, and so was Charlie Torres on timbales, but they didn't have that sound. They had tried to work 'Lady I Love' from the *Malo V* album as a single release; but while everybody on the album got paid, Arcelio never got financially taken care of by Traq Records. The album's sales never were accounted for saleswise and the company and people were never heard of again. I guess they went off-Traq!" Curious to see if Malo still had drawing power, the trio proceeded with plans for a San Francisco concert at the Fort Mason Center in November of 1985.

Initially, the plan was to hire the father-daughter team of Pete Escovedo and Sheila E. Sheila was the only female percussionist to stand out in the male-dominated Latin-rock scene, but "she could slam and she could bury most guys," Sansoe points out. "It wasn't too hard for her in that macho world not being a man." She was also a hot property, nationally known for her work with Prince; in fact, the week before the show she was

Photos: Courtesy Pete Garcia

Buddy Braille, drummer on Malo's *Coast to Coast* album.

Gary Maggio on guitar on *Coast to Coast.*

Bob Bellucci plays saxophone on *Coast to Coast.*

offered, and accepted, a gig on the comedy show "Saturday Night Live." Pete Garcia came to the rescue by bringing in Tower of Power vocalist Lenny Williams as a special guest.

Personnel concerns were only one of the promoters' problems. "Ticket sales were slow," says Gonzalez. "That day the show was sold out by five o'clock. There was a big crowd outside and we didn't have electricity yet. One of Ron's friends, Curtis Jackson, an electrician, got us wired up and we finally got electricity. If we hadn't, I think there would have been a riot."

Arcelio Garcia: "I came back to California after the RAP (Real Alternative Program) show at Fort Mason. I did the comeback show with Pete Escovedo and Tower of Power. It was around that time that Gloria and Emilio Estefan named Malo as one of their influences. That was when they won the Grammy. At first there were only 1500 tickets sold and the place held 5000. So Ronnie Sansoe was having a nervous breakdown. I was saying 'Don't worry about it, I've got a big following here,' but they were worrying. Bill Graham had three concerts on that night. I remember Bill Graham showing up and saying 'Great show!'

Malo's security team wouldn't let Bill Graham backstage because he had no backstage pass, until Bernie saw him being hustled. Bill says, 'I didn't know you guys had the balls or the money to do this.' Bernie just laughed."

Their hunch had paid off. Malo was about to rise from the ashes. The trio's next move was to work out a recording deal with the Blue Heron label. The new album would be entitled *Coast to Coast*. "I still had the New York band on that recording," says Garcia. "We did some of the first songs again, 'cause people really wanted it! The New York band split after that because I was moving back west

Malo band—"New York" version.

Photo: Courtesy Arcelio Garcia

Pete "Pele" Garcia

Photos: Courtesy Malo Archives

Arcelio Garcia, Jr.

and they weren't going to move here. Then I started developing the nucleus of the current Malo band: Gabe Manzo, Tony Menjivar, Roberto Quintana."

In San Francisco, Pablo Tellez had assembled a performance version of Malo that included Richard Bean, Leo Rosales, Abel Zarate, and, occasionally, Rico Reyes. "They did a lot of shows, but out of respect for Arcelio, they let that go," says Sansoe. "Leo Rosales was also in a band called Uno Malo, also with Abel Zarate. We had a couple of [Malo] shows lined up; we see this Uno Malo shows advertised, but we had to get attorneys on it to sort it out. Funnily enough, after it happened, Leo joined the band again when Arcelio was putting it together. Luis Romero played with them for awhile, a timbalero and percussionist who was with the Fania All-Stars. Tony Menjivar was in there [on congas] and I think he brought Gabe [guitarist Gabriel Manzo] into the group."

Both Manzo and Menjivar had been part of Tellez's own band, Searching. Both had been educated in the Mission district's school of the streets. "I'm a Mexican-Indian from Arizona, but I was raised out here in California," says Manzo. "I was a field workers' kid. My grandmother played a lot of Mexican music; she played from her heart and she influenced me to play. As time went on my relatives would play. There was no TV, so music was real important. My cousin played guitar; I thought, 'I want to do that.' I started out playing bass, learning chords and songs around the age of eighteen. I played in a band anywhere—labor camps, weddings, anything. The sixties were going on, so I'd go to Haight Street to hang out. Being out there tripping, smoking pot; I was still a kid but I wanted to experience the scene. That whole scene on Haight was really open musically. There was a lot of blues around: Charlie Musselwhite, John Mayall, Paul Butterfield, and Mike Bloomfield was, like, the cat in San

Francisco. I started to learn how to jam. I ended up playing with Bo Diddley for about a year and a half."

After opening for It's a Beautiful Day, John Lee Hooker, Country Joe and many other 1970s-era bands, Manzo left Bo Diddley to tour Canada with a soul black band called Pure Gold, decked out in "platform shoes and big Afros." When he returned to the Bay area, he joined the house band at Bajones nightclub.

Menjivar, whose parents were from El Salvador, grew up in San Francisco listening to New York salsa a la Willie Colon, Ray Barretto, and Eddie Palmieri. His cousin played timbales, and Menjivar got his first pair of congas when he was seven years old. The Santana album was released the same year and "I practiced along with that," he says. He played with Chepito's All-Stars "without any training. He made his solo album and was playing around town, his bass player was a friend of mine; I was about thirteen years old." He played with Chuck Rainey in Dallas and with Mexican-American pop singer Trini Lopez and his brother before returning to San Francisco in 1986 to join Searching. "I came in and Francisco went down to LA. They had Karl Perazzo on timbales; they'd used Chepito, and when I came in, they had Leo on timbales. There was Richard Bean singing, Abel Zarate on guitar, Pablo Tellez on bass, in this version of Malo—all but Arcelio.

"It turned out that Arcelio was coming back to San Francisco with another Malo band. We had a bunch of deals on the table with Budweiser, Corona, and Coors. We stopped what we were doing because Pablo realized that the group was Arcelio's baby. Our last gig was at Alma Park in San José. I hooked up with Richard Bean, Abel Zarate, and Leo Rosales after this and we had the bands Suave and Uno Malo, but we got a letter from Ron Sansoe about that. The interesting thing was Gabriel, who was auditioning for the Malo band at the time, came from Pablo Tellez's band, Searching." Timbalero Roberto Quintana began playing at age eight in a group called the Ghetto, organized by his brother. By age fifteen he had graduated to traditional Afro-Cuban music and patterned some of his style after Orestes Vilato, who shaped the sound of Ray Barretto's New York salsa band before moving west and joining Santana.

Ronnie Sansoe

Poster for the Fort Mason show.

Pete and Arcelio Garcia

Photos: Courtesy Malo Archives

Instead of shipping his own East Coast band to the Left Coast, however, Garcia decided it was time to return emphatically to his roots. Says Sansoe: "Arcelio asked the New York band if they wanted to relocate, around the time *Coast to Coast* was coming out. They felt abandoned, I think; but when Arcelio heard what it sounded like out here, he didn't want to go back there. The guys all got paid after the album, but we really never heard from them after that."

The *Coast to Coast* album sees Malo and Garcia in transition. It relies heavily on the first album's favorites: "Suavecito," "Café," and "Nena," plus a reworking from *Malo V* of "I Found You Out." "Good Tasting Stuff" from *Malo V* becomes "Good Taste of Life," and from the same album "Young Man" has morphed into "Big Brother." The production on *Coast* is better, clearer, and less dank than on *Malo V*; however it is an album attempting to re-establish the band and, as such, plays it safe. Richards Kermode is back, albeit temporarily, on keyboards for "Nena," "Café," "Big Brother," "I Found You Out," and "Save the Children."

Photo: Courtesy Richard Bean

Rico Reyes, Richard Bean, and Abel Zarate play with Pablo Tellez's version of Malo, which disbanded when Arcelio came back to the Bay Area.

Photo: Courtesy Malo Archives

Gabriel Manzo wails with a new Malo West Coast lineup in Oakland.

Auditions and rehearsals for the new Malo band took place in a back room at Tip Top Inn on Mission and 26th Streets, which was owned by Ron Sansoe and Jim Susoeff. Garcia produced the recording with help from his brother Pete, Ron Sansoe, and Bernie Gonzalez. The album again sported an image by Jesus Helguera, illustrating his passion for Aztec warrior imagery.

Tony Menjivar plays congas with Malo in Oakland.

Photo: Courtesy Malo Archives

Photo: Arcelio Garcia

Roberto Quintana plays timbales onstage with Malo.

Photos: Arcelio Garcia

Tony Menjivar, a series of shots displaying his exuberant, wild conga style.

The Tip Top Inn. Located at 26th and Mission Streets.

Photo: Courtesy Ron Sansoe

SALSA DE SAN FRANCISCO

The early Latin music scene in San Francisco and the Bay area blossomed in the late 1940s and 1950s; Oakland dance halls were a thriving concern. The Escovedo Brothers had a sound based on Tito Puente's band, and a lineup which included Al Bent on trombone, Willie Colon on congas, pianist Carlos Federico, Coke Escovedo on timbales, Phil Escovedo on bass, and Pete on vocals and percussion. They could be found playing up an Afro-Cuban storm at Sunday afternoon tardeadas, during the mambo sessions in the Gold Room at the California Hotel. Other hot spots were Maria's Club and the El Patio in San Jose. Benny Velarde was playing timbales in Cal Tjader's band at the Black Oak in San Francisco's North Beach district. Velarde had Cliff' "El Chino" Anderson on congas before his stint with the Malibus.

DM Reed, a white congero (unusual in the Bay Area at that time), played with Cesar Ascarrunz in early salsa bands. Los Locos was one band featuring Cesar on piano and vocals. They could be found playing six nights a week at Lucky Pierre's at Broadway and Columbus in San Francisco. Los Locos became New Los Locos and eventually Cesar's Men. Guy Hoffman's (a timbales player from Peru) Latins could be found playing the El Cid club over the street. Wally Chilcott, another Panamanian pianist, and Lalo Reyes, a Mexican bassist, were both praised for their high musical professionalism.

Carlos Federico moved to the Bay from Panama in 1948, just before the mambo craze hit in the 1950s (the musical form known as "salsa" did not exist then). His career straddles the entire length of the Latino music phase in the Bay. He contributed to both Chepito Areas's solo album and played on Malo's *Evolution* recording. Chato Gutierrez, who, for over twenty years has hosted her Saturday salsa show "Con Clave" on KPOO, also represents salsa on the radio in the Mission.

Music from Africa, the Caribbean, and the East Coast of the US has always made its way to San Francisco; but in the 1970s, the city's Latin music scene benefitted from an explosion of interest in New York salsa music. One of its disciples and best-known exponents is percussionist and educator John Santos. "There was always music in the house. When I was twelve years old, I played congas in my grandfather's band. I trained first on the clarinet, then left music for a while to play baseball. The Latin-rock thing and Santana got

Carlos Federico plays piano at Bimbo's, San Francisco, 1991 with the Conjunto Chano Pozo. This band was put together by John Santos for the San Francisco Jazz Festival.

De Pie: JOE ELLIS, Trompeta; FRANCISCO (Pancho) Zabala, Cantante; DAN REAGAN, Trombón, DAVID BELOVED, Bass: ROGEI PAIZ, Bongoces; BENNY VELARDE, Timbales y Director; WILLII COLON, Congas. De rodillas: STEVE BUSFIELD, Guitarra. Ausente e la foto SAMMY GOLDSTEIN.

Benny Velarde's Super Combo, 1979.

Photo: John Santos

Orquesta Batachanga, 1983.

Back row:
David Belove (bass), Bill Ortiz (trumpet),
John Santos (director, percussion),
Juan Ceballos (flute).

Middle row:
Harold Muñíz (congas),
Rebeca Mauleón (piano, arranger),
Mike Spiro (timbales),
Ismael Rodriguez (coro).

Bottom row:
Chris Cooper (2nd violin),
Anthony Blea (1st violin),
Rick Rangel (lead vocals).

Photo: John Santos

Orquesta Tipica Cienfuegos,
outdoor festival, Mission district, 1977.

(L to R) John Calloway, Rick Rangel, Harold
Muñíz, Mike Madrigal, John Santos.

me back into the music. My older brothers and cousins were at Mission High with Carlos. We were in tune with his development, before Santana hit. I learned largely playing in Dolores Park. Most of the good drummers here on the West Coast played by feel. They were mostly Mexican or Central American, [although] the traditions were more from Cuba and the Caribbean. The Escovedos, Carabello, players who played by feel, inspired me."

In the mid-seventies, Santos joined Santana, along with Raul Rekow. "I was only with them for a couple of weeks; I was playing timbales before Chepito came back," he says. Eager to start his own band, he began studying the Cuban and Puerto Rican origins of Latin music: "I wanted to find out about the roots, the folkloric groups like Emikeke from Matanzas. Others like Los Papines, Grupo Folklorico Afro Cuba. These all preserve the traditions of rumba, the Congolese, things like palo, macuta, the stuff from Yoruba, the bembe, guiro, bata, and the abakua traditions. Next, he organized a band called Ritmo '74.

"That was about the time New Yorkers were coming in bringing in more salsa," says Pete Gallegos. "All of a sudden you'd hear Tito Rodriguez, Machito, Willie Colon, Ray Barretto, a lot of the Cuban stuff. The salsa stuff came into popularity then. The younger players—John Santos, John Calloway, Karl Perazzo—cut their teeth in that scene, so did Leo Rosales and Tony Menjivar; it was like wildfire in the seventies.

"I was playing in a band called Tipica Cienfuegos at the time with Mike Rios and a lot of the young players in the Mission. Mike and I were good friends and involved in many different art projects at the time as well. In May of 1975 we were invited to be part of an artists' delegation to visit artists in Cuba through the Venceremos Brigade. When we returned from Cuba, John Santos and John Calloway had revamped Tipica Cienfuegos and brought the band to another musical level. I decided to leave the band but Mike continued playing. Tipica Cienfuegos morphed into a geat band known as Batachanga.

A few years later Mike and I joined a new band called Alma del Barrio with Gibby Ross, Joe Ross, Mario Fortin, Chris Velasquez, Ramon Garcia, and Johnny Castaing. We recorded a salsa tune called 'San Francisco Salsa All the Way.' It was a local hit in the Bay Area, and there was my fifteen minutes of fame.

"The Mission had a lot of great musicians. I remember one time Eddie Palmieri called John Santos 'The Encyclopedia,' because of his knowledge of Latin Music."

Photo: Courtesy Malo Archives

Cover painting for Malo *Coast to Coast* by Jesus Helguera.

I FOUND YOU OUT

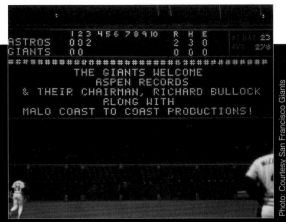

Promotional evening at Candlestick Park for the release of the Malo's *Coast to Coast* album.

Photo: Courtesy San Francisco Giants

Ron Sansoe and Jeff Trager backstage at a Malo benefit in Marin County.

Photo: Courtesy Malo Archives

The biggest problem with *Coast to Coast* was the record company, Blue Heron. Blue Heron was founded by Richard Bullock who'd sold his Odyssey record stores (a Bay Area chain) and had entered the recording business as a kind of serious avocation. His jazz label, Blackhawk, was known for its gem-like releases, such as Billie Holiday's *Live at Monterey* (her last recording), and material by Maynard Ferguson, Stan Getz, and Kenny Barron. But the company had sunk too much money into start-up costs, and once salaries were paid there was little in the budget for promotion; Blackhawk would remain a collector's label rather than a mainstream commodity. Still, there were plans for New Age label with Elmer Robinson, one of Frank Sinatra's writers, and Blue Heron was intended to be the company's pop division according to music promoter Jeff Trager, a veteran of the Bay Area music scene before working with Blue Heron in the mid-1980s.[36] "[Bullock] loved 'Suavecito'; he released it as a twelve-inch single with a dance remix of 'Big Brother' on the flip side, along with the album. He loved Malo but they were the last group to be signed, as Blue Heron was running out of money."[37]

---

[36] Trager worked with Kool and the Gang at Polygram and broke out Ike and Tina Turner's first record, "I've Been Loving You Too Long." He's a source of endless stories, such as this illustrative tale about Ike Turner: "We got him on white pop radio for the first time. They'd send me out to ride shotgun with the artist. Ike picks me up in Beverley Hills in a brand new Rolls. 'If you see any cops' [he says], 'the gun is in the glove compartment in front of ya.' Later, Captain Beefheart and Arthur Lee from Love were hangin' out at the studio, people who had their own planets going on. In walks Ike. He reaches in his pocket, pulls out a huge wad of cash, throws it down on the table, then pulls out his gun, saying, 'I dare anyone to pick it up!'"

[37] Carlos Santana appeared on the *Dance to the Beat of My Drum* album by Michael Olantunji, released in 1986 by Blue Heron. It received almost no promotion.

With almost no money to promote *Coast to Coast*, Sansoe and Gonzalez called on personal contacts and creativity to get the word out. The album release coincided with a San Francisco Giants baseball game. Sansoe was friends with Giants pitcher Vida Blue, who in turn referred Sansoe to the team's promotions staff. In the middle of the game's seventh inning, a welcoming message to Blue Heron and Malo management was posted on the scoreboard, and "Suavecito" rocked over the loudspeakers throughout the stadium.

Sansoe and Gonzalez had invited Bullock to share their VIP box at the game, hoping they'd also teach him a thing or two about local record promotion. They weren't sure he would actually show up, as relations were, at that point, somewhat tense (the production team still hadn't been paid for the album's expenses). To their surprise, Bullock arrived and took a seat near the window in the front row of the box. Every time Gonzalez or Sansoe moved to open the window, however, Bullock moved back a row. "He was afraid we might bodily throw him out," says Sansoe, laughing. "That's why he was re-christened 'I-Won't-Sit-in-the-Front-Row Bullock.'"

As the situation worsened, Bullock had a right to feel fearful. "As time went by and he still owed us money, one of the things Ron and I could do was the good guy/bad guy routine," says Gonzalez. "Bullock would talk to me but Ron would go down there and rattle his cage. But I could see we weren't getting anywhere. He'd closed up, not taking our calls. He had one secretary left; he was living in a security condominium above Max's Diner on Third Street in San Francisco. We were getting really pissed with this guy. He was very secluded, an older guy with a very attractive secretary, so I guess we knew what his weakness was.

"At that time, I was going out with this very nice young girl. We used to go to Max's Diner for a few drinks. We knew Bullock's secretary was called Pam. Anyway, we got my girlfriend to go ask for him and [to say] that Pam said for her to look him up, if ever she was in town. I'm standing behind this tall plant [in the lobby] and here he comes. I've been drinking scotch. He opens the door and he sees this beautiful girl and he's walking towards her and I jump out from behind this plant, I'm saying, 'Hey dude.' I grab his neck and we go downstairs to Max's Diner. I'm poking him in the chest and I walk him over to a pay phone and call Ron. I say to Ron, 'Guess who I've got here?' I hand Bullock the phone and he's stuttering and spluttering. We go outside and I'm still hanging on to his jacket. Finally, the waiter from the restaurant says, 'The police are on the way.' So I throw Bullock, WHAM!, straight to the ground. As I was taking off, Jim Susoeff picked me up. The long and the short of it is, we didn't get our money."

Dr. Bernie Gonzalez

Photo: Courtesy Dr. Bernie Gonzales

With zero tour support, travel was a similar nightmare. On the weekend of Cinco de Mayo, 1991, the band was booked to tour San Diego and Los Angeles in California and then continue to Denver, Colorado. Cinco de Mayo, a Mexican holiday celebrating the victory of Mexican troops over the invading French army, can be a rowdy holiday in the American West, and this one was no exception.

"The Friday night show was fine," says Sansoe. "We got to San Diego, did the show, got back to the hotel. We were about one hour and twenty minutes from LA. It was about one-thirty or two in the morning and we had to be up about seven in the morning in order to set up to play at noon. Needless to say, nobody got much sleep. We loaded up the vans and the bus, got to LA, did our show. The place was out of control. People were drinking; the place was packed. They loved it but we see there were going to be problems with the amount of people—had to be about thirty, forty thousand people there. There was no security throughout the park." (Roberto Quintana adds: "Boy, that gig, after we left, it became total mayhem; people got shot, there was a huge gang fight. Pete and Sheila E. were coming in a limousine and they never played.")

"Everybody's signing autographs after the show, and me and Bernie are [insisting]: we need to get in the bus and get going," Sansoe continues. "So we're on the way to Los Angeles airport and we're hitting heavy traffic. We finally get to the airport. Our flight is at two and we get there at five minutes to one. I had everybody get in line to get ticketed. The line wasn't moving, so I get this woman from the airline and how she ever got a job as a customer service for United Airlines, I'll never know. She informed us we wouldn't be able to make this flight. And we didn't make that flight. Next flight's at seven o'clock.

"I'm trying to get a hold of the promoter; they finally get us on a Continental flight about 3:30. We sat on the tarmac for another hour plus. There's no way we're going to make the show. Plus, it's Arcelio's birthday. We're all sitting around in our Malo tour jackets. We got there eventually at 7:30—we were real late. We couldn't go home, we couldn't call the promoter to get our rooms for the night. We start looking for rooms. The radio stations were saying Malo didn't show up, Malo's a no-show. We turned our jackets inside out at the airport, so people couldn't see the logos.

"I call Bernie, he's already heard from the promoter's attorney. We need to stop this whole thing from collapsing. So what ended up happening was we talked to the radio stations the next morning, the guys told them exactly what happened and we did the show in August; we had to do a lot of damage control. The band, in its whole history, had never missed a show. If I or Bernie died tomorrow, sooner than we should have, it'll be because of that."

Photos: Jim McCarthy

Roberto Quintana at Ron Sansoe's house, on Potrero Hill, in San Francisco, 1995.

Pete Escovedo at the Fort Mason show.

Sheila Escovedo plays timbales.

There were three distinct festivals in the Mission that capture the spirit of pride reflected in Latin-rock music. Cinco De Mayo started in 1966 as a community parade down Mission Street. The 24th Street Fair (later re-named Festival of the Americas), organized by the merchants, launched in 1978. It takes place in September to celebrate the Independence Days of eight Latin-American countries. Carnaval, a Rio-style festivity held at the end of May or early June, includes a massive parade and weekend street fair with bands on several stages. It started in 1979 with a small group of musicians, dancers, and artists gathering in Precita Park.

"The second year it tripled in size and it just kept growing in leaps and bounds," according to Pete Gallegos. The early events drew as many as 60,000 people, but today Carnaval attracts ten times that many over the weekend.

Photo: Courtesy El Tecolote

24TH Street Fair in the Mission, 1982; organized by MECA and the 24th Street Merchants Association.

Bernie Gonzalez remembers the first 24th Street Fair. "They got in trouble the first year for not having the right permits. One guy was making carnitas out in the open in a huge cauldron. The Health Dept. turned a blind eye, but told them they needed to get more organized. I helped them the second year, and then I worked with them for ten years.

"Roberto Hernandez was running the Bernal Heights Neighborhood Center. We pooled our resources and began Mission Economic Cultural Association [MECA], in 1984 with Hernandez as director. The initial board of directors included Real Alternatives Project's Mitchell Salazar, Sam Ruiz from Mission Neighborhood Center, George Suncin from Horizons Unlimited. They used to call us the 'Mission Mafia,' thinking we were pocketing the cash, but actually we were turning the cash back into the community. Hernandez got all the different associations and merchants together; the events were coordinated to maximize the economic impact in the community."

When Carlos Santana agreed to do a free concert for the community, organized by MECA in 1987, Gonzalez greeted him with the words: "Welcome back to the neighborhood." He responded: "I never left!" Thousands of people came to see the show. That notable year also saw Pete Escovedo opening for Malo, with Santana topping the bill; Michael Rios, the artist behind Santana's graphic identity, was painting a mural on South Van Ness and mounting a retrospective show honoring Santana at the Mission Cultural Center.

For better or worse, the festivals put the Mission district on the map and helped make it a tourist destination while contributing to the neighborhood's sense of worth. "It all became a little more corporate as time went on," notes Gonzalez, "as the commercial world realized the Hispanic dollar was just as green as anybody else's."

Photo: Courtesy El Tecolote

Children enjoy hanging out under the 24th Street painted mural by Michael Rios, which features depictions of Carlos Santana, Armando Peraza, and Eddie Palmeiri.

Photo: Ron Sansoe

Mission Cultural Center

217

Arcelio Garcia Jr., Jorge Santana, and Johnny Valenzuela.

Photo: Malo Archives

THE BEST OF THE BEST

The 1980s found veterans of Santana, Malo, and their various spin-off bands older, wiser, and more sober; in a position to be reflective of the good (and bad) old days of the previous decade and their roles as creators of the Latin-rock sound.

Photo: Malo Archives

Pablo Tellez and Richard Bean play as Malo.

Photo: Jim Welch

Gregg Rolie in performance.

Gregg Rolie: "When we rehearsed for the Santana 20th Anniversary show in 1986, we played for about eight hours; it went by so fast. We rehearsed the day before at SIR rehearsals in San Francisco. It was really fun; it all just came back." Herbie called me up and it was, 'What did we do to screw this up?' He was eating it up. David Brown was in jail in San José for some stupid thing and [when I told him] Herbie says, 'Never mind, now I remember how we screwed it up! It all comes back to me.'

"The chemistry of that original band is undeniable and was totally intact; that music was created by that band. But there's more to music than just notes."

In 1978, Greg Errico,[38] Sly Stone's first great drummer finally got Mike Carabello's 1971–72 Attitude sessions released under the title Giants through War's LA International label. Errico finished off the vocal tracks on the album and it stands as a curio, a sense of what Santana could have sounded like, 1971 vintage, with a heavy Sly Stone influence. There's a version of "Fried Neckbones" in which Carlos and Neal Schon burn in *Santana 3* style. Die-hards can spot the place where Neal takes over the guitar solo from Carlos on "In Your Heart," a great example of their telepathic interplay. "Attitude," the title track, is a raw, burning funk-out with Dougie Rauch's excellent bass and Errico's drums pushing the track upward. The most fascinating piece is a drum-led instrumental called "Kilimanjaro," in which Carabello, Pantoja, Reyes, Chepito, and Errico, all riffing under a velvety coat of harmonica melodies dropped down by Lee Oskar of War.

---

[38] Errico has produced many Bay Area releases, including Lee Oskar's solo albums and recent work with Many Faces and Bueno, two projects led by Tony Menjivar and Gabe Manzo, who also are co-partners in Bueno, San Francisco's first Christian-Latin rock-gospel band.

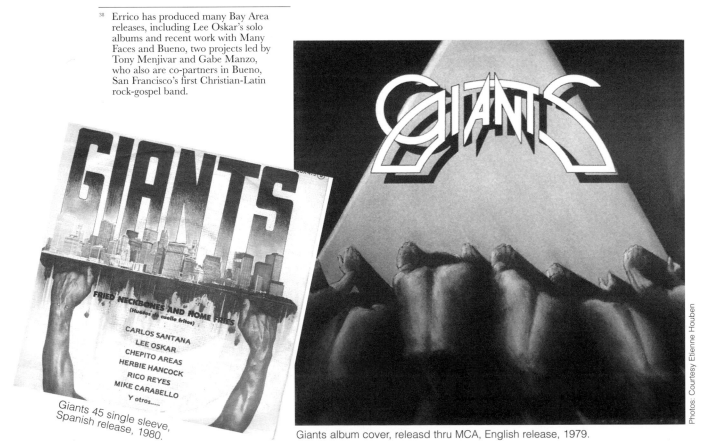

Giants 45 single sleeve, Spanish release, 1980.

Giants album cover, releasd thru MCA, English release, 1979.

Photos: Courtesy Etienne Houben

A release that started to re-cement interest in Mission-style Latin and Malo's fortunes in the nineties was *The Best of Malo*, released in 1991 on GNP Crescendo, a label with strong roots in the LA music scene. Gene Norman originally owned the GNP Crescendo label, and he ran it out of an office on Sunset Boulevard. Norman was an influential promoter and radio disc jockey with years of experience, particularly in the jazz-end of the business. His radio show helped the careers of Stan Getz and Gerry Mulligan, among others, according to his son, Neil Norman of GNP Crescendo: "My father was a famous disc jockey. He ran the Crescendo and the Interlude clubs concurrently. He put on acts like Woody Allen, Ella Fitzgerald, Stan Kenton, Lenny Bruce, Bill Cosby; he'd also tape some of these [shows, and] some have come out on the label. He was also recording Latin legends like Tito Puente and Rene Touzet. I grew up with a lot of Latin music. We also put out a Cold Blood album and we released the first Azteca album.

"I was digging Malo in the seventies and I realized they hadn't had a compilation out, so we did that and it's been one of our best sellers.[39] I also approached them about a new album, which we also did, called *Senorita*."

Culled from Malo's first four Warner Bros. releases, *The Best of Malo* serves as a solid reminder of the breadth and scope of those entirely unique records. "[When] GNP Crescendo called us to say they were doing a compilation, I don't think they knew if the band was still going," says Arcelio Garcia. "Warner Bros. was licensing the first album to a company called Line Records out of Germany. We found out that Crescendo had negotiated the rights to the *Best of Malo*. They were surprised there was a band that could tour this thing. At that point Neil Norman had the choice of the short radio edits that David Rubinson had done, because they couldn't mess around with the Warner masters."

[39] Best of Malo has sold more than 95,000 copies to date.

Azteca debut album CD release on GNP Crescendo, 1994.

Tito Puente *Now* CD release.

Jack Constanza, *Mr. Bongo* CD release.

Photos: Courtesy GNP Crescendo

Photo: Courtesy GNP Crescendo

The release helped "Suavecito" get more airplay than the first time around. "Hit singles are few and far between, but good songs are timeless," says Jeff Trager. "Malo found a song that lasted for years. They had three minutes of what people wanted to hear. Warner Bros. had a knack for picking hit singles on Top 40 radio. Sly happened because Sly wrote hit songs for AM radio, black radio, underground radio—he crossed all the way. 'Suavecito' did the same thing because black radio embraced it because it was a street record. The sound was still different from Santana's sound; these kids were from the Mission, Santana were from different backgrounds, [including the wealthier] Peninsula, although Michael and Carlos were from the neighborhood."

And *Best of Malo* ensured the band stayed on the road, if somewhat haphazardly. "When the album first came out in 1991, Arcelio and me realized there was no tour support, no nothing," says Ron Sansoe. "So Arcelio, myself, and Bernie sat down and arranged tours from here to Texas, and it was quite successful. We've been out on the road a lot. The highlights were the Greek Theater in Berkeley, also the House of Blues shows. I remember seeing Robert Palmer really digging the show at the House of Blues."

In 1991, an apparently good prospect was a tour to Mexico, arranged by a woman who was managing a Mexican band. Malo and the management team had reservations about the tour when advance payments arrived late, but the woman insisted she would set up the shows and they would be paid in US dollars. The band was to be flown from gig to gig. After a hellish airport journey they arrived to find the woman burnt out before the tour began; she had been partying all night with friends.

As the band set up for the first gig, Bernie Gonzalez noticed soundman Chris Solberg[40] urgently beckoning from the restroom. Apparently, the club owner and a couple of cops had caught Solberg indulging in cocaine in the bathroom. Solberg didn't speak Spanish and they didn't speak English; it looked as though they were ready to haul

The Best of Malo CD release, 1991.

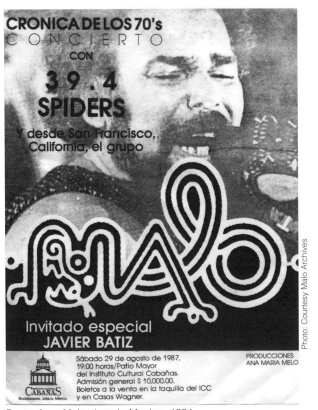

Poster from Malo show in Mexico, 1991.

---

[40] An excellent soundman and musician, Chris appears on and co-wrote songs for Santana's *Inner Secrets* and *Marathon* albums.

him into jail. Amazingly, after Gonzalez's handling, they let Solberg go. Gonzalez maintains that every time he sees Solberg, he throws his arms around him, shuddering at the thought of the potential "Midnight Express" horror of it all. He didn't forget that incident in a hurry.

Despite their suspicions about the promoter, the show that Malo did at Specio Cabana in Guadalajara was one of the best shows on the tour. They played in a renovated former orphanage to a capacity crowd. Later, Sansoe and Gonzalez confronted the woman about her financial responsibilities for the tour. She began to cry. The next date was six hours away; everybody had been up all night and the equipment truck had proceeded ahead. Asked about transport to the next show, the promoter replied "I have plenty cars." After the band departed in a convoy of cars, Gonzalez and Sansoe followed by taxi. Arriving at the town, they found no audience at the venue, and no lights. The promoter and club owner were arguing and the equipment hadn't arrived when about forty people showed up for the concert. To top off the shambolic mini-tour, the woman paid in Mexican peso currency. The hotel bed after was awash with cash. The scenario was repeated over the next five days.

In 1995, Malo went back into the studio to record *Senorita*, their second GNP Crescendo release.[41] The title track, "Senorita" opens side one and sets the stage for the entire album—an uneasy mix of electronic percussion overlaid with Latin percussion, synthesizer, and horn stabs. "Senorita" the tune is a confection, with Latin percussion underscoring an essential pop tune. "Everybody Let's Dance" is an

[41] Bob Margouleff, called in to do the remixing, was responsible for the early '70s innovative synthesiser work on Stevie Wonder's albums, including *Music of My Mind* and *Talking Book*.

GNPD 1410

Malo CD reissue of their debut album release on Warner Brothers.

Photo: Courtesy Warner Brothers Records

Photo: Ron Sansoe

A stash of Mexican pesos currency and a picture of the Three Stooges on a hotel bed sums up feelings about Malo's mini-tour of Mexico.

223

Photo: Courtesy GNP Crescendo

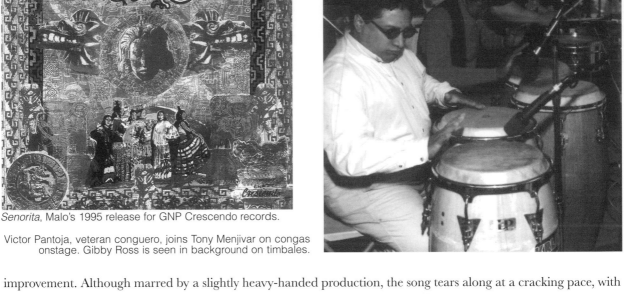

Photo: Malo Archives

Senorita, Malo's 1995 release for GNP Crescendo records.

Victor Pantoja, veteran conguero, joins Tony Menjivar on congas onstage. Gibby Ross is seen in background on timbales.

improvement. Although marred by a slightly heavy-handed production, the song tears along at a cracking pace, with Garcia providing an impassioned vocal and Manzo's piercing guitar breaks sliced and diced by Gibby Ross's furious timbales blowouts. Manzo lets rip on the first unbridled example of his individual addition to the Latin-rock guitar field in "Malo Ya Llego." A rumble from the barrio streets, it reminds the listener forcibly of the music's roots and features strong congas from Menjivar over a percussion-driven chant. "Ghetto Man" is a slice of R&B with an interesting "jump" in the drum programming. The electronics here manage to add to the excitement, but essentially the song is a reworking of "Young Man" from *Malo V*. The album is encased in artwork by Michael Rios, who was also responsible for Santana's stage backdrops and T-shirt designs.

Between the release of *Best of Malo* and *Senorita* in 1995, Arcelio Garcia continued to develop the band. Wayne Carter held the drum chair until sidelined by a back injury; David George took his place and has remained with Malo. Guitarist Manzo and conguero Menjivar began to come into their own, bringing their own sensibilities to the retooled band. "I'm part of the Mission sound, that culture," says Manzo. "Carlos was the first Mexican player. [He] and Neal, I really enjoyed their playing. I loved John McLaughlin, Al DeMeola, all that fusion stuff. I picked up bits from all those players and then you learn to express yourself. I learned from playing with Arcelio to play melodic, so people in the audience can identify pieces in the playing, not just riffing."

Menjivar brought an understanding of the African roots of Latin drumming, which he'd picked up from listening to Mongo Santamaria and Francisco Aguabella. "I had a real open-handed style at first. Also, I'd say Leo Rosales really gave me a lot of basics. Victor Pantoja's stuff I'd also absorbed—his playing was like old-school Puerto Rican style. When he played in Malo in the early nineties, he showed me a lot of his stuff. Mingo Lewis showed me a lot of flashy styles on congas.

"I once saw a show with the young Mingo, young Raul Rekow, and Sheila Escovedo at the Mission Cultural Center. The way Sheila played was really low to the drum and really fast. Raul was fast and a little bit higher. Mingo was really high from the drum but also really fast. When he started ripping it, that was the way I wanted to play. I remember the way he'd cross his hands, and I'd look around and people would be like 'Wow, this is so intense!' I think I've achieved a lot of that. I may not be a technician on the level of Giovanni Hidalgo, [but] I can strike an audience. I feel you can pick up a person's spirit through their playing. I'm a people's conga player. I'm a real physical player." One of Menjivar's favorite memories is of world heavyweight boxing champion Roberto Duran, a great fan of Latin music, who witnessed Menjivar's "crazy solo" during a show with Raul Rekow. "Roberto walked up [and] said, 'After that I don't want to go near those congas.' He was called the 'Hands of Stone.' He says to me, 'You really are the Hands of Stone,' which was a great compliment."

James "Mingo" Lewis, Leo "Pepe" Rosales, and Jose "Chepito" Areas backstage.

Photo: Courtesy Martin Cohen at Latin Percussion

Photo: Malo Archives

Gibby Ross drums up a storm on timbales, seen here with Malo. Drummer David George provides the hothouse backbeat.

Photo: Courtesy Richard Bean

Richard Bean onstage with Malo.

Photo: Malo Archives

Ron Sansoe backstage at Malo performance.

Since the mid-eighties, Malo have used a pool of percussion players, but the three main timbaleros were Leo Rosales, Gibby Ross, and Roberto Quintana. Ross, an Oakland native, is the half-brother of Santana drummer Karl Perazzo and the son of Joe Ross, well-known in the drum world for his work as a sideman and in the Bay Area band Alma Del Barrio. His other influence was his godfather Mario Fortin. A child prodigy, Ross sat in with Malo at a Winterland gig when he was six years old (Tito Puente and Celia Cruz also were on the bill). "They did a jam at the end, Tito, Malo, and Azteca," recalls Johnny Valenzuela. "Tito came out, Leo Rosales came out, Coke Escovedo came out, and Gibby came out. They set up four sets of timbales and they just jammed, a real drum-off! I remember that show like it was yesterday. When he was about ten years old [in 1975], Tito took him back to New York to play at Shea Stadium, that's how good Gibby was! Tito gave him his timbales. Gibby has lightning speed; he's got two right hands." He put them to good use in the Malo format: "When I first started with Malo, Tony had to show me the approach to timbales, as playing salsa-style was a softer feel," says Ross. "This is a much more high-energy style."

Photo: Courtesy Richard Bean

Richard Bean performs live with current lineup of Sapo.

Menjivar was instrumental in bringing Richard Bean back to the lineup. Bean and Garcia had had a falling out over artistic and financial concerns. "I got a call from Tony Menjivar in early '91 [asking,] 'Do I want to come back into Malo?' I said, 'Well, Arcelio and I don't really talk.' So, Arcelio calls me up and we worked it out: 'Let's get Malo back to where it was.' I was with them again from 1991 to about 1994. We were always having problems with that damn tour bus. One of my last gigs with Malo was at the Boathouse, down on the lake. We were also doing Sapo material, 'Can't Make It,' 'Sapo's Montuno,' stuff I did with Jorge like 'Love the Way,' and new stuff like 'Could It Be.' The show was very diverse."

KARL PERAZZO / MISSION HARDCORE

Percussionist Karl Perazzo joined Santana in 1991, after a stint touring with Sheila E. during her "Glamorous Life" era. Perazzo is another Mission-schooled musician of Mexican-Italian background with a strong, identifiable style.

"I was playing on any surface from the age of two. I was known as Harvey Wallbanger due to my constant rhythmic tapping. I played a lot of cumbia and salsa early on. I started performing at Cesar's club when I was thirteen years old. I go back to the Benny Velarde days; he had the number-one salsa band then. I was playing congas back then. One of the first shows was with Mongo Santamaria and Azteca. When I was in twelfth grade I got to sit in with Cal Tjader. I was gigging with Jorge Santana by then also, while I was at John O'Connell trade school. At that time the Mission had a serious vibe; music was everywhere. The salsa scene was a hip thing in the city.

"When I was a young kid I used to play in Dolores Park. I had an incredible split on my finger from playing—it was just wide open. As much as it hurt I couldn't stop, because the feeling of playing was so great. I remember this skinny guy with an Afro sitting next to me. He asked me if he could play. I'd been playing for about two hours straight. The way he asked was so a cariño. He started to play, and as I was listening to his chops and I looked at his face, I realized it was Mike Carabello. I totally froze and we talked; he told me he been in rehab. I told him what a big influence on me and the other percussionists in the city [he was].

"He called me a couple of weeks later to join Attitude. I was with them for a year and change. He had David Brown on bass—this was before Abel Zarate—they had Mike Suzaki [from Cold Blood] on guitar. I was playing timbales, and they had Danny Holmes on vocals. The band was hot and I thought I'd made it to the big time.

"In the Mission, we're not so refined. People ask me 'What drum corps did you study at?' I say, 'I'm from the Mission, I studied hard core.'

"If you didn't know how to play, it wasn't so much about technique; it's: you got to be able to make somebody dance! My style is an amalgam of everybody. I am Nicky Marrero, Chepito, Changuito, Orestes Vilato, Bobby Allendes, and all the guys coming up; I'm going to be part of their soup.

"I do believe we have a West Coast sound that is very street, very multicultural, very diverse. You can almost smell it.

"If you listen to the first Santana or Malo albums it's till five years ahead—I don't care how out of tune or how analogue it is. I'll tell you what it is. It's Precita Park, it's Mission, it's Golden Gate Park, it's the Fillmore. You can't deny it. I don't think it could ever be done again; people are too refined now. I think Santana is one of the last garage bands to have survived the feeling. When Santana and Malo happened, the whole Mission district was percolating, bubbling. It was amazing. You could almost taste it."

Karl Perazzo performs with Cal Tjader at Edison Elementary School in San Francisco around 1973. Karl here is just 11 years old.

Photos: Karl and Debi Perazzo

Karl Perazzo:
timbales and percussion with Santana.

Photo: Joan Chase

David Brown, resplendent in his stage finery, a shining star and symbol of
the multiracial hues of the original Santana group.

UP FROM 24TH STREET

Years on from that first blaze of talent, Santana retain their place in the upper hemisphere of the business. Malo also retain their large fan base, but many talents have fallen prey to the usual music business snares and the frailties of human nature. The Mission has had its fair share of casualties in the wake of that first rumble from the barrio.

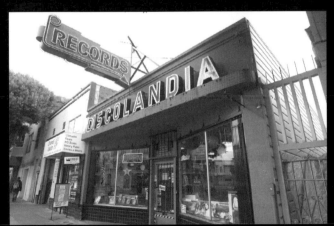

Views from the Mission: Discolandia, a record store on 24th Street.

The old Victoria Theater site, Mission district.

Photos: Courtesy El Tecolote

Photo: Joan Chase

Dougie Rauch, who died in the late seventies.

Photo: Diane Balck, Jan Cameron

David Brown, seen here in later times.

Dougie Rauch, the young bassist from the Voices of East Harlem who replaced David Brown in Santana, got caught up in the web of heroin addiction in the late 1970s and died of an overdose in his Nob Hill home. Alberto Gianquinto, the troubled talent that lent his signature cascades of rippling piano notes to *Abraxas*, died in the 1980s after falling on concrete in a Kansas City doorway. Richard Kermode eventually moved to Colorado but died after a long fight with alcoholism. (Malo performed a benefit for his remaining relatives.) Coke Escovedo also passed in July 1986 on the way to a Tierra gig; years of partying had finally taken their toll.

Ron Estrada, Santana's former road manager, also passed away due to alcohol-related problems in 1997. Ron DeMasi, the talented Malo keyboardist, and Tony Smith, the outrageous funk drummer on Malo's third and fourth albums (he also pops up on Santana's *Welcome* album on the "Samba de Sausalito" cut, and with the Jeff Beck and Jan Hammer *Live* album), have both passed on.

Sadly, David Brown also lost an off-and-on, thirty-year battle with addiction, succumbing to liver and kidney failure in September 2000. The charismatic bass man, who represented the Afro-American face of Santana's music, thankfully was around to receive his Santana Hall of Fame award in 1998, although he was too ill to play. David's funeral service, although small, was ministered by both Freddie Stewart (Sly Stone's brother) and Leon Patillo. Patillo sang and played with Brown and Santana in the *Borboletta* days. David was most remembered for his shy and laid-back nature, which kept him calm despite the storms that raged through his personal life. As he once said, "When I'm on the road, I'm in a hotel room studying and reading, you know. And I feel free inside 'cause that's what it took me to get to play in the first place."

Jan, his sister, remembered: "David lived the life of a rock star in his own way. A couple of months before David passed, we were coming back from the local barbeque place he liked to eat at in Oakland. We were listening to a cut from BB King and Eric Clapton. He looked at me and said, 'I could have been great like that.' He never really realized his own talent."

232

José "Chepito" Areas has also seen better days. The tiny powerhouse timbalero is generally credited with igniting the flame of Mission Latin rock. You only have to listen to the killer cut "Ya Llego" on the album *Abraxas Pool* by Abraxas Pool, a band featuring members of the original Santana lineup, to realize none of Chepito's percussive, razor-sharp genius has left him. His timbales solo is a masterpiece of dynamic beauty. Areas is a strong contender for the crown of one of America's musical treasures—a true original. As Herbie Herbert remembers him: "When we did Tanglewood, Dave Holland [Miles Davis's bassist] and Chepito were playing congas backstage. Chepito had impossible chops, I swear to God; at that moment he was the best percussionist in the world and with all deference, that includes Tito Puente." Adds Johnny Villanueva: "After he had the aneurysm, when he came back, he was a totally different person, a real prankster, but he can still play his ass off." Chepito is currently fronting his new band, doing a complete Santana set and the old fire is still there.

Abraxas Pool comprised the original Santana band with Brown and Carlos absent. Alphonso Johnson took David's bass position. Formed in late 1995, before the recent upsurge in Latin music, the band played their first gig at the Marina, San Francisco, in a nod to the days of free, open-air concerts. Combining the raw sound of the original Santana with new compositions, they showed the old fire was there. The self-titled album released in 1997 on Miramax has some killer cuts: "Bailar Mi Cha Cha," "Guarijona," both from Chepito, "Szabo," a sensitive tribute to Gabor, and a heavy version of "JingoLoBa," with an African drum intro segueing to the heavy percussion section of Shrieve, Areas, and Carabello and with some fiery swoops from Neal Schon on guitar. Gregg Rolie is on hand to supply his great Hammond B3 style and still-strong vocals.

Jose "Chepito" Areas holds on to his sticks.

Photo: Skip Shuman/Sacramento Bee

Abraxas Pool debut CD release, 1997.

Photo: Courtesy Miramar Records

233

These days Chepito's son, Adrian Areas, is a fine conga and timbales player, carrying on his father's tradition. He can be heard on Gregg Rolie's new recording, *Roots*, which celebrates Rolie's strong vocal and Hammond style, which along with Carlos's guitar, stamped the Santana sound of the first three classic albums. Gregg's record features his rarely heard Hammond B3 to great effect again, and shows both his Santana and acoustic Spanish influences. Adrian Areas can also be caught around town playing with Mike Carabello, among others. Gregg Rolie notes, "If you want to hear the Santana music the way it was written, then I think my band is as near as it gets; the band really smokes. Ron, myself, and Alphonso just let the percussionists go, but nobody overplays.

Mike Carabello has recently recorded some great dance track, with a project called the BB Club, again with Neal Schon laying down some blistering guitar parts, and drum loops courtesy of Mike Shrieve. A song about poverty and homelessness, "Live 4 Today," particularly stands out, sung in a way that would be a perfect match for Madonna.

Luis Gasca hasn't released a record in years; apparently having burnt many bridges (he once threw a beer can in the face of Fantasy Records' president Saul Zaentz, who was not promoting an album to Luis's satisfaction). Seemingly, Gasca appears to have little catalogue available at present.

Gabor Szabo, the guitarist who influenced Carlos, Schon, and the Latin-rock scene generally, attempted to escape heroin addiction by enrolling in NarcAnon, a Scientology rehab program. However, by 1980 he felt Scientology was yet another trap. Gabor yielded to his heroin habit and was hospitalized finally after a final trip home to Bucharest, Hungary. He passed away in 1982. Abraxas Pool's debut album features a fine tribute to the master guitarist, simply entitled "Szabo."

Last known pictures of Richard Kermode, who added so much to the sounds of Santana and Malo.

Photo: Malo Archives

Michael Carabello, 2004.

Photo: Janice Hughes

234

Stan Marcum, who turned Carlos onto jazz and helped put together the original Santana lineup, is occasionally seen around town, but appears to be still struggling with problems in connection with substance use.

Errol Knowles, who sang with Azteca and Willie Bobo, dropped out of the music scene. "Errol Knowles was good singer," says Abel Zarete, "but I think he's doing time now. I heard he'd fallen in with the wrong people and is in prison for armed robbery. To me, he was such a loving guy, very street smart; I find it hard to believe."

More recently Rico Reyes, the soulful vocalist from the Mission neighborhood, who sang with Santana and Azteca, passed away in San José in May 2002, with substance related problems.

A lot of these musicians, in the early days of the Mission music revolution, didn't comprehend the increasing payback from the encroaching drug culture, which consumed their lives and those of their families. Ghettoes were flooded with these unwelcome narcotic temptations and thirty years on, the results speak for themselves.

Addiction—difficult to understand from the outside but equally difficult to escape from the inside—has devastated many talents in the music world. In keeping with it's spread worldwide, drug and alcohol problems have left their legacy in the Mission.

However, Mission-flavored Latin-rock, although seeming dormant to the recording industry, was due to have its very public renaissance.

Photo: Courtesy Warner Brothers Records

AMERICANOS

Latino Life in the United States
La Vida de los Latinos en Estados Unidos

A Musical Celebration
Una Celebración Musical

Rubén Blades, Willie Bobo, Celia Cruz, Paquito D'Rivera with The Orchestra of St. Lukes, Pedro Luis Ferrer, Flaco Jiménez with Ry Cooder, Lhasa, Los Lobos, Malo, Frankie Negrón, Ozomatli, Eddie Palmieri, Tito Puente, Marc Ribot y Los Cubanos Postizos, Santana, WAR

Americanos CD release on Warners
tied in with their sumptuous photo book publication.

Photo: Jim Welch

The Gregg Rolie Band hang out backstage.

Just before Carlos Santana's huge comeback with *Supernatural*, which utilized the talents of many of today's young chart talents, Malo also hit a home run when Sugar Ray, self-described as a "a bunch of boneheads from Orange County," included music from "Suavecito" in the track "Every Morning," a track culled from best-selling album *14:59*. (The title is a pun on Andy Warhol's famous dictum that in the future everybody would be famous for fifteen minutes.) The song sold more than two-and-a-half million units, stayed Number 1 for ten weeks on *Billboard*'s chart, and was nominated for both MTV Song of the Year and MTV Video of the Year.[42] Sugar Ray's Mark McGraw explained to MTV News: "We referenced 'Suavecito' because growing up in California, it was just, like, the lowrider anthem. Any car show or swap meet you'd ever go by you'd always hear 'Suavecito' and it just stuck in your mind."

Santana, Malo, and Latin-rock have also been well represented by a slew of compilation CDs currently in the racks. The Chicano Alliance double-release on the R-Town label features "Lady I Love" from *Malo V*, with other cuts from El Chicano, the Village Callers, and Tierra, among others. Also released in 1998 was *Raza Rock*, with excellent liner notes by Chuy Varela and Ruben Guevara. "Suavecito," the Malo cut, is in company with Los Lobos, Santana's excellent "Oye Como Va," Cold Blood, Azteca, Sapo, Tower of Power, War and many others.

[42] When I visited San Francisco in the course of writing this book, we were having the usual barrel of laughs, sitting in Ron Sansoe's office, when a package arrived from Warner Brothers containing a cassette of "Every Morning." Warner was requesting that Ron assess the copyright boundaries on the song. I remember Ron, Roberto Quintana, and I driving in the city and taking a relaxed listen to the tape. It's a blast, in retrospect, to be listening to a future Number 1 hit.

Photo: Courtesy Rhino Records

Ay Califas! Raza Rock, CD release on Rhino Records, 1998.

In 1998, British label Soul Jazz released *Chicano Power*, containing Malo's "Street Man" (previously unreleased on CD) plus "Pana" from the debut album. Strong sleeve notes, with the emphasis on Chicano politics, supported by hot cuts by Benitez, Sapo, Chango, Santana, and others make this an excellent package. In 1999, Atlantic put out *Americanos*, along with an accompanying documentary. "Suavecito" again is Malo's featured cut along with a broad range of new and older Latin material, such as Willie Bobo's "Fried Neckbones," Santana's superb "Guajira," and tracks by Ruben Blades, Eddie Palmieri, and Los Angeles-based band Ozomatli.

Photo: Courtesy Gabe Manzo

Dolores Huerta with Malo guitarist Gabe Manzo.

Photo: Courtesy El Tecolote

Photo: Courtesy Etienne Houben

Raul Rekow and Karl Perazzo, percussion team of Santana.

Erecting Cesar Chavez Street sign, replacing older Army Street sign.

237

Santana *Shaman* CD cover artwork, 2002.
Superb illustration by Rudy Gutierrez.

Photo: Courtesy Santana and Artista Records

SUPERNATURAL/SHAMAN

Carlos Santana sports a Michael Rios shirt design, which features Armando Peraza.

Photo: Courtesy El Tecolote

Supernatural was the brainchild of Clive Davis, the then–head of Arista Records who'd originally signed Santana to Columbia in 1968. The *Supernatural* project combined classic Santana guitar work with guest artists representing 1990s rock permutations, such as Everlast, Lauryn Hill, and Dave Matthews. Wyclef Jean of Fugees fame penned "Maria Maria" almost entirely in the studio and generated one of the album's two Number 1 hits on the *Billboard Hot 100* chart. "Smooth," the other huge hit, featuring Rob Thomas of Matchbox 20, introduced a nineties take on cha-cha-cha with its clever, dry-processed vocal and Carlos's exuberant, thrilling solo. It became the flagship single for the *Supernatural* album. The release went on to win eight Grammy awards and stayed in the Number 1 slot for more than ten weeks; sales topped the 21 million mark worldwide, allowing Santana's Latin-based rock to reach a new, huge international, crossover (and young) audience.

Photo: Tana and Arista Records

Santana's *Supernatural* CD, 1999.
Cover artwork by Michael Rios.

239

Supernatural rumors abounded as to which guest stars and songs would appear on the release. Under consideration were a tune written by Mick Jagger and Dave Stewart, "Blind Lead the Blind," and Lauryn Hill singing a cover of the Beatles' "And I Love Her" (Carlos had guested with Hill at the 1999 Grammies, performing "To Zion" on both acoustic and electric guitars). Prince was rumored to be part of the project; so was Sting. Would Aretha Franklin also appear? The resulting album was as good as the rumors, unfounded or not.

Supernatural opens with "(Da Le) Yaleo," a rousing chant-based number originated by Mama Sez with additional Santana music and delicate guitar by Carlos to spice up the intro. He then cranks up the wah-wah as Billy Johnson on drums rouses the music by constant beats on the four. An electrifying middle eight allows the percussion to open up with solos by Raul Rekow on conga and Karl Perazzo on timbales, until Johnson flips round the drum kit with spectacular double drum fills.

"Love of My Life" is co-penned with guest singer Dave Matthews and features members of his band. Carter Beuford's drums set the tone with a heavy break beat over which Matthews delivers a caressing vocal performance. Just before the recording, Carlos's father had passed away, and Carlos's main guitar melody, derived from Brahm's "Third Symphony," reveals his feelings at the time. The tune is excellent with a seamless performance and an exciting outro with Carlos blowing with controlled passion.

"Put Your Lights On," in tandem with Everlast, is a departure from the Santana sound completely—a trawl through inner-child terrors and real or imagined evils lurking "under my bed"; it is also a call for spiritual protection. Everlast's gravelly vocal and Carlos's power chords make this an exciting original. "Africa Bamba," a song originally called "Guerilla," is from the West African Toure Kunde band with an added Spanish vocal and a salsa-style coda; a majestic cool sweep through the main song with Cuban supremo Horacio Hernandez on trap drums. It segues hotly into the dramatic outro with Karl Perazzo singing his heart out.

"Smooth" gave Santana their first hit in a long time: an insistent commercial cha-cha-cha with rousing guitar and a beautiful joyous solo from Carlos. "Do You Like the Way," features Lauryn Hill collaborating with Carlos over a rolling, programmed R&B groove. The end passage features singer Cee-Lo on some great husky Otis Redding-inspired vocals. The second hit, "Maria Maria," follows a cartoon-style *West Side Story* vignette made up in the studio by Wyclef Jean; this is a sparse, open romp that is loads of fun. Tasty acoustic guitar by Carlos decorates the groove. In "Maria," Wyclef gives Carlos his props: "Yo Carlos, man, you're making that guitar cry."

Photo: Courtesy Santana and Arista Records

Santana "Maria Maria" cassette-single cover artwork.

"Migra" follows, with penetrating lyrics about Californian immigration policy. The song, by Algerian artist Rachid Taha, allows Santana to broaden the Latin palette. Heavy tom-tom beats open the tune, and joyous unison playing by Carlos and producer KC Porter on accordian give it real fire. Carlos plays some seriously fluid wah-wah with a vigour and freedom that has always enchanted followers of his guitar style.

"Corazon Espinado" joins Santana with Mexican rock en español stars Maná for a flinty-hard groove with lyrics about an unforgiving heart. Again produced by whiz KC Porter, the song both grooves in a Latin vibe and rocks with hard playing by Carlos accompanied by Perazzo's crisp timbale rolls and Maná's superb vocal chorus.

"Wishing It Was," produced by the Dust Brothers (of Beastie Boys, Beck, Boo Yah Tribe, and Mellow Man Ace fame) features singer Eagle Eye Cherry in a sinous Latin-flavored lope thru a low-key outing. "El Farol" follows, and is a beautiful lilting guitar-led instrumental with a quietly passionate fadeout. Keeping up the Latin vibe, the CD continues with "Primavera," a song about rebirth with KC Porter both singing and playing strong rhythm guitar. This has an explosion of searing guitar flourishes by Carlos, and captures his stunning guitar solo performance—his best (recording-wise) in ages; it is backed by a kicking drum part by guest Jimmy Keegan.

"The Calling" showcases guest Eric Clapton, who jumped on board at the last minute, playing his guitar parts over a swampy, electro-based shuffle. Clapton and Carlos fail to really catch fire here; instead they trade luxuriant licks before the song rolls into a double-time rhythm with band singer Tony Lindsay chanting "One love, Lord God Almighty." The album concludes with a 'secret' track, "Day of Celebration," a feature of Santana's live sets with its rolling time signature, searing and rasping lead guitar (displaying Carlos's infatuation with Sonny Sharrock's free-form fretwork); a strong example of fusion, Santana style.

Carlos Santana in the *Caravanserai* era.

Photo: Courtesy Sony Records

The album was a triumph; with Clive Davis of Arista at the helm, everything seemed to fall into place. Excellent performances and hook-filled arrangements allied to contemporary production meant the album superceded all previous estimations.

"[*Supernatural*] worked beyond anybody's expectations," says Jeff Trager. "It was a great record. Carlos's record sales went down over twenty years. I mean they used to sell sixteen, seventeen million records worldwide; the sales went down but Carlos could still pack 'em in. Now he's got a brand new audience."

Two contemporary bands that perform under the banner of the Latin rock created by the Mission groups opened the triumphant touring shows that promoted Carlos Santana's 1999 release, *Supernatural*. Ozomatli and the Mexican pop-rock superband, Maná, reflected the divergence and commercial potential of an all-Latino bill, and the legacy of the 1970s Latin-rock era.

Released in October 2002, *Shaman* is the studio follow-up to *Supernatural*, which has sold in excess of 24 million copies worldwide. Shaman entered the *Billboard* chart in its first week at Number 1, with sales of 300,000. The strategy of *Supernatural* is repeated with a stellar guest lineup plus a few Santana-style offerings on *Shaman*'s generous sixteen tracks.

The album opens with "Adouma," a song by African artist Angelique Kidjo, with a well-realized, almost fully electronic backing. Carlos plays some quicksilver guitar flurries over a vocal by Tony Lindsay. From there it's straight into "Nothing at All" sung by Musiq, which sets the tone for most of the remaining album. Written by Rob "Smooth" Thomas, it's a pretty tune. Sung beautifully by Musiq, it became the second single release from the album. It leads up to the track that was the first single release, "Game of Love."

"Game of Love" was a guaranteed hit out of the box. With its acoustic guitar, a feel similar to "Harvest for the World" by the Isley Brothers, and a joyous vocal by newcomer Michelle Branch, it features Carlos's great intense lead lines. It deserved its instant entry to the US charts. (The "enhanced" CD single included the hit song, a video and two tracks that didn't appear on the LP. "Come Into My World," featuring vocals by Andy Vargas, has a modern Latin feel, and "Curacion" is a shimmering guitar instrumental produced by the hot KC Porter. Both are welcome additions to the material on the CD). "You Are My Kind," featuring Seal on vocals, is again adequate but unremarkable.

Santana "Game of Love" CD single (with Michelle Branch) cover artwork.

Photo: Courtesy Santana and Arista Records

Photo: Etienne Houben

Carlos Santana overdubs guitar parts for Africa Bamba (Guerrilla) at Fantasy Studios, Berkeley, 1997.

Photo: Ron Rinaldi: Courtesy Mike Shrieve

Micheal Shrieve co-wrote "Aye Aye Aye" on *Shaman*, the only track featuring a full-on Latin vibe.

"Amor (Sexo)" features the great vocals of Macy Gray, and an interesting Latin intro with modern production. Most of the tracks do not feature Santana as a band. "Foo Foo" does. A romp through a merengue-style tune with groovy horns, even with the monster Dennis Chambers on drums and the percussion section, it feels restrained. Another live favorite follows: "Victory Is Won," a thoughtful and redemptive guitar piece by Carlos, which was featured in their live act for some time. "America" combines Carlos with POD and has real fire in its belly—a full-on thrash with Carlos blowing his balls off on a great rousing solo. "Sideways" is a bluesy lope with Citizen Cope (Clarence Greenwood) on vocal. Some heavy bass by Me'Shell Ndegocello anchors it mightily. "Why Don't You And I" has Chad Kroeger from best-selling Nickleback on vocals; it passes by pleasantly but doesn't ignite any fire. It is also the third single-release from the album. Currently climbing the US *Billboard* chart, the single-release version is a revamp of the album track with Alex Band from the Calling, handling the vocals. This move is no doubt due to record company infra-politics.

"Feels Like Fire" is a combined effort with Dido, another pretty piece, produced in England and the US, with Sister Bliss from Faithless supplying keyboards. "Let Me Love You Tonight" is a forgettable piece of fluff with a big atmospheric intro and reminiscent of a lot of current "boy band" pop—the worst cut on the record.

"Aye Aye Aye" reunites original Santana member Michael Shrieve and Carlos for the only real Latin salsa-style track on the CD. Shrieve, tho co-wrote the song with Carlos, supplies drums on the middle eights and some electronically enhanced horn stabs to beef up proceedings. It has guitar histrionics from Carlos (engineered by Hendrix producer Eddie Kramer) and some crisp percussion breaks from Rekow and Perazzo. Karl Perazzo remembers, "Michael came down; he plays drums on the bridges on the song and I play the rest. He was really open."

"Hoy Es Adios," a bolero featuring singer Alejandro Lerner, is almost fully acoustic with a strong Spanish vocal. "One of These Days" with the mighty and exuberant Ozomatli looks at the common man's alienation and deprivations; it contains an excellent vocal by JB Ekl, who brings some weight to the album. This is the only track that feels like it originated somewhere near the street. Beautifully aggressive wah-wah guitar by Carlos pulls this groove along. "Novus," written by Carlos with a credit to Gabor Szabo, is a large orchestral piece with Carlos's charged guitars, both acoustic and electric, soaring along with Placido Domingo's vocal to make this a fitting track to close to the album. It's an evocative ending to a restless album, which doesn't gel quite as well as *Supernatural*.

Santana's current mega-success has prompted a flurry of re-releases and compilations from longtime label Columbia. The first three groundbreaking albums have been remastered and repackaged with extra sleeve notes by Ben Fong Torres. Of more interest to die-hards is the inclusion of extra live cuts on all three.

Santana features "Fried Neckbones," "Savor," and "Soul Sacrifice" live from the 1969 Woodstock appearance. "Savor," particularly, features a hot timbale outing from the mighty Chepito.

Abraxas features live bonus cuts from their 1970 Royal Albert Hall appearance in London, England. Here, we have a work in progress: look at "Se A Cabo," and a pre-recording version of "Touissant L'Overture," again featuring tight interplay between Carabello and Chepito. Again, it features Cheppy, laying down the heat on a stirring timbale solo. The set is completed with the *Abraxas* hit "Black Magic Woman/Gypsy Queen."

Santana 3 bonus cuts feature the last official live appearance of the 1971 original Santana group. Starting off their live set and these bonus tracks is "Batuka." "Jungle Strut," with Carlos and Neal wailing follows; it closes with the unreleased but crowd-pleasing, favorite, "Gumbo."

Columbia also released *Best of Santana, Volumes 1 and 2. Live at the Fillmore 1968*, followed—an interesting look at the infant Santana band with its Afro-style grooves supplied by Marcus Malone on congas and Doc Livinston on drums. Gregg, Carlos, and David Brown supply surprisingly sinous topping on early versions of "Jingo," "Treat," and "new" stuff such as "Conquistadore" and "Freeway Jam."

The Essential Santana soon followed—another remastered package which featured selections by Carlos himself.

Of further interest to their fan base, Columbia remastered *Caravanserai*. No bonus cuts here, and none are needed; just the recording with a new pristine mix.

Santana *Caravanserai* CD reissue, 2003.

Santana *Live at The Fillmore '68* CD release, 1997.

Michael Shrieve, mastermind, along with Carlos of the *Caravanserai, Welcome, Lotus* album trilogy.

Photo: Courtesy Sony Records

Photo: Joan Chase

Photo: Courtesy Sony Records

Photo: Joan Chase

Carlos Santana, 1973.

Santana *Welcome* CD Reissue, 2003.

Photos: Courtesy Sony Records

Welcome is another gem, and features the outtake "Mantra," with pulsating waves of keyboard sounds anchored by Dougie Rauch's stuttering bass and Michael Shrieve's outrageous 4/4 drum pattern—featuring some of Shrieve's off-the-wall fills as the track deepens and intensifies—with possibly Leon Thomas intoning, "Joy, Joy" towards the fade out. "Mantra" can also be heard on the *Lotus Live in Japan 1974* release, and another version featured on *Blessings in Disguise*, Shrieve's unreleased recording from 1974. David Brown is credited on the *Welcome* sleeve with a bass contribution. I think I can hear him on "Mother Africa," maybe?

Love, Devotion, Surrender, the second solo outing from Carlos, sees him paired with Mahavishnu (or just plain John McLaughlin to his folks back in Yorkshire, England). This release is an intense heatwave of Coltrane-inspired and penned pieces that feature both musicians from McLaughlin's band and Santana—notably Armando Peraza on congas to supply a Latin flavor and again, the redoubtable Michael Shrieve, and Dougie Rauch on bass. This disc is served with alternate takes of "A Love Supreme," and "Naima," the meditative, acoustic guitar piece from John Coltrane's hand, which, coupled with "Meditation," is a peaceful aside from the sheer sonic blast of the other cuts.

Carlos Santana and John McLaughlin,
Love, Devotion, Surrender CD reissue, 2003.

On the Malo front, the double-CD package *Latin Legends Live* was recorded at two sold-out shows at the Hop in Puente Hills, twenty minutes east of Los Angeles, in 1996. The show featured Malo on the majority of songs, the reunion of Bobby Espinosa and Mickey Lespron for El Chicano's set, and a concluding set, by East LA favorite Tierra. Thump Records, an LA label associated with Latin, hip-hop, and R&B, released the CD in 1997. "Malo, El Chicano, and Tierra were three acts that had continued to flourish in the Hispanic community," says Thump Records' Peabo Rodriguez, a former DJ from San Juan, Puerto Rico, who'd started a small label called ElectroBeat; its first two artists were Ice T and Kid Frost. They also had a band called Stop, which earned a gold record in South America. "Thump started doing compilations called *Low Rider* videos. *Low Rider* magazine is the number one Hispanic magazine in the nation. I also started to put together compilations for the Hispanic population here in the Southwest. Along with that, we started to talk about the live album. We did the *Latin Legends* tour and also the *Low Rider* tour. *Latin Legends* has done really well."

The *Latin Legends* disc features the established favorites, but blasts into "Techno Rumba," (written by Menjivar and Manzo) after Tony Menjivar's enthusiastic MC opening. Sebastian Ponti and Paul Benividez ably back Arcelio Garcia here on vocals. Leo Rosales provides a rousing timbales solo over a son montuno played on the piano by Gary Fisher. The other new cut, "Ritmo Tropical," by Manzo, Menjivar, and Garcia, opens with moody piano atmospherics. Everybody's favorite, "Suavecito," is here, of course. A balanced, clear remix by Garcia, Manzo, and Menjivar ensures the best-recorded sound, with just minor vocal overdubbing.

El Chicano's trademark Hammond B3 organ sound is fully represented in a set put together by Bobby Espinosa and Mickey Lespron with just a fifteen-minute rehearsal. "Canteloupe Island," from their first record, starts proceedings; Espinosa's Hammond cooks and simmers over a sultry tumbao rhythm. Mickey Lespron on guitar throws in some languid jazzy chords for good measure. Aaron Ballesteros from Tierra firms up the heat on drums. "El Ojo Rojo," which has a passing resemblance to the "Oye Como Va" riff, vamps on a mid-tempo jaunt. Their big crossover hit, "Viva Tirado," features an instantly recognizable organ riff.

Sebastian Ponti, singer with Malo, who is making interesting Latin hip-hop material.

Photo: Malo Archives

Leo Rosales on timbales, playing on Malo's *Latin Legends* CD.

Photo: Joan Chase

Tierra are well represented with seven cuts. The band shifts the gears up with "Celebrate with Tierra," a Latin shuffle with their lead vocalist Rudy Salas exhorting the audience. Also ripping on this cut is a hot conga solo by Johnny Valenzuela. The song smokes with sax by Victor Cineros and excellent guitar from Rudy Salas. The band hit many styles on this short but intense set, through the "Tierra Medley" ("Gonna Find Her," "La La Means I Love You," "Are We in Love?"), in a showcase of the massed-harmony vocals of this excellent band, which ranks among the best soul acts. "Memories/Latin Disco" has Valenzuela firing again on timbales. "Margarita" is a hot slab of Latin funk propelled by a slinky salsa piano figure, a hold-tight tribute to a foxy señorita. The closing encore, "Together," was Tierra's big hit, reaching Number 18 in the US Top 40.

Rocks the Rockies, recorded live in Colorado by Daniel Deaguero and released on his Night Beat Records, is an overdub document of a 1998 Malo show. "My link to Malo started with Richard Kermode," Deaguero says. "We had done a recording together that got two Mexican awards. He played on a cut called 'Caliente.' In fact it was his last recording; he died a month after this."

"For the *Rocks the Rockies* CD we taped Malo's first and second shows but we ended up with the second show recorded at about one in the morning; so it tells you a lot about the energy of this group. They have a lot of fire." Again the disc opens with the two newer Malo songs, "Techno Rumba" and "Ritmo Tropical." "Sapo's Montuno" shows Manzo's fire as a player and he really comes into his own. With its distinctive piano intro, this is a killer and the particular jewel on this disc. The music heats up until Manzo cools the pace to allow his languid solo to breathe, then gradually fires off a few McLaughlin-esque flurries. He continues to bring the pressure up; the solo takes on a more fervent spirit from here, starting to seriously smoke, complete with feedback. Then, unbelievably, his solo hits another plateau and the band takes off once more. Romero Amidor's bass playing is the perfect foil for Gabe Manzo's stellar guitar. "Pana" features some serious congas from Tony Menjivar. The music goes into a spin to allow Roberto Quintana to build an intense timbales flight as he plows and spins over Menjivar and David George's percussive backing.

Tony Menjivar, musical director and white-hot conga player for Malo.

Gabe Manzo, Malo's guitarist, puts it out live onstage.

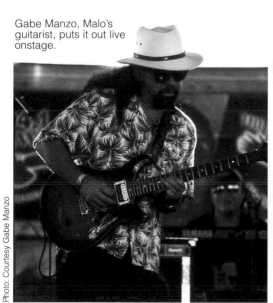

Photo: Courtesy Gabe Manzo

Photo: Courtesy Tony Menjivar

247

FUTURE PRIMITIVE

Players from Santana in particular but also from Malo, Azteca, and their ilk, placed Afro-Caribbean music in people's ears all over the world. This overlooked piece of music history is part of a jigsaw puzzle of rhythm and sound that has exploded over the last thirty years with the widespread interest in world musics.

Cuban hip-hop, courtesy of Orishas for example, reflects many influences from rap to roots. The band, composed of musical brothers from Havana who started out in Amenaza, one of the leading groups in the first wave of Cubano-style rap, had an international seller with their first release in 2000, *A Lo Cubano*. The phenomenal success of the Ry Cooder-produced Buena Vista Social Club, featuring the cream of veteran Cuban musicians, has opened the door for the great back-catalogues of Cuban music to be properly revisited.

New-wave salsa, as represented by Marc Anthony, whose debut featured Eddie Palmieri and Tito Puente and the songs of India Caballero, Masters at Work, Nuyorican Soul, plus Dark Latin Groove (DLG), all fused trip-hop, salsa, rap, reggae, and house to great effect. Dark Latin Groove did a great job of updating Celia Cruz's "Quimbara" into a heavy, shuffling, electro-based dance piece. Their joyous version of Cuco Valoy's hit "Juliana" is astounding—an infectious song with over-the-top rap-style breaks and a soaring falsetto. "Acuyuye," another great dance hit with a boss conga solo by Richie Flores, is featured on DLG's 1998 release *Gotcha*.

A London-based band, Sidestepper, mix up cumbia, sampled dub bass, and live horns with the timbales of Roberto Pla on the *More Grip* release (a standout track is "Hoy Tenemo").

Orixa and Los Moscosos are musically representing current Latin culture in the Mission. Both bands have recorded for the independent label Aztlan Records. Los Mocosos are influenced by an amalgam of sources—ska, hip-hop, bugaloo, Mexican corridas, and Latin rock—and English and Spanish lyrics are combined into the verbal fusion known as "Spanglish." Their album *Mocos Locos* features current Santana timbalero Karl Perazzo[43] on "Somos los Mocosos" (their set-opening signature tune) and "Latinos with Soul." This new wave of Mission sound is creating a musical blend being tagged as "Latin Groove."

[43] Malo timbalero Roberto Quintana also plays with the group.

Photo: Courtesy Manny Martinez

Los Mocosos

"Right now, I think we have the same mentality that bands in the past had, which is to incorporate our culture into the rock scene," says Manny Martinez, vocalist with Los Mocosos. "With us, its not just about rock; it's got ska, hip-hop, R&B, soul. I believe that the music industry in general is going to see a lot of these cultural bands, born and raised here, or born elsewhere and raised here, that incorporate lots of American influences. I believe the West Coast is a totally innovative spot right now." Los Mocosos's 2002 release *Shades of Brown* sold about 10,000 copies in California and has been released in Europe; it earned a California Music Award for Best Latin Album.

Martinez also plays in Azabache along with his brother Rafael "Ray" Martinez. Azabache is a Mission-style salsa band with a great self-titled album release. One track, "Montuno Street," with its madly groovy bongo solo by Roman "Ito" Carillo, is a constant play in London and other regional English salsa clubs. The album deserves to be heard for its West Coast slant on the salsa sound with other excellent tracks such as "Batman and Spiderman," "Simplemente Complicada," and the cool ballad "Surrender." Roberto Quintana (from Malo and Michael Franti's Spearhead) can often be found playing percussion in their ranks.

"The earlier Mission sound is still prominent in the landscape," says Raul Pacheco, Ozomatli's guitarist and vocalist. (Carlos Santana emphasizes the connection by noting: "San Pacu were like the first Ozomatli; we thought they could have been big, but they was too much tension in the band.") The group's bass man, Wil-Dog Abers, offers: "We definitely try to put consciousness into our music. We have conscious people in the band; a lot of us grew up being into different social causes. Issues around things like National Day of Protest against police brutality in Los Angeles, every October 22, and Mumia Abu Jamal's imprisonment. In LA there's a group called the Watts Drum Corp. They got together to just play at demonstrations; we went down there to meet them and taught them a lot of drum patterns that we knew. We did things together, marches and stuff. We be singing, 'Who let the pigs out, oink, oink, oink" [a play on the 2002 pop song "Who Let the Dogs Out?" by the Baha Men].

Azabache CD, 2000: superb salsa, Mission style.

Los Mocosos CD, 1998: excellent Latino, hip-hop, ska concoction with Karl Perazzo from Santana.

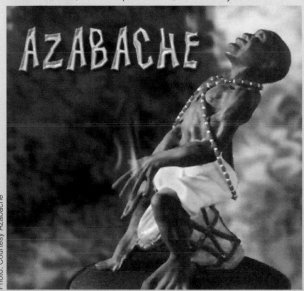

Other bands carrying the torch include Beans and Rice, although "they're a band that didn't get out past LA; [ex-Mandrill] Tommy Trujilla was in that band," says Pacheco. "Tommy is a Chicano kid from Highland Park; he has a funky Latin-rock style on guitar. [Another band] Firme are doing similar stuff to Ozomatli and us. Quetzal, out of LA, is touring with Cubanismo at the moment. Bands like Los Jaguares would be very innovative, from total pop to really hard rock. They've been around for years and they got a really loyal following."

The East Coast and West Coast sounds are forever mutating, and one band of renegades from the New York area, King Shango, on David Byrne's Luaka Bop label, have a hard-line frenetic danceable energy on their two CD releases, *King Shango* and *The Return of El Santo*.

Over on the West Coast, one band with a different slant on the Latin and R&B style is Cecilia Noel and the Hot Clams. I had the good fortune to see them perform at a Hollywood Bike Jam weekend party at Paramount Studios in Hollywood in October 1997, and they were a blast. Cecilia Noel fronts an all-dancing troupe of beautiful sisters whose music is a blend of soul and salsa styling. They call their blend "salsoul."

Orixa (not to be confused with Orishas from Cuba) from the Mission district, have a more abrasive, guitar-heavy sound, with pointed political lyrics on songs like "Latino Culturizate," the anti-suicide song "The Trigger," "Carioca," and "Sacudete." Orixa, popular on the college circuit, have a few independent releases, including *Siembra* (2003). Their front man and vocalist Rowan Jimenez mixes socially aware commentary with a no-holds-barred

Cecila Noel, the red-hot salsoul sister who fronts the Hot Clams.

All Photos: Curtis Harrison; Courtesy Cecilia Noel

Photo: Joan Chase

Ozomatli,
the superb
LA-based band.

sound that incorporates heavy hip-hop, soul, funk and nu-latin grooves. The band also comprises Michael Cavaseno on guitar, Mark Caipo on bass, and Juan Manuel Caipo on drums. Their live show is a full-on blast with Jimenez providing a charismatic visual focal point.

The thread between all of these expressions is the willingness to experiment, to add a range of spice to the musical mix. "Musically we've accomplished new stuff by breaking rules. We mix congas, timbales, tablas, a DJ, many influences," says Asdru Sierra, Ozomatli's trumpet player, who acknowledges: "The early Mission style was my influence as a kid. If it wasn't for Carlitos, we wouldn't be around." Pacheco adds: "Every culture looks for affirmation; what we are about is affirming our roots, our culture."

Andy Mendoza

Asdru Sierra

Orixa CD cover, released 1995.

Photos: Joan Chase

SONGS
1. latino culturízate   (4:08)
2. la roca   (5:10)
3. el bebé   (4:48)
4. sacúdete   (2:47)
5. música del alma   (4:25)
6. el gatillo
7. exit
8. canción de cuna   (4:12)
9. 500 years   (1:59)
10. mentiras
11. carióca   (4:05)
12. cariño   (2:44)
13. xicano   (3:09)

© ℗ Aztlan Records S.F.
P.O. BOX 347376 SAN FRANCISCO, CA 94134
(415) 821-7559 / fax (415) 821-8464
peermusic, Ltd. / El Faro Music (BMI)

AZTLAN
RECORDS

Photo: Courtesy Aztlan Records

Justin "Nino" Poree   Jiro Yamaguchi   Kanetic Source   Raul Pacheco   Ulises Bella   Wil-Dog Abers

Photos: Joan Chase

251

Neal Schon, from teen prodigy with Santana to Journey to current solo work.

Photo: Steve Jennings; Courtesy Neal Schon

CAN'T TAKE THE FUNK OUTTA ME

Santana are one of the few acts to have had hit records in the 1960s, '70s, '80s, '90s, and 2000. With the current record, *Shaman*, they have had a five-decade run. The market for Latin music, in ever-increasing styles and categories, continues to grow. Santana's appearance at Live Aid in 1985 was important in that they were about the only "black" act on the bill. The set was notable for Armando Peraza dancing the "funky Cuban shuffle" at the outro to their set.

The original Santana band was inducted into the Rock and Roll Hall of Fame in 1998. Karl Perazzo was pleased to play timbales during Chepito's absence. "It was really their moment, to get recognized for their contribution to American music. It was one of the highlights of my life. Playing with those supreme cats, to play with Carabello and Shrieve, their swing on it. Peter Green also played with us on 'Black Magic Woman.'"

Photos: Courtesy Jan Cameron

Mike Shrieve with Jan Cameron (David Brown's sister) at the Rock and Roll Hall of Fame, at Santana's induction.

Jan Cameron with Carlos Santana at the Waldorf Astoria New York. The event: Santana's induction to The Rock and Roll Hall of Fame 1998.

253

Carlos individually has been recognized for his music at the Grammies and was been presented with a star on the Hollywood Walk of Fame, Hollywood Boulevard, Los Angeles, on August 17, 1998. In many respects, the once-marginalized music is now mainstream.

Neal Schon sums up the nostalgia that remains for the late, great era of Mission district Latin rock and roll. "The original Santana was the coolest band of all. To this day, I felt if the original Santana band got together, the magic would flow again. Not everyone in the original Santana was an amazing musician, but the chemistry was just right there. Now that the bad habits are past, it could be a great experience." Yet the times, inevitably, have changed; the veterans of those days wonder if the recording and distribution environment can support the street music that captured their generation. "Radio is such a toilet now," Schon declares. "It's all playlists and payola. Kids only learn what they hear. When the first Journey album came out, Tom Donaghue on KSAN played the entire fucking record on his show. It's not like we play two seconds of this and you can phone in and tell us whether to smash it, bash it, or trash it. To me the music business seems really fucked up. I was never a pop-meister; I've always been a musician," he says, adding hopefully, "but I think Carlos has helped tremendously with the success of *Supernatural*."

"I feel very grateful that I've had almost two lifetimes of musical knowledge just coming to San Francisco and being in America at this point in time," Carlos Santana said in an interview with Chuy Varela. "Nowadays [commercialism] is dangerous—you want Coca Cola or Pepsi? That's it. So when radio people consciously and deliberately program forty songs for you to cram in your brain for a month and those forty songs already sound like themselves, you're shortchanging everybody.

Carlos Santana getting his star at The Walk of Fame, Hollywood. Boulevard, August 17, 1998.
(Leo Rosales, with beret, can be seen in the background crowd.)

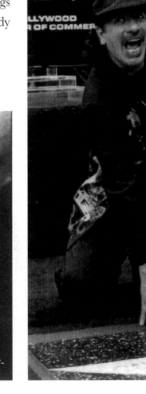

Neal Schon, a versatile and underrated guitarist, and a perfect foil for Carlos.

Photo: Karen Harris; Courtesy Neal Schon

Photo: Reuters

"Everything is a struggle in finding your own identity and what you need to do. The key word is 'crystallizing.' Where do I see myself in the world? What kind of music do I want to be playing? How do I want to play it and whom do I want to play it for? Like Jimi Hendrix said before he died: 'I like electric church sky music.' It's the same as street social music. Right now I'm interested in bringing in the spiritual side to the politics in music. The big corporations need to know that, without inspiration, they're dead. The only thing that makes a person come alive is when you're doing something for somebody else. That's where music comes in. It's the ultimate way for me to serve on this planet and serve in a way that a lot of generations, not just mine, can say, 'You know what? I heard that and my hair stood up, I heard a bell ring, I can do that.' I want to live for that. My platinum hours are when people write in and say, 'You move me with the way you play.' Commercialism is only bad when people who program the music only hear the cash registers ringing, and not the music.

"John Coltrane, the supreme musician, was really humble. Arrogant people can't play for shit. I think a lot of people need to assess their existence, to go forward with their music. Otherwise you become a caricature of yourself. To me, everyone has to get out of that loop. If they want to thrust forward, they have to shed their skins and embrace new things.

Tony Lindsay, soulful lead vocalist for Santana.

Photo: Courtesy Etienne Houben

Photo: Courtesy Santana

Santana *Shaman* tour VIP pass, 2003.

"Some music is passé and some is forever. Afro-Cuban music to me is the spice in life. Rhythm is spice; melody is the tranquillizer. I say melody is the female and rhythm is the masculine and we always try for a good marriage, a good balance. All this music can be used to seduce somebody or to uplift somebody to God. The more I learn, the more I realize that all music comes from Africa. Even classical music with polytonality and polyrhythms draws from African musical textures. I respect tradition but I love transition. A lot of people say, "Why don't you play Mexican music, like a huapango?' Well, huapango isn't Mexican music; it comes from Veracruz and that music comes from Cuba and Africa.

"That's what I'm trying to give to the Latin community. There's very little that's new except for people like Eddie Palmieri or Ruben Blades who take chances and stick their necks out. We're going to be criticized. If Richie Valens hadn't died he would have been playing with everybody! As Dexter Gordon would say, 'The cream always rises to the top.' Rock and roll has to go through certain things to have an impact. Sometimes it's preconceived arrangements. I like jazz because it's the ultimate in being naked. You're not hiding behind a melody, an arrangement, or a certain hit. You can take something like 'Oye Como Va' and play it with someone like McCoy Tyner and every time you do it it's going to be different. Jazz is the purest form of music. It's the purest water."

After playing the *Sacred Fire* tour and album in 1989, Jorge Santana joined Carlos's management team. Jorge Santana is as philosophical as his brother: "Latin rock has never gone away. It's evolving and also mutating." Others in the industry are equally hopeful that the music will prove to be as resilient as the generation that produced it.

"As far as I'm concerned, with Latin music, its best days are ahead of it," says promoter Jeff Trager. "Without a doubt, between Latin, world, and dance, it's always infusing new ideas and people. 'Suavecito' is going to be around for another twenty years. The baby boomers remember the song and new people hear it on soundtracks and you have [the appreciation of] a huge, huge Latin population."

"If you check the current *Billboard* charts, you'll see that in the Latin charts that 35 to 40 percent of the chart is full of salsa," says Peabo Rodriguez of Thump Records. "Latin music has seen the largest increase in sales in any music genre over the last five years. It continues to do so. It's on the edge of crossing over. A lot of rap acts are using Spanish lyrics and samples. The whole rap en español thing that has blown up out of the Caribbean and Mexico is a huge, burgeoning, underground market. The timing is ripe for Malo to reach back into their Latin roots and tie in with the salsa side and compete in that market. The great thing is they are very exciting live."

Says Neil Norman of GNP Crescendo, "Everything recycles every seven years. People are just getting hip to Latin again; a new generation is discovering Latin music, and Malo are one of the best Latin bands. They're a really hot live band and people get real excited with their act. Whenever I see their gigs, I'm always astonished how much they affect me."

That's because, says Gabriel Manzo, "In Malo, it's real versatile in terms of including Latin, blues, funk, rock—and that's why it doesn't get old. It's open playing, from the heart. Some people think they can do this stuff but they can't do it. This current band sounds like it's supposed to sound, in a Mission way. We just go out there and kick it."

"Arcelio is molding the future with the young guys in his band," agrees Chuy Varela. "The future is coming on from the eighties sampling culture now. We are headed toward a new way of consuming music. I'm noticing bands getting their chops from Santana and Malo, the barrio bands in their garages, learning all these great songs. We have all the turntable-ism and more synthetic stuff, but the essence of this music is people interacting together, in a big way; we don't want to lose that heartbeat. With Malo getting involved in education, it may get kids back into instruments." And according to Pete Gallegos, it's happening: "I see the kids turning back to a more instrument-based view of music, not just the sampling culture; it's like instruments as an extension of their personality."

That's where it all started. It's fitting that Arcelio Garcia, the whiz-kid baseball player who threw in his glove for a shot at the stage, should have the last word. "The way I see it is like my mother says: 'Always go ahead, never look back.' I've never looked back, even through the times of turmoil."

How the Latin scene in the Mission became apparent from the music on the streets.
John Santos remembers, "Two great Cuban rumberos, Eugenio 'Totico' Arango and Francisco Aguabella at Precita Park in San Francisco's Mission district, Oct 1978. The park is three blocks from where I lived for 17 years and a place where I'd come to see older drummers like Mike Carabello and others in the 1960s."

Photo: Courtesy John Santos

A

FRANCISCO AGUABELLA Master conga drummer, played with Tito Puente and briefly with Santana in 1976. Appears on Malo's *Dos, Evolution,* and *Ascension* albums. Consistent solo career.

VICTOR ALEMON Photographer, took early Malo shots.

ADRIAN AREAS Son of Chepito Areas. Following in his father's footsteps, an ace timbalero, currently with the Gregg Rolie Band.

JOSÉ "CHEPITO" AREAS Ignited the flame of Mission-style Latin rock. Joined Santana (from the Aliens) in time to record their debut album. Released solo album in a salsa-style for Columbia in 1974.

B

RICHARD BEAN Native of San Francisco, original member of Malo, supplied them with "Suavecito," a US Top 20 hit. Formed Sapo in 1974. Appeared with Jorge Santana Band; also in the Wizards (with Abel Zarate) and Jet.

JORGE BERMUDEZ Conguero who appeared briefly with Malo on the *Dos* album. Records on his own Bermudez Triangle label.

WILLIE BOBO Legendary timbalero/band leader, came through Tito Puente's bands. Appeared with Santana in Africa, 1971. Supplied band with first hit, "Evil Ways." Long solo career. Died in Los Angeles in 1979.

DAVID BROWN Original Santana bassist, brought the Afro-American face to Santana's music with a strong bass style and charismatic visual appeal. Died in 2000.

C

MICHAEL CARABELLO Original Santana conguero of Puerto Rican origin. Carabello introduced the sound of the conga drum, with a hypnotic rhythmic signature, to the rock world.

FRED CATERO Veteran producer who worked in tandem with David Rubinson and engineered all four Malo releases. Produced Santana's classic album *Abraxas.*

JOAN CHASE Resident photographer on Santana payroll, documented much of the band's early activity. Current whereabouts unknown.

CESAR CHAVEZ Founded and led United Farm Workers union. Awarded Aguila Azteca, Mexico's highest honour. Second Mexican-American to receive Presidential Medal of Freedom. Family created Cesar Chavez Foundation. Died in 1993.

JOHNNY CORTADE Co-owner of the influential Nite Life club, booking the Aliens, Malo, Tower of Power.

D

ANGELA DAVIS Leading African-American political prisoner, once on FBI's Ten Most Wanted list. Member of Black Panther party. Malo played 1972 concert in Berkeley to benefit international movement for her release. Currently professor at University of California, Los Angeles.

CAST OF CHARACTERS

RON DeMASI — Excellent keyboard player/arranger who appears on Malo's *Evolution* and *Ascension* albums. Along with Tony Smith, brought an exciting rhythmic foundation and solo verve.

GREG ERRICO — Mission district resident, went on to fame as original drummer with Sly and the Family Stone. Worked with Santana, Attitude, Chepito Areas, and War, among others. Currently with Bueno, Many Faces, and the Family Stone.

PETE ESCOVEDO — Timbalero/percussionist. Older brother of Coke, they joined forces as the Escovedo Brothers; worked briefly in Santana in 1971 and recorded two albums with Azteca. Joined Santana in 1977 for the *Inner Secrets* and *Moonflower* albums. Has had a long recording and live-dates career; ran Mr. E's Night Spot in Berkeley until recently.

SHEILA ESCOVEDO — Daughter of Pete Escovedo. Influential conga/timbales player. Perhaps best known for stint as Prince's drummer by name of "Sheila E." Has recorded solo albums with Pete.

THOMAS 'COKE' ESCOVEDO — Timbales/conga player, drafted into Santana in 1971 during Chepito's illness and toured with the band. His strong personality is said to have caused rifts within the group. Formed Azteca and had four solo albums released. Died July 13, 1986.

RON ESTRADA — Part of the original Santana management team until 1971. Partners with Stan Marcum. Died in 1997.

CARLOS FEDERICO — Influential salsa pianist from Panama. Played the early SF Latin scene. Featured on Chepito solo and Malo *Evolution* releases. He died in 1996.

BEN FONG-TORRES — Rolling Stone journalist, responsible for first major article on Santana in 1972 (currently available in *Not Fade Away* reprint) Provided liner notes for CD reissues of the first three Santana albums.

ALEX GALLEGOS — Co-owner of Nite Life with Johnny Cortade.

PETE GALLEGOS — Educator, musician, and graphic artist; longtime Mission district resident.

ARCELIO GARCIA, JR. — Lead singer of Malo with a dynamic stage presence; has led the band to the current day.

CARMELO GARCIA — Extroverted timbalero, played with Mongo Santamaria, Luis Gasca, and Richard Kermode.

PETE "PELE" GARCIA — Brother of Arcelio Garcia.

WILLIE "G" GARCIA — Singer from the East LA scene with Thee Midniters and Cannibal and the Headhunters. Lead vocals for Malo's 1974 *Ascension* album.

LUIS GASCA — High-octane trumpet player with Janis Joplin and Mongo Santamaria. Recorded on *Santana 3*, plus *Carlos Santana & Buddy Miles Live*. Played on Malo debut album. Has released many solo albums. Contrary to reports of his death, he is still alive and based in Texas.

D
E

F

G

ALBERTO GIANQUINTO Tumultuous pianist from the Mission, arranged on Santana first album. Co-wrote "Incident at Neshabur" with Carlos Santana for *Abraxas*, a Santana classic. Died in the eighties in Kansas.

DR. BERNIE GONZALEZ Played a significant part in Malo's relocation to San Francisco in the mid-eighties, and a large role in guiding the band's business affairs. Has been involved with the 24th St Fair and the Cinco De Mayo celebration in San Francisco.

BILL GRAHAM Possibly the most important rock promoter in the USA. Opened the Fillmore's East and West. Championed the original Santana band, for whom he had a particular love. Died October 25, 1991.

TOM HARRELL Expert jazz arranger/horn player, arranged for Malo *Dos* and appears on both Azteca albums. Worked on *Every Step of the Way* for Mike Shrieve and for Santana on the *Caravanserai* sessions.

HERBIE HERBERT Came from Fruminous Bandersnatch to road-manage Santana. Stayed till starting hugely successful Journey project with Neal Schon and Gregg Rolie. Runs Nightmare Productions. Extremely influential in the US rock business.

ROBERTO HERNANDEZ Instrumental in setting up Mission Economic and Cultural Association; freelance concert producer.

DOLORES HUERTA Co-founded United Farm Workers union. Today is union Secretary and Treasurer. Lobbyist in support of civil rights of Latino workers and the poor.

MIKE JUDGE Creator of "Beavis and Butthead" cartoon. Played briefly with Abel Zarate in Wizard.

RICHARD KERMODE Superb pianist on *Malo* and *Malo Dos* who also contributed to Santana's *Welcome* and *Lotus* albums. Equally at ease nailing down a montuno as he was playing dexterous, swinging solos. He died in 1996.

GREGG LANDAU Member of Arcelio Garcia's Zorro after the early Malo days. Recently produced excellent Carlos "Patato" Valdes CD, which received a Grammy.

ROBERT LAZANEO In Jim and the Gents and SUBB with Jorge Santana until 1969; wrote Malo's "Everlasting Night" cut.

JACK LEAVITT Promoter of early Latin-rock shows; still active in California music business.

JAMES "MINGO" LEWIS Conguero picked up on Santana's 1971 tour in New York. Recorded on *Caravanserai*, then sessions for Billy Joel, Buddy Miles, and Al Di Meola. Released solo album, *Flight Never Ending* on Columbia in 1976.

MARCUS MALONE First Santana conguero with a pronounced African playing style. Can be heard on *Santana, Live from the Fillmore 1968*. Jailed on manslaughter charges in 1969.

GABRIEL MANZO Lead guitar with Malo since mid-eighties. Plays with a rousing lead style. Co-fronts Many Faces and Bueno with Tony Menjivar.

STAN MARCUM Original Santana manager. After attending barber college; he helped assemble the first Santana aggregate.

MANNY MARTINEZ	Lead singer with the Los Mocosos band; also plays with his brother Ray in the West Coast-style salsa band, Azabache.
TONY MENJIVAR	Conguero with Malo since mid-eighties with a wildly explosive solo style. Currently fronting Many Faces and Bueno.
BUDDY MILES	Drummer-singer with the influential Electric Flag. Part of Jimi Hendrix's *Band of Gypsies*. His long solo career was punctuated by the *Carlos Santana & Buddy Miles* album release in 1972. Returned to Santana for the *Freedom* album and tour in 1986–1987.
GLENDON MISKEL	Attorney whose clients include Herbie Herbert, Aynsley Dunbar, and Nocturne Productions.

VICTOR PANTOJA	New York-born veteran conguero of Puerto Rican origin. Played with Santana, Malo, Azteca, and Willie Bobo, among many others.
LEON PATILLO	Vocalist/keyboard player who joined Santana in 1974 for tour and *Borboletta* album. Presently a minister with a long career in the Christian music market.
ARMANDO PERAZA	Veteran conga master with long pedigree; worked with Machito, Charlie Parker, and Mongo Santamaria, among many others. Joined Santana in 1972 through 1990.
BILL PERASSO	As Warner Brothers' product manager, worked a lot of the Latin-rock releases for Bay Area radio.
TOM POOLE	Superb trumpeter/arranger who joined Malo for the *Dos* recording. Also performed with Boz Scaggs, currently with Etta James.
ROBERTO QUINTANA	Malo timbalero during the 1980s and nineties. Has a Cuban salsero style. Also appears with Los Mocosos and Michael Franti's Spearhead.

DOUG RAUCH	Bassist from Voices of East Harlem, entered Santana after David Brown's departure. Slap-funk bass style innovator along with Larry Graham. Played on Santana's *Caravanserai*, *Lotus*, and *Welcome* releases. Also with Loading Zone, Gabor Szabo, Lenny White, Cobra, Betty Davis, and Attitude. Died in the late 1970s.
RAUL REKOW	Exciting conguero originally with Soul Sacrifice, moved to Malo, then Sapo. Joined Santana in 1976 for *Festival* album and has stayed almost continuously to present day.
RICO REYES	Supplied beautiful, soulful Spanish vocals to Santana's "Guajira" cut from their third album, a Santana classic. Contributed percussion, backing and lead vocals to the *Abraxas*, *Santana 3*, and *Caravanserai* albums by Santana. Vocalist with Azteca and Quicksilver Messenger Service. Led the short-lived San Pacu group. Died in April 2002.
GEORGE RODRIGUEZ	Latin rock photographer/chronicler. Brother of Rudy.
RUDY RODRIGUEZ	Photographer/chronicler of the Los Angeles rock scene. Died 2001.
BRIAN ROHAN	Attorney responsible for signing most of the San Francisco bands (starting with the Grateful Dead), including Santana.

GREGG ROLIE Co-founder, original singer, and organist/arranger for Santana. Rolie's grooving, carousel Hammond B3 playing was the perfect foil for Carlos's guitar work and a major part of Santana's early success. Later joined Neal Schon to found hugely successful Journey. Current release, *Roots*, celebrates his influential Santana heritage.

LEO "PEPE" ROSALES Timbalero with a pulverizing style based on Chepito Areas, his early mentor. Played on *Malo Dos* and *Latin Legends Live*.

GIBBY ROSS Child prodigy timbalero, who, at age eight, appeared on stage with Tito Puente. Currently playing with Malo.

DAVID RUBINSON Hot-shot producer from New York. Prolifically produced Herbie Hancock, Mongo Santamaria, Malo, Santana's *Amigos*, *Festival*, and *Moonflower* albums, and more.

ABEL SANCHEZ Leader, vocalist, and guitarist of seminal Mission district outfit Abel & The Prophets.

RON SANSOE Responsible for Malo's return to West Coast.
Instrumental in originating this book's creation.

CARLOS SANTANA Beautiful, lyrical, stinging guitar solos allied to innovative funk, soul, Latin, and rock rhythm playing makes Carlos one of the great modern American stylists.
Massive comeback with his *Supernatural* and *Shaman* releases.

JORGE SANTANA Carlos's younger brother; lead guitarist with Malo. Brought a burning, intense guitar style to the young band. Also played and recorded with Fania All-Stars. Released two solo albums plus *Brothers* album with Carlos Santana and his nephew Roberto Hernandez (not to be confused with the MECA event promoter).

CHIORI SANTIAGO Well respected San Francisco Bay Area music and entertainment journalist and freelance writer.

JOHN SANTOS Started by playing congas in the parks. Respected ethnomusicologist and fluent conguero, leads his own Orquesta Batachanga and Machete Ensemble. Played with Santana briefly in 1976. Ongoing solo career.

NEAL SCHON The 15-year-old Schon jammed throughout the *Abraxas* sessions and joined Santana to record *Santana 3* and *Caravanserai*. Schon's savage, exciting solo guitar playing and unison lines complemented Carlos perfectly. Went on to major success with Journey.

JOEL SELVIN Pop music critic for the *San Francisco Chronicle* since 1972. Selvin is the author of the popular Ricky Nelson, Monterey Pop, Sly and the Family Stone, and the Summer of Love books.

MICHAEL SHRIEVE The most creative and musical of all the Santana drummers, his fiery style relentlessly drove the original Santana band. Famous for their appearance at Woodstock, Shrieve also turned the Santana group towards a more jazz-influenced sound. Solo career has included Automatic Man, Novo Combo, Go, Klaus Schulze, plus many experimental/jazz based recordings and guest appearances.

JOSÉ SIMON Bass player with Sapo. Now a well-known comedian.

Tony Smith   Drummer and vocalist with flair, style, and great funk-fusion chops. Appears on Malo's *Evolution* and *Ascension* albums. Went on to appear with Jeff Beck and Jan Hammer. Appears on Chepito's solo album. Recorded on Santana *Welcome* album (on "Samba de Sausalito").

Richard Spremich   Original Malo drummer, joined with Roy Murray and Abel Zarate from Naked Lunch.

Carol Steele   Mission district resident and one of the first female congueros; played many street fairs. Credited with coming up with the name "Malo."

Freddie Stewart   Guitarist brother of Sly Stone in the glorious Sly and the Family Stone. Distinctive; rhythm-scratch style innovator. Currently is a minister in Vallejo, California.

Sylvester "Sly" Stone   Soul-funk legend with the incredible Sly and the Family Stone. Wrote and/or arranged all their greatest hits. Heavy, hip influence on Santana, Miles Davis, Jimi Hendrix, and Prince. Career derailed by cocaine usage. Now lives in North Hollywood.

Gabor Szabo   Influential guitarist on the burgeoning Mission Latin-rock scene. Santana used his song "Gypsy Queen" on *Abraxas* album. Died in 1982.

Pablo Tellez   Superb original Malo bassist, wrote and arranged for the first four albums. Appears on Santana *Festival*. Currently a minister based in San José.

Cal Tjader   Renowned vibes player and band leader. Recorded many classic Latin-jazz albums on Fantasy. Candido Camero, Willie Bobo, Victor Pantoja, and many others went through his ranks. Died in 1982.

Doug Tracy   Tour manager/manager of Malo until 1975. Originally with Tower of Power.

Jeff Trager   Has been in music promotion since Santana were rehearsing on Fillmore Street.

Benny Valarde   Conga drummer/timbales player in the Mission district Latin-jazz scene. Played with Willie Bobo in Tito Puente's band and with Cal Tjader. Until recently, led his own ensemble in the San Francisco Bay Area.

Johnny Valenzuela   Conguero who started out with Soul Sacrifice (which became Dakila); released two albums on Epic. Plays with War, Tierra, and promotes Latin shows.

Jesse "Chuy" Varela   DJ and writer on the San Francisco Latin music scene. Music director at jazz station KCSM FM 91 and contributing writer to the *San Francisco Chronicle* and *Latin Beat Magazine*. Public Affairs and later Music Director at KPFA Radio where he co-hosted the weekly lowrider show, "La Onda Bajita" for 18 years.

John "Zopi" Villanueva   Herbie Herbert's friend during their days in barber college. Roadie with Santana through the early glory years; went on to work with Journey and with Herbert's Nightmare Productions.

Chris Wong   Original Malo manager until release of *Evolution*. Managed the Basin Street West club; at present designs nightclubs and sports bars.

Abel Zarate   Lead guitarist with Malo on debut album. Fluent jazzy style earned him spots with Coke Escovedo, Willie Bobo, Attitude, Sapo, and more.

GLOSSARY

Abakua A secret Cuban religious sect of West African origin and the rhythms associated with its practices.

Acid A term for the hallucinogenic substance LSD (lysergic acid diethylamide).

Afro A sculpted, bubble-style hairdo worn by many African-Americans as a sign of Black pride; emulated by Mission Latinos such as Arcelio Garcia and Mike Carabello.

Afro-Cuban Musical term for a meld of Cuban-style Spanish vocals with African rhythmns and dance attitude; an aggressively self-confident demeanor.

Bajo Bass

Barrio Spanish word for "the neighborhood," specifically a Spanish-speaking neighborhood.

Bata A set of three drums sacred to santeria worship and its accompanying music.

Beatnik Term applied to purveyors of 1950s counterculture as expressed by writers Jack Kerouac, Allen Ginsberg, and fans of bebop jazz ("Crazy, man!").

Bembe A religious celebration involving music and dance; of Afro-Caribbean origin.

Blue beat Early reggae.

Bolero A slow, romantic tune.

Bongocero One who plays the bongo drums.

Boogaloo A 1960s musical hybrid of R&B and and Latin rhythms, devised primarily by New York promoters in a quest for a crossover audience.

Bosh British slang for "a complete disaster."

Bugalú Spanish spelling of "boogaloo."

Carnitas Mexican-style roast pork.

Cascara A rhythm played on the outer metal rim of the timbales.

Cha cha cha Latin dance style and rhythm derived from Cuban son.

**Chicano/
Chicanismo** Originally a disparaging term for an American of Mexican descent, "Chicano" came to symbolize Mexican-American ethnic pride during the 1970s; Chicanismo is the expression of that pride.

Cholo Slang for a street tough or gang member.

Conguero Conga player.

Conjunto A musical ensemble.

Conk A form of hair straightening ("conking") popular for a while with Latinos and Afro-Americans; the conk is the finished result.

Corridas	A story-telling ballad of Mexican origin.
Cumbia	A dance and musical style of Columbian origin.
Danzón	A graceful, elegant form of dance and music developed in Cuba and orginating in the French contradanse or ""country dance."
Descarga	Literally, "to unload"; connotes a musical jam session.
Do-rag	A head scarf used to keep one's "conk" in place.
Doo-wop	A harmonized street corner-style of vocalizing that evolved in the 1950s; it influenced the early Mission sound.
Dopester	One who likes to travel stoned while listening to music.
Fatback	Literally, a piece of fatty pork used to season beans, greens, and other dishes. Denotes a style of drumming as defined by James Brown and King Curtis; a solid, heavy groove, "on the one." Related to the more current term, "phat."
Glomming	To take advantage of.
Griot	A storyteller.
Guaguanco	One of three basic rumba rhythms originating in Cuba; fundamental to modern salsa and popular Latin dance music.
Guajira	Cuban-style dance, originating from the hill farmers.
Guaracha	Cuban song and dance of Spanish origin, performed in 2/4 time.
Guiro	A Caribbean rhythm instrument fashioned out of a hollow gourd; prominently used in Latin music.
Hispanic	Of Spanish origin; also a term refrring to a Spanish-speaking person.
Huapango	A musical form from the Huastec region of Mexico; a foundation of modern mariachi.
La Raza	Spanish term for "the race."
Latin groove	Term for new Latino soul derived from the music of the San Francisco Bay Area.
Latinismo	Exaggerated Latin style.
La vida loca	"This crazy life."
Liquid Owsley	Potent form of clear LSD.
Lowriders	Term for aficionados of cars with chassis modified to ride low to the ground; the cars usually are superbly restored and decorated.
Macuta	A rhythm of African origin popular in religious practices.
Mambo	A popular Latin dance adopted in the United States in the 1950s.
Mano-a-mano	Literally, "hand-to-hand."
Mariachi	A musical style originating in 19th-century Mexico, performed at first by a simple string ensemble; now can encompass full orchestra with brass.
Merengue	A fast-paced dance style considered the national dance of the Dominican Republic; from the word for meringue, as in "whipped to a froth."
Mersey beat	A 1960s wave of bands from Liverpool, England; the most visible of which was the Beatles.

265

Mozambique	A complex Afro-Cuban rhythm. 
Onda nueva	Refers to the "new wave" of urban Cuban music.
Pachuco	A tough guy; specifically, a term originating in 1940s zoot suit culture.
Palo	Another secret religion of African origin.
Pasteles	Puerto Rican tamales; an entrée of meat-filled soft dough.
Peruvian Marching Powder	Cocaine.
Phat	Extremely funky.
Pompadour	Hair piled high and swept back.
Process	*See* "conk."
Quinceaños	A celebration of a girl's fifteenth birthday; a coming out party in Spanish-speaking countries.
Quinceñeras	The girl celebrating her fifteenth birthday; a debutante.
Quinto	A high-pitched conga drum.
Ranchera	Mexican folk music; literally "of the ranch."
Rare groove	English term for sought-after Latin, funk, soul, and R&B vinyl releases.
Rudy	A young, bold Jamaican boy, living in England; derives from "rude boy." 
Rumbero	Someone who dances or plays the rumba rhythm.
Salsa	Literally, "hot sauce"; applies to modern Latin dance music.
Ska	Early form of blue beat and reggae.
Skin	An English term for skinhead; originally a 1960s working class youth—a sharp dresser interested in Motown.
Son	A form of popular music that originated in eastern Cuba.
Son montuno	A style of son; literally "from the mountain."
Speeding/ whizzing	Being cranked up on amphetamines or speed.
Spliffed-up	On a marijuana high.
Taqueria	Restaurant that sells tacos and other Mexican dishes. 
Tardeada	An afternoon dance.
Timbalero	A timbales player.
Toast	To reach a state of total exhaustion.
Trompeta	Spanish word for "trumpet."
Tumbao	A rhythmic congas pattern.
Wanker	An English term of abuse meaning a masturbator; also known as puller, stroker, tosser, or plonker; generally someone who is feeble or socially inept.
Weed	A slang term for marijuana. 
Zoned out	To be taken to a higher place by music.

REPRESENTAR / RESOURCES
MUSIC SITES

www.VoicesofLatinRock.com
THE OFFICIAL SITE FOR THIS BOOK.

www.santana.com
THE OFFICIAL SANTANA WEBSITE.

www.greggrolie.com
GREGG'S SITE WITH FREQUENT NEWS/TOUR UPDATES.

www.jorgesantana.com
FEATURES AN INTERESTING TIMELINE AND RARE PHOTOS.

www.santanaworld.com
EXCELLENT SANTANA FAN SITE BASED IN HOLLAND.

www.monarecords.com
KARL PERAZZO-RUN WEB SITE, WITH PERCUSSION VIDEOS
AND ADVANCE CDS AVAILABLE FOR PURCHASE.

www.elchicanomusic.com
OFFICIAL WEB SITE FOR THE INFLUENTIAL EAST LA
GROUP.

www.johnsantos.com
HIGHLY RESPECTED PERCUSSIONIST AND
ETHNOMUSICOLOGIST.

www.journeytheband.com
NEWS ON THE BAND FORMED BY GREGG ROLIE AND
NEAL SCHON.

www.malomusic.com
MALO OFFICIAL SITE: LATEST NEWS, TOURS, ETC.

www.mandrillis.com
WILSON BROTHERS-LED SITE WITH CURRENT NEWS
ON THE REVAMPED MANDRILL BAND.

www.orixazone.com
MISSION-BASED BAND WITH A STRONG LIVE SET, FEATUR-
ING A HARD-CORE POLITICAL SLANT.

www.ozomatli.com
SUPERB LIVE NEW WAVE ACT FROM EAST LA; HOSTS
EXCELLENT WEB SITE.

www.spearheadvibrations.com
MICHAEL FRANTI, A MISSION RESIDENT LEADS THIS
EXCELLENT ENSEMBLE.

www.syklopps.com
HERBIE HERBERT'S INCOGNITO/BAND; WITH SUPERB
GUEST MUSICIANS.

www.PassionsJustLikeMine.com
MORRISSEY'S SITE; EXCELLENT ENGLISH SINGER BASED IN
LA, WITH A HUGE HISPANIC FOLLOWING.

www.wildclam.com
EXCELLENT SITE FOR THE SALSOUL TROUPE LED
BY CECILIA NOEL.

www.buenotheband.com
CHRIST-FILLED LATIN-ROCK BAND WITH SUPERB DEBUT
CD FOR SALE.

members.tripod.com/~KingRhythm/id72.htm
NEFTALI SANTIAGO'S SITE; FUNK DRUMMER PAR EXCEL-
LENCE FOR MANDRILL AND MORE.

www.congahead.com
MARTIN COHEN'S SUPERB SITE ON ALL THINGS PERCUS-
SIVE WITH GREAT FILM AND VIDEO CLIPS.

www.bumpcity.com
THE ONE AND ONLY TOWER OF POWER,
LIVE AND KICKING!!

www.coldblood.biz
LYDIA PENSE AND COLD BLOOD WEB SITE.

www.kramerarchives.com
EDDIE KRAMER'S SITE HAS RARE PICTURES OF THE ORIG-
INAL SANTANA BAND
RECORDING THE 3RD ALBUM IN 1971.

Expansions

www.disinfon.com
De-centralize, de-corporatize, avoid the coming meltdown. Everything you know is wrong (apart from what you read in this book!).

www.breakingopenthehead.com
A modern journey through cynicism to shamanism.

Photo: Bob Sansoe

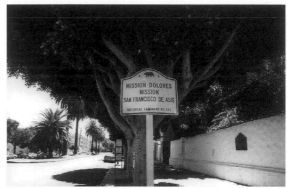

Mission Dolores park

Drug & Alcohol resources

Alcoholics Anonymous,
www.alcoholics-anonymous.org
Aimed at those who may have a problem with alcohol misuse.

Narcotics Anonymous
www.na.org
Sister fellowship to AA: for those who may be experiencing difficulties with substance misuse.

Cocaine Anonymous
www.ca.org
Specializes in helping those whose primary difficulty is cocaine or crack misuse.

Also recommended is…
The Stanton Peele Addiction web site.
www.peele.net/

Latino magazines, news, and resources

www.eltecolote.org
www.accionlatina.org
www.lowridermagazine.com
www.LatinBayArea.com
www.descarga.com

Photo: Johnny Valenzuela

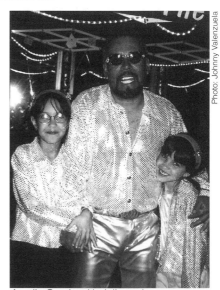

Arcelio Garcia with Julie and Christina Valenzuela.

Photo: Bob Sansoe

Mission High School.

Photo: Courtesy Arcelio Garcia, Jr.

Pete and Arcelio Garcia at the Bravo Awards,
Los Angeles.

LATINO EVENTS

www.carnaval.com

www.salsasf.com

RADIO STATIONS

www.kpfa

www.kcsm

POLITICAL RESOURCES

www.black panthers.org

CATHOLIC CHARITIES OF THE EAST BAY

CALIFORNIA YOUTH CRISIS LINE

LA CLINICA DE LA RAZA,
www.laclinica.org

www.mumia.org/freedom.now

www.Milagro foundation

oeop.larc.nasa

UNITED FARM WORKERS UNION,
www.ufw.org

FURTHER READING

SALSA, MUSICAL HEARTBEAT OF LATIN AMERICA; SUE STEWARD
Excellent history of salsa, well designed, and lavishly illustrated.
Published by Thames & Hudson, 1999.

www.mictlan.com
THE OLD BARRIO GUIDE TO LOW RIDER MUSIC
1950–1975 BY RUBEN MOLINA
NEW BOOK IN LIMITED EDITION EXPLORING THE ROOTS OF HISPANIC,
DOO-WOP, AND R&B MUSIC IN EAST LOS ANGELES.

www.chiorisan.com
CHIORI SANTIAGO IS THIS BOOK'S EDITOR AND A
WRITER/AUTHOR IN HER OWN WRITE (SIC!)

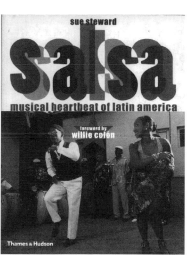

DISCOGRAPHY

ESSENTIAL LISTENING COMPREHENSIVE LATIN ROCK DISCOGRAPHY (WEST COAST-BASED)

SANTANA	*Live at the Fillmore 1968*	Columbia	1997
SANTANA	*Santana*	Columbia	1969
SANTANA	*Abraxas*	Columbia	1970
SANTANA	*3*	Columbia	1971
SANTANA	*Caravanserai*	Columbia	1972
MALO	*Malo*	WB	1972
MALO	*Dos*	WB	1972
MALO	*Evolution*	WB	1973
MALO	*Ascencion*	WB	1974
MALO	*Best of Malo*	GNP	1991
MALO	*Celebracion*	Rhino [4cds]	2001
AZTECA	*Azteca*	Columbia	1972
AZTECA	*Pyramid of the Moon*	Columbia	1973
DAKILA	*Dakila*	Epic	1972
EL CHICANO	*Viva Tirado*	Kapp	1970
EL CHICANO	*Revolucion*	Kapp	1971
EL CHICANO	*Celebration*	Kapp	1972
EL CHICANO	*El Chicano*	MCA	1973
EL CHICANO	*Cinco*	MCA	1974
EL CHICANO	*Pyramid of Love & Friends*	MCA	1975
EL CHICANO	*Chicano Chant*	MCA [cd]	1997
TIERRA	*Tierra*	20th Century	1973
SAPO	*Sapo*	Bell	1974
JOSE CHEPITO AREAS	*Chepito*	Columbia	1974
LUIS GASCA	*Little Giant*	Atlantic	1969
LUIS GASCA	*Luis Gasca*	Blue Thumb	1971
COKE ESCOVEDO	*Coke*	Mercury	1975
COKE ESCOVEDO	*Comin' at Ya*	Mercury	1976
COKE ESCOVEDO	*Disco Fantasy*	Mercury	1977
WILLIE BOBO	*Do What You Wanna Do*	Sussex	1972
WILLIE BOBO	*Bobo*	Columbia	1979
CHANGO	*Chango*	ABC	1975
MACONDO	*Macondo*	Atlantic	1972
ARMANDO PERAZA	*Wild Thing*	Skye	1969
DANIEL VALDEZ	*Mestizo*	A&M	1974
GIANTS	*Giants*	MCA	1978
ABRAXAS POOL	*Abraxas Pool*	Miramar	1997
GREGG ROLIE	*Roots*	33rd Street	2001

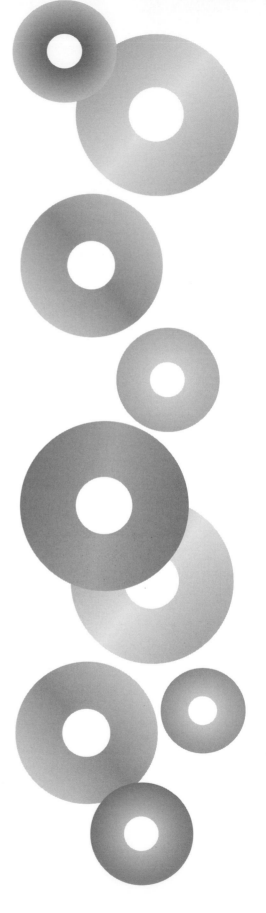

JIM MCCARTHY (AUTHOR) AND
LANDY GRAY, ENGLAND, 2004

Photo: Richard Mann

**RUDY GOES AFRO GOES RASTA
SKIN GOES LATINO GOES SALSA**

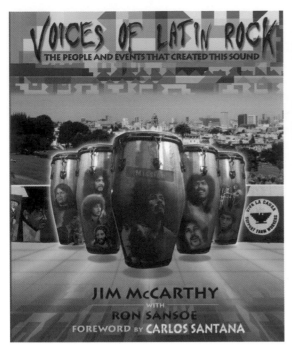

Congas at Dolores

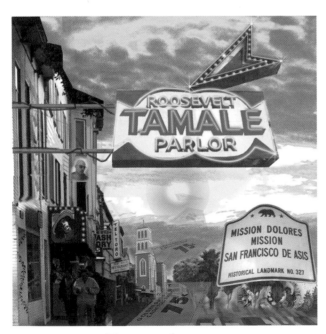

Ghetto Nite Life

Tamale Sunrise

Up from 24th Street

Digital Poster Artworks by Richard Mann and Jim McCarthy
Copyright: VOLK inc. 2004

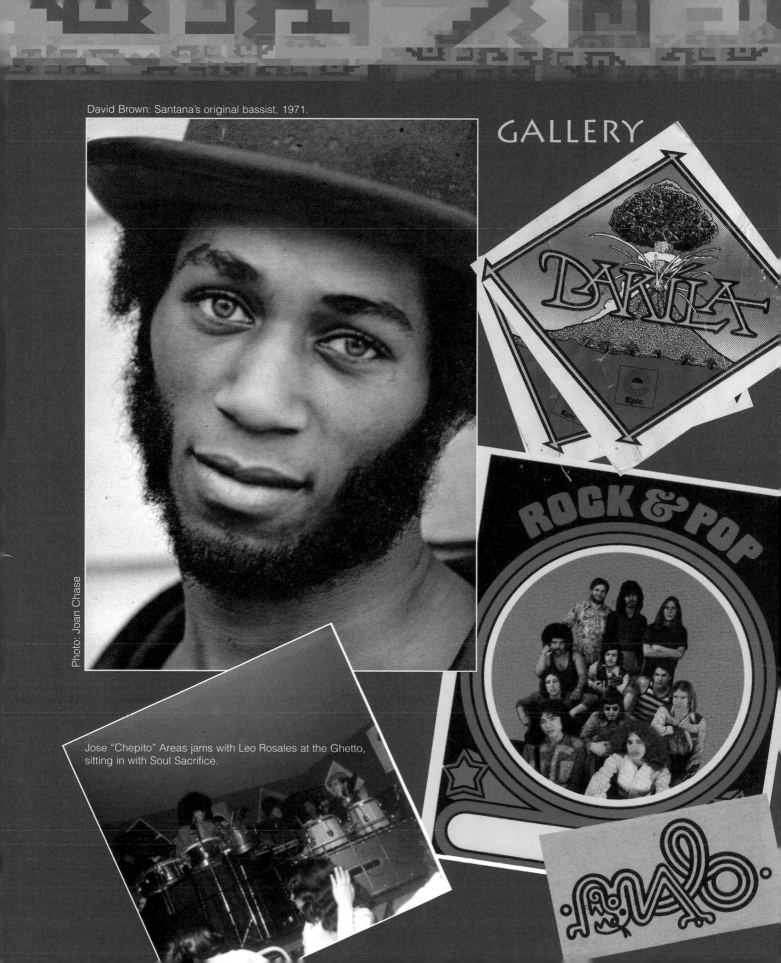

David Brown: Santana's original bassist, 1971.

Photo: Joan Chase

GALLERY

Jose "Chepito" Areas jams with Leo Rosales at the Ghetto, sitting in with Soul Sacrifice.

Photo: Joan Chase

Carlos Santana and David Brown

Carlos Santana onstage in Africa, Accra, Ghana:
Soul to Soul celebrations in 1971.

Photo: Ron Reisterer. Oakland Tribune.

Santana fall about in an outtake from the
3 album photo sessions, 1971.

Malo on "American Bandstand,"
1973. Latino Rock spreads to
nationwide television.

Photo: Courtesy Malo Archives

ÁZTECA

Stereo
CBS
CBS 1191

Mamita
Linda

Peace Everybody

Azteca 45 vinyl single sleeve, Holland, 1972.
Courtesy CBS/Sony Records.

Carabello art by Jim McCarthy

Jorge Santana with a beautiful Gibson guitar.

Photo: Rudy Rodriguez
Courtesy: Warner Brothers records

suavecíto 16 155

Malo

WB 16 155

SUAVECITO / NENA

Malo

WB

STEREO

WB P-1148W

脅威のブラス・ロック・グループ マロの2枚目シングル、ドカーンと登場！

カフェ CAFE

B面：平和/PEACE

歌・演奏：マロ/MALO

WB 16 194 (7605)

WB

Malo

CAFÉ   PEACE

* Cafe Sans Cola
  A mi me canta el cafe.
  No me gusta cafe prieto
  Damelo, mira como va
  Primo ese conjunto
  Oyeme, Mamie
  Pasame el azucar
  Porgue yo quiero
  Tomar me otra taza
  Cafe Sans Cola (5x)
  * (Repeat)
  Que, que, que, que
  Mira como va
  Primo ese conjunto
  Con eso nosotros

Malo 45 vinyl single sleeves x 4.
Courtesy Warner Brothers
Records.

【Stereo】
CBSA
82128

CBS
SONY

FLY WITH CBSA AIR-PLAY
AIR-PLAY
SERIES 45 RPM
CBS SONY RECORDS

新しい世界
EVERYBODY'S EVERYTHING

サンタナ
SANTANA

C/W グアヒーラ GUAJIRA

Courtesy CBS/Sony Records

Santana 45 vinyl
single sleeve,
Japan, 1972.

Photos: Joan Chase

ntana 45 vinyl
gle sleeve,
xico, 1972.

Courtesy CBS/
Sony Records

Santana on the road in 1971.

sin depender de nadie
tabú SANTANA

Courtesy CBS/Sony Records

Santana 45 vinyl single
sleeve, Spain, 1972.

Santana 45 vinyl single
sleeve, Spain, 1972.

Photo Joan Chase: Courtesy Julio Sanchez

Santana pictured at
Gregg Rolie's Mill Valley
home in 1971.

Leo Rosales plays timbales with Malo.

Photos: Rudy Rodriguez

o Rosales

Abel Zarate,
in the Malo days.

ぼくのリズムを
聞いとくれ

OYE COMO VA

サンタナ ──────── SANTANA

C/W 君に捧げるサンバ
SAMBA PA TI

Stereo
CBSA
2101

FLY WITH CBSA AIR-PLAY
AIR-PLAY
SERIES 45 RPM
CBS SONY RECORDS

¥400

SANTANA

BLACKMAGICWOMEN GYPSY QUEEN
OYE COMOVA SAMBA PATI

SANTANA
NO ONE TO
DEPEND
ON

Stereo
CBS
CBS S 7812

TABOO

SANTANA

OYE
COMO
VA

SAMBA
PA
TI

Stereo
CBS
7046

Top) Santana 45 vinyl single sleeve, Japan, 1970.
Bottom) Santana 45 vinyl single sleeve, Germany, 1970.

(Top) Santana 45 vinyl single sleeve, Thailand, 1972.
(Bottom) Santana 45 vinyl single sleeve, Germany, 1971.

Courtesy CBS/Sony Records

Photo: Joan Chase

Mike Carabello plays congas with Santana at Altamont. The concert, said to define the end of the '60s dream, was staged by the Rolling Stones. Santana played first on the bill, well away from the Stones, who always feared being blown offstage by Santana's superior firepower. Mick Jagger and his "Satanic Majesties," truly invoked the American nightmare on this ill-fated day. The young Meredith Hunter was murdered in the audience during the concert and ugly scenes involving the Hell's Angels (there providing security at Jagger's request) were rife. A bad trip man!!

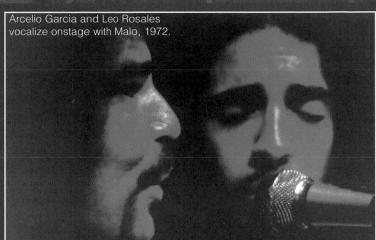

Arcelio Garcia and Leo Rosales vocalize onstage with Malo, 1972.

Photos: Rudy Rodriguez
Photo Courtesy Malo Archives

Raul Rekow plays congas with Malo, 1972.

Raul Rekow with a "jazz" cigarette.

APPEARING IN CONCERT AT WINTERLAND
FRIDAY AND SATURDAY   FEBRUARY 4 AND 5

Gregg Rolie: "Roots" promo shot.

Photo: Jim Welch, Courtesy Gregg Rolie

Raul Rekow onstage with Malo.

Photo: Rudy Rodrigue

Malo backstage passes

Many Faces CD sleeve, featuring members of Malo, with Gregg Errico, and a fantastic guitar solo from Jorge Santana on the fabulous "Esta Bien."

MANY FACES

SALSA CON TIMBA
& WORLD MUSIC
2 DJ'S

FRIDAY, APRIL 26, 2002
IL PIRATA 2007 · 16 th st. San Francisco

Photo: Julio Sanchez

Richard Kermode sits in at the Keystone Korner, San Francisco.

EL mexico canta
COLECCION PRIMAVERA

Photo: Beatriz Deonbi: Courtesy Pete Gallegos

Impromptu street jam in celebration of the annual Carnaval in the Mission, circa 1980.
Early incarnation of "Alma del Barrio" with Pete Gallegos playing bass, Mike Rios, cuatro,
Harold Love, congas, Jamon Balberan, bongo, Ramon Garcia, flute, and Angelo Pagan, maracas.

Photos: Jim Welch. Courtesy Gregg Rolie

Gregg Rolie promo shots for *Roots* release.

Johnny Villanueva, Jackie Villaneuva, and
Herbie Herbert.

Carlos Santana jams with John Santos and Machete Ensemble.
(L to R) Singers Ismael Rodriguez and Willie Ludwig, pianist
Rebecca Mauleón, timbalero Orestes Vilato, John Santos on bell
and Harold Muñiz on congas at the Great American Music Hall,
April 1989 at the "Tribute to Armando Peraza."

BLACK AND WHITE PICTURE GALLERY

Photo: Jim Marshall

Santana at the Woodstock festival, 1969.
Pictured are Gregg Rolie (back to camera), Mike Carabello, Jose "Chepito" Areas, Carlos Santana, David Brown, and Michael Shrieve.
In the background behind amps are road crew: Johnny Villanueva and Herbie Herbert.

THE METEORIC RISE TO FAME OF THE ORIGINAL SANTANA BAND WITH THEIR APPEARANCE AT THE WOODSTOCK FESTIVAL IN 1969, AND THE SUBSEQUENT RELEASE OF THEIR FIRST RECORDING, GALVANIZED THE FESTIVAL AUDIENCE AND PUT GUAGANCO, RUMBA AND THE RHYTHMNS OF TITO PUENTE, WILLIE BOBO AND RAY BARETTO ON THE WORLD MAP.
SANTANA WERE RESPONSIBLE FOR THE FIRST WAVE OF WHAT MAY NOW BE DESCRIBED AS "WORLD" MUSIC, SELLING MILLIONS OF RECORDS AND POSITIONING THEMSELVES IN THE ARC OF HISTORY AS A PIVOTAL, POTENT, CREATIVE AND SIGNIFYING FORCE FOR YOUNG, ASPIRING LATINOS IN THE USA. REPRESENTAR !!

The house where it started; the Santana sound had its birthplace here on 21st and Potrero Streets, San Francisco, which was Danny Haro's old house. The Santana lineup then consisted of Carlos, Mike Carabello on congas, Gregg Rolie on keys, Gus Rodrigues on bass, and Danny Haro on drums.

Photo: Ron Sansoe

An early Santana bootleg, featuring a performance from the Fillmore West with amusing cover artwork.

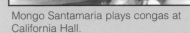

Mongo Santamaria plays congas at California Hall.

Photo: Julio Sanchez

Photo: Courtesy Michael Shrieve

Up Against The Wall, Motherfuckers! (4th from left, Rico Reyes; 6th from left, Mike Carabello; 8th and 9th from left, Ron Estrada and Mike Shrieve; 10th and 11th, Herbie Herbert and Joan Chase, in white fur coat).

Herbie Herbert: " Stan Marcum opened the Santana office about then. The location is called Levi Plaza; now you can't afford to be there. We were on 1375 Greenwich, a half-block dead-end on Sansome Street, where our offices were, in a poultry company building. Right across the street was this torn-down building. I think Jefferson Airplane took a famous photo there; it was for their *Volunteers* record. It reads, 'Up Against The Wall Motherfuckers.' About two blocks away was a real greasy spoon, the Bottom of the Mark. The greasiest cheeseburgers ever, it was like post-war Dresden; now it's called The Fog City Diner."

Malo backstage: Raul Rekow, Leo Rosales, Pablo Tellez, and Tom Poole.
Whisky a Go Go, Los Angeles, 1972.

Photo: Rudy Rodriguez

1988 Dinner to campaign
for Orlando Cepeda's
induction to Baseball
Hall of Fame.
Left to Right: Dusty Baker
(manager of Chicago
Cubs), Michael Shrieve,
Marc Gibson (ABC TV
broadcaster), Mike
Carabello, Nate Thurmond
(NBA Hall of Fame),
Orlando Cepeda.

Photo: Jeff Trager

Malo backstage: Leo Rosales,
Jorge Santana, Pablo Tellez,
and Tom Poole.
Whisky a Go Go,
Los Angeles, 1972.

Photo: Rudy Rodriguez

olores Park
as quejas de los vecinos han acallado el repiqueteo de las congas que se tocaban
re libre—y llevado a los músicos ante la corte.

_atinos' right of free expression is be-
ng jeopardized. *Conguero* John San-
os has no doubts on the matter:
'The drum has been the voice of the
heritage of the Black and Brown people since the beginning of time. We
cannot afford to let its voice be si-
enced. It is of utmost importance that
our ancestral ties be preserved, particularly because we live in a system
that is designed to demoralize and di-
vide us in so many ways." But for the
moment, the Dolores Park drums remain quiescent.

—*Juan Gonzales*

On the steps of SF City Hall
to protest arrest of John
Santos and Raul Rekow for
playing congas in the
Mission's Dolores Park, 1973.
Musicians L to R:
Rafael Ramirez (conga)
John Santos (conga)
David Virelli (voice)

Orquesta Típica Cienfuegos, outdoor festival, Mission district, 1977.
L to R: John Calloway, Rick Rangel, Harold Muñíz,
Mike Madrigal, John Santos.

Salsa Caliente in 1987. Top three L to R: Dan Regan (trombone), Tony (trumpet),
Bill Ortiz (trumpet). Bottom L to R: Oscar Soltero (bongos), Angelo Pagan (vocals),
Eric Rangel (timbales), Gary Flores (piano-leader), Mike Spiro (congas),
Coco Pagan (vocals), Ricky Encarnacion (bass), Jose Flores (conga).

RITMO '74 · EXCLUSIVE ARTISTS OF BENNY RECORDS ·

Ritmo '74 (1974) straight out of the Mission.
L to R:
Edgar Cabezas (trombone)
Frank Torres (guitar)
Roberto Quintana (timbales)
Ted Strong (bongos)
John Santos (coro-percussion)
Gregory Gomez (leader-cantante)
Raul Guerra (congas)
Patricia Thumas (piano)
Jorge Chinchilla (bass)
Victor Quintana (cantante—Roberto's brother)
Frank Rodriguez (1st trumpet)
Gary Flores (2nd trumpet)

Santana onstage at
Muenster, Germany, 1971.
(Pictured L to R)
Gregg Rolie in shadow,
Coke Escovedo, Mike Carabello,
Carlos Santana, Mike Shrieve,
and Neal Schon.

Photo: Jurg Buschmann, Courtesy Etienne Houben

Photos: Joan Chase

Mike Carabello onstage, 1971.

Neal Schon:
CBS Studios,
Folsom Street,
1971.

Carlos Santana onstage at Muenster, Germany on Santana European Tour, 1971.

Photo: Jurg Buschmann, Courtesy Etienne Houben

Photo: Joan Chase

Jose "Chepito" Areas plays at
the Altamont festival, 1969.

Photo: Rudy Rodriguez

Malo's Richard Spremich on drums.

Carlos and Debbie Santana backstage at the 1974 Winterland show, with Ralph Mercado from Fania Records, plus Armando Peraza and Mongo Santamaria (with backs to camera).

Jorge Santana cooking onstage with the Fania All-Stars.
Johnny Pacheco (vocalist) fans the flames of Jorge's guitar solo. Winterland, 1974.

Photos: Ray Cotter, Jr.

Carmelo Garcia and Arcelio Garcia

Jorge Santana and Richard Spremich

Photo: Rudy Rodriguez

Pablo Tellez smokes a blunt with Abel Zarate.

Photo: Rudy Rodriguez

Doug Rauch: Santana bassist with his Citroen at Butler Aviation, 1973.

Carlos Santana, SIR rehearsals, 1973.

Michael Shrieve on drums with Carlos Santana. SIR Rehearsals, 1973.

Dougie Rauch: sadly-missed exponent and innovator of slap and fluid funk bass styles.

Photos: Julio Sanchez

Gregg Rolie and Chepito Areas,
SIR Rehearsal Studios,
San Francisco, 1973.

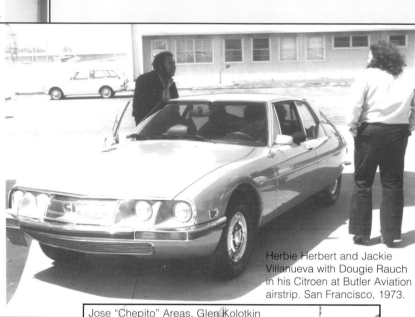

Herbie Herbert and Jackie
Villanueva with Dougie Rauch
in his Citroen at Butler Aviation
airstrip. San Francisco, 1973.

Jose "Chepito" Areas, Glen Kolotkin
(Santana sound engineer and producer),
and Richard Kermode outside
SIR rehearsals, 1973.

Johnny Villanueva at
SIR Rehearsals, 1973.

Photos: Julio Sanchez

Carlos plays the drums.

Carlos watches Neal Schon during early Journey rehearsals in the next studio at SIR Rehearsals, 1973.

Neal Schon jams with Prairie Prince (from the Tubes) on drums and Richard Kermode on keyboards.

Neal Schon and Richard Kermode

Photos: Julio Sanchez

Malo in the studio for the Malo *Dos* recording.
Pictured: Tom Poole (background), Leo Rosales, Richard Spremich, Pablo Tellez, Raul Rekow, and Jorge Santana.

Malo backstage at the Ike and Tina Turner show, 1973.
Pictured (Back, L to R) Richard Spremich, Pablo Tellez, Mike Atwood, Leo Rosales with bongos, Raul Rekow, Tom Poole, Mike Heathman and Richard Kermode playing guiro. (Front) Jorge Santana plays bass and Arcelio Garcia enjoys the sounds.

Photos: Rudy Rodriguez

Armando Peraza,
Chepito, and Dougie Rauch,
SIR rehearsals, 1973.

Carlos Santana:
SIR rehearsals.

Chepito plays some hot
timbales at SIR rehearsals
during Santana's *Welcome*
rehearsals.

Carlos Santana:
SIR rehearsals.

Photos: Julio Sanchez

Sheila E. and Pete Escovedo onstage at Berkeley Community Theatre in 1976.

Photos: Ray Cotter, Jr.

Carlos and Jorge Santana hang out backstage at the Berkeley Community Theatre, 1976.

Dougie Rauch on bass and
Carlos Santana on drums.

Neal Schon and Prairie Prince at early
Journey rehearsal at SIR studios, 1973.

Dougie Rauch with
Carlos Santana on drums.

Neal Schon with Ross Valory on bass
and Prairie Prince on drums at early
Journey rehearsals.

Doug Rauch, Michael Shrieve,
and Carlos Santana rehearse.

Photos: Julio Sanchez

Photo: Courtesy Mike Shrieve

Todd "Bayete" Cochran and Michael Shrieve (wide awake) in the Automatic Man days, London, 1976.

William Lee Brent seen here at a Black Panther rally in Oakland. Later he got involved in a gun battle outside the Hall of Justice and wounded three police officers. On June 17, 1969, Brent hijacked a TWA flight to San Francisco and re-routed the plane to Cuba, where he has lived since that fateful day.

Photo: Ron Reisterer, Oakland Tribune

Film star Marlon Brando also supported the Black Panther party and was a hipster student of Jack Constanza, from whom he learned to play bongos.

Photo: Ron Reisterer, Oakland Tribune

Mike Shrieve of Santana.
Photo: Joan Chase

Series of shots from Malo's 1987 Carnaval gig in the Mission. The bill also featured Pete Escovedo and Santana.

Photos: Courstesy Malo Archives

Photo: Malo archives

Arcelio Garcia sings with Malo at the 1987 Carnaval Festival in the Mission District, San Francisco.
In the background: Leo Rosales and Luis Ramirez (ex Fania All-Stars) on timbales.

Ron Sansoe, Gregg Errico, and Jeff Trager onstage at Malo's Carnaval gig in the Mission, 1987.

View from the stage as Arcelio Garcia, lead singer with Malo, works the huge Mission crowd at Carnaval.

Photos: Malo Archives

Malo on-the-road pictures:

Doug Tracy and Pablo Tellez from Malo.

Tom Poole with a senorita.

Ron Smith, Malo's trumpeter, with a friend.

Dave Garibaldi, drummer with Tower of Power and Rich Spremich, drummer from Malo, on the plane to another gig.

Jorge Santana on the baggage carousel.

Pablo Tellez

Forrest Buchtel looms in the window.

Arcelio Garcia and Jorge Santana on the plane.

Arcelio Garcia, Tony Smith, and Jorge Santana.

Photos: Malo Archives

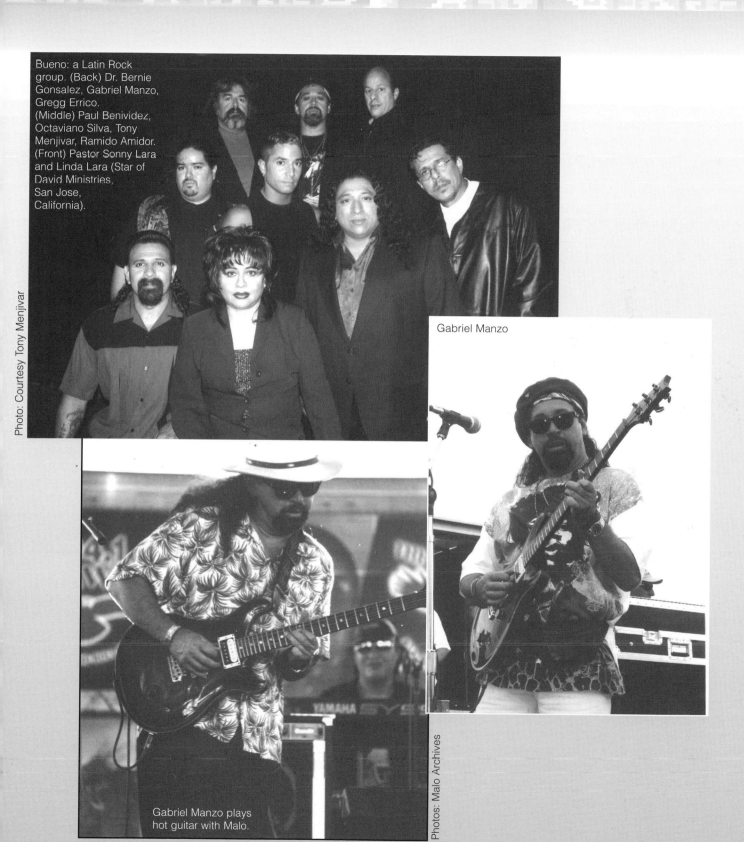

Bueno: a Latin Rock group. (Back) Dr. Bernie Gonsalez, Gabriel Manzo, Gregg Errico. (Middle) Paul Benividez, Octaviano Silva, Tony Menjivar, Ramido Amidor. (Front) Pastor Sonny Lara and Linda Lara (Star of David Ministries, San Jose, California).

Photo: Courtesy Tony Menjivar

Gabriel Manzo

Gabriel Manzo plays hot guitar with Malo.

Photos: Malo Archives

Miles Davis gigs at the Keystone Korner in San Francisco. Seen in the background: Michael Henderson on bass and Dave Liebman on saxophones.

Photos: Julio Sanchez

Digital bollocks:
Miles head shots: Jim McCarthy

James "Mingo" Lewis: Santana conga player for *Caravanserai* period, 1972.

Giovanni Hidalgo, conga player, shows Johnny Valenzuela a conga pattern.

Photos: Johnny Valenzuela

Percussionists Marcos Reyes, Victor Pantoja, and Johnny Valenzuela hang out.

Photo: Rudy Rodriguez

Leo Rosales on timbales with Malo.

Dave Brown and Gerry Bell in martial arts pose.

Photo: Rudy Rodriguez

Raul Rekow, congas, with Malo in 1972.

MALO
~with~
JORGE SANTANA

CARSON HI. GYM
$1.00
APRIL 29, 1971 - 6TH PERIOD
$1.00
PROMOTION ASSOCIATES

Courtesy: Jorge Santana.

DAKILA
GÓZALA

Epic
EPC 8497

EL DÚBI

Courtesy: Epic/Sony Records

Jorge Santana and
Fania Record label
boss Jerry Masucci
backstage at
The Winterland,
San Francisco, 1974.

Gibby Ross, at the tender age of nine, jams on
timbales with Tito Puente at St. Francis Hotel,
San Francisco in 1976.

Photos: Ray Cotter, Jr.

Photo: Jim Marshall

Santana jam on percussion during their performance at Woodstock, 1969.
Pictured are Jose "Chepito" Areas playing tambourine, Carlos Santana also with tambourine, and Mike Carabello playing conga drums.

INDEX